Discourse and Institutional Authority:

Medicine, Education, and Law

edited by

Sue Fisher
Wesleyan University
Middletown, Connecticut

and

Alexandra Dundas Todd
Suffolk University
Boston, Massachusetts

Volume XIX in the Series
ADVANCES IN DISCOURSE PROCESSES
Roy O. Freedle, editor

ABLEX PUBLISHING CORPORATION
NORWOOD, NEW JERSEY 07648

i

Library of Congress Cataloging-in-Publication Data
Main entry under title:

Discourse and institutional authority.

   (Advances in discourse processes; v. 19)
   Includes bibliographies and indexes.
   1. Sociolinguistics. 2. Discourse analysis. 3. Social interaction. 4. Social structures.
I. Fisher, Sue, 1936–   . II. Todd, Alexandra Dundas. III. Series.
P40.D5127   1986   401′.9   85-22888
ISBN 0-89391-282-4
ISBN 0-89391-367-7 (pbk.)

Ablex Publishing Corporation
355 Chestnut Street
Norwood, New Jersey 07648

Contents

A special thanks to all those who were willing to be observed, taped and analyzed without whom this book would not have been possible.

Acknowledgements: To Bud Mehan for his continuing support as friend and colleague. To the faculty and staff of Suffolk and Wesleyan Universities for their encouragement of us as scholars and teachers. And to our sons Drew Todd and Bob, Jeff and Mike Warner.

Preface to the Series

Roy O. Freedle
Series Editor

This series of volumes provides a forum for the cross-fertilization of ideas from a diverse number of disciplines, all of which share a common interest in discourse—be it prose comprehension and recall, dialogue analysis, text grammar construction, computer simulation of natural language, cross-cultural comparisons of communicative competence, or other related topics. The problems posed by multisentence contexts and the methods required to investigate them, while not always unique to discourse, are still sufficiently distinct as to benefit from the organized mode of scientific interaction made possible by this series.

Scholars working in the discourse area from the perspective of sociolinguistics, psycholinguistics, ethnomethodology and the sociology of language, educational psychology (e.g., teacher–student interaction), the philosophy of language, computational linguistics, and related subareas are invited to submit manuscripts of monograph or book length to the series editor. Edited collections of original papers resulting from conferences will also be considered.

Volumes in the Series

Introduction: Communication in Institutional Contexts: Social Interaction and Social Structure

Sue Fisher

Wesleyan University
Middletown, CT

Alexandra Dundas Todd

Suffolk University, Boston

The social sciences share an interest in explaining and understanding patterns in the mosaic of social life. For the most part, language has been treated as an unexamined background resource, rather than as a researchable topic in the social sciences. The relationship between language and human society is so pervasive, it has hardly been noticed. Yet researchers from many social science disciplines have come together to understand the structure of language and the functions such structures serve. From linguistics, sociology, anthropology, psychology, and philosophy, scholars have reached a similar conclusion: Language is an organized, patterned, social activity. The work in this book continues in that tradition by exploring the relationship between the structure of discourse and the institutional context in which it occurs.

DISCOURSE AND INSTITUTIONS

When discourse has been studied as a social activity, the most striking finding is the persistence of recurrent patterns of behavior. An examination of ordinary, everyday conversations displays an overwhelming similarity. There is an expectation of balanced participation which is, in most cases, realized. Speakers take turns and change topics in an orderly fashion. They ask and answer questions, exchange greetings, and interrupt each other in equal measure. However, status and power have been shown to wreak havoc with this symmetry. For example, Zimmerman and West (1975) point out that when women are talking with women, or men are talking with men, they interrupt each other in roughly equal fashion. But when men and women are conversing, men interrupt women more frequently.

Zimmerman and West conclude that status and power differences disrupt the more normal state of balance even in everyday conversations. This asymmetry is heightened in institutional contexts. The structure of the institution is organized so as to lend those in power the authority to pursue defined goals. This authority is reflected in the forms and functions (structure and content) of educational, legal, and medical discourse. For example, the educational system gives teachers the authority to control students' behavior and motivate them to learn. Doctors' power, consistent with our current medical model, is organized to control medical resources and influence patients' health. Similarly, lawyers and judges derive power from the legal system—a power reflected in the physical arrangement of courtrooms as well as the management of legal discourse and expert testimony. Clients, like students and patients, are dependent. They lack the technical information and skill to be partners in the legal process. This authority is generally understood by all the participants—students, patients, and clients usually accord teachers, doctors, and lawyers respect. In the courtroom, all rise when the judge enters.

Our point here is not that doctors, lawyers, and teachers have all the control and always act out institutionally predefined roles, or that patients, clients, and students are powerless. We do not intend to suggest that any of the participants in institutional events are "judgmental dopes" (Garfinkel, 1967), passively enacting normative scripts. Rather, our goal is to shift the focus of analysis from individuals lifted out of the context of their interactions to active participants embedded in a nexus of the organizational, structural, and cultural arrangements of their society. Such a shift in focus highlights the negotiated nature of interaction while displaying it as both a social and political, or, as Henley (1977) suggests, a micropolitical activity.

A REFORMULATION: BRIDGING SOCIAL INTERACTION AND SOCIAL STRUCTURE

Since medical, legal, and educational work primarily occurs during face-to-face interactions and is an infinitely practical activity performed by doctors, lawyers, and teachers with patients, clients, and students to accomplish the tasks at hand, it is social. Medical, legal, and educational work also reflects, helps sustain and reproduces status relationships and in that sense is micropolitical. In the process of doing their work, doctors, lawyers, and teachers have the power to control resources and to act as gatekeepers, allowing options to some while denying them to others.

An analysis that is both social and micropolitical has the potential to increase our understanding substantively, methodologically, and theoretically by adding new designs to the mosaic of social life. With such an analysis it becomes possible to make connections between approaches normally seen as incompatible. Communication during institutional events displays the negotiated nature of the content and structure of participants' strategies for eliciting and transmitting information and for reaching decisions. It also offers researchers an occasion for making visible the communicational patterns participants use to accomplish activities. These spoken interactions supply the data to begin building a theoretical link which connects social interaction with social structure.

The call to link approaches traditionally seen as disparate grows out of long-standing debates. In linguistics the focal issue has been the relationship between language and context. Sociolinguistic research has been an outgrowth of this debate. Whether focusing on linguistic rules (forms or structures) and exploring linguistic variation, or examining the content and functions fulfilled by speech, sociolinguists recast language use in the social context of the speech community and work to develop both a method for capturing and a theory capable of accounting for the relationship between language and context.

There is a similar debate in sociology. Traditionally, sociologists—whether supportive or critical of the status quo—have engaged in research at one of three levels of analysis—interactional, organizational, or structural—while simultaneously engaging in a rigorous debate on the relative merits (or lack thereof) with each mode of analysis. Recently, an effort has been made to reintegrate what Knorr-Cetina and Cicourel (1981) call "macro- and micro-sociologies." In this effort language is used as a critical link in the bridge between social interaction and social structure. In the introduction to this book, Knorr-Cetina states:

> Macro-social theories and methodologies have generally focused their interest on the interrelationship of social action. They have promoted conceptions of (macro) social order which start from an interrelation hypothesis and employed notions such as social system and social structure to deal with this interrelation. In contrast, micro-social theories and methodologies favour conceptions which start from the ontological and methodological primacy of micro-social situations. While this has resulted in a long-standing challenge of macro-approaches to social reality, attempts to *reconstruct* macro-sociology from a microsociological perspective are new. (1981:40)

She identifies three hypotheses for *reconstructing* the macro from micro insights. First, in the aggregation hypothesis stemming from the work of Collins (1981), Knorr-Cetina asserts that the macro-realm of social order and structure are composed of aggregations of micro-moments in everyday life. This is the most extreme of the micro-theories as it posits that *all* understanding of macro-phenomena are aggregated from *in situ* micro-data. In other words, the whole is the sum of the parts.

Second, in the hypothesis of unintended consequences suggested by the work of Harre (1981) and Giddens (1981), Knorr-Cetina claims that there are unintended as well as intended consequences of micro-experiences. Micro-events must be studied in order to know the macro-world. But unlike the aggregation hypothesis, the entire global (macro) picture cannot be fathomed from the intended (micro). There is an acknowledgement that there are influences on social life that transcend empirical evidence. One can try to understand the unintended by study of micro-action and one can study unintended consequences to see the emergent macro-world, but there is no assurance that this will provide all of the answers. In this case the whole is more than the sum of its parts but only the parts are researchable topics.

Third, in the representation hypothesis drawn from the work of Cicourel (1981), Knorr-Cetina suggests relationships and connections between situation and the construction of accounts or the represented and the representation.

> The macro emerges from such work not as the sum of unintended consequences of micro-episodes nor as their aggregate or network of interrelations, but rather as a summary representation actively constructed and pursued within micro-situations. In other words, the macro appears no longer as a *particular layer* of social reality *on top* of micro-episodes composed of their interrelation (macro-sociologies), their aggregation (aggregation hypothesis), or their unforeseen effects (hypothesis of unintended consequences). Rather, it is seen to reside *within* these micro-episodes where it results from the *structuring practices* of agents. (1981:34)

The macro-order becomes a part of micro-action, an integral meshing rather than the emergence of macro from micro as espoused in the earlier two hypotheses.

Although we join in the call for a reintegration between micro- and macro-sociologies, there are distinctions between our conception and Knorr-Cetina's on the status of social structure and social interaction (what she refers to as their ontological primacy), and therefore, of necessity, with our suggestions, for how the gap should be bridged. Since proponents from both macro- and micro-sociologies have tried to make these connections, perhaps a comparison between their proposals will illuminate this distinction.

Habermas (1970, 1981), a traditional macro-theorist, has been one of the leaders in the call for integration. Although Habermas addresses interre-lationships and linkages, for him macro-structures (institutional arrangements) have priority. Social integration is rooted in a historical location in the political order: macro-institutional arrangements are interrelated with micro-social ac-tions. However, since he is interested in social change, he posits a micro-process for creating new forms of social integration. He suggests that alternative in-terpretive systems develop in marginal groups and spread to other societal mem-bers. Once spread, they create a shared cognitive potential for reorganizing society. Institutions change by embodying this shared interpretation. Language and interaction are, of course, central features of this interactive transformation. Although it appears that Habermas is calling for an integration between macro-structures and micro-processes, the weaving of these micro-processes into the larger picture is weak. Habermas' forté is social systems—a theory of language and interaction remains underdeveloped.

By comparison, the representational hypothesis put forth as the most viable of the micro-positions, turns Habermas's vision on its head. Where for Habermas the macro—institutional arrangements—takes priority, for the representational hypothesis the micro has primacy. Macro-structures reside within "micro-epi-sodes" and are accomplished through the social activities of the participants in these episodes. The forté of this work is the detailed analysis of the ways individuals accomplish events or create social realities. Power, structures, and social order are all alluded to, but when the hypothesis has been fully unveiled, the strength lies in the development of the micro-world—the larger concerns of social structure remain vague.

Taking power as an example, as does Knorr-Cetina, two opposing arguments can be made: Power is depicted as a macrophenomenon arising out of concrete social relationships. Here, power is truncated from interpersonal relationships and individuals' actions. Or, power is seen as something accomplished through the actions of individuals. Here, power is isolated from concrete institutional arrangements. We suggest, by contrast, that power is both a micro- and macrophenomenon. If one were to break the law, get arrested, be tried and sentenced, the power of police, law enforcement agencies, and the courts would be both interactional and institutional. Although aspects of this power would reside in micro episodes of social action, the reality of power could not be captured totally in these micro-scenes. Power is more than a summary representation. It is a political reality realized and reflected in social actions which in turn often help to support the status quo.

The statement that the macro resides within micro-episodes, established by people's actions, leads to a possible conclusion that individuals control their activities abstracted from concrete social reality. A "blame the victim" ideology, useful to maintaining status relationships is the logical conclusion of this view. Once again we do not mean to imply that human beings are passive robots moving solely to society's song; but neither are they free agents. To borrow from Marx, individuals make their own society and history, but not just as they please.

Unlike the micro-focused hypotheses posed by Knorr-Cetina and the macro-based theories of Habermas, Fisher (forthcoming) suggests a contextual web as a heuristic device for reintegrating language with context, social structure with social interaction. Picture communication between the participants of medical, legal, or educational events at the center of this web. However, since neither medical interviews, classroom lessons, nor courtroom scenes occur in a vacuum, the web extends from these micro-episodes of interaction to the organizational, structural, and cultural contexts in which they occur and folds back again to shape interactions and communication.

We use this model, posing social interaction and social structure in a reflexive relationship in which each influences the other, and giving priority to neither level of analysis. However, we also agree in part with some of the recommendations from both micro- and macro-sociologies. With Knorr-Cetina we envision macro-influences reflected in micro-episodes of interaction, rather than conceptualizing the macro as a layer of reality on top of these interactional events. With Habermas we see social reality as rooted in an historical location in the political order. To do otherwise would leave us unable to address the continued existence of social inequalities or to suggest remedies. The persistence of inequalities and a widespread resistance to change speaks to a pattern of power and control that extends from interacting individuals through the institutions of medicine, education, and law, and on to the structural and cultural arrangements of society.

If the relationship between social structure and social interaction is reflexive, how do we conceptualize social change? Again, we draw on some of the insights of macro- and micro-sociologies. We agree with macro-theorists who see the hierarchical arrangements of society mirrored in the organizational structure of institutions (see, for example, Navarro, 1976) and recapitulated in language (see, for example, Henley, 1977). We concur with the micro-theorists who display how individuals acting in concert accomplish events, producing social reality in the process.

Drawing from the strengths of both perspectives we, nevertheless, recognize the difficulties of mapping macro-issues with micro-episodes. Again, examples may clarify. Scully (1980) talks about how poor women are used as teaching material by doctors-in-training, and Todd (1983) and Fisher (1983) display conversational strategies used by medical professionals to control and persuade women patients interactionally. The empirical evidence speaks eloquently of inequities. Anyone who has spent any time in an outpatient clinic, has little doubt that the practical problems of a teaching hospital influence residents to impose treatments on patients who are less powerful, in these cases women, for the learning experience such treatments provide. Yet, while many sociologists have argued that the structure of our medical system and our society demand ''teaching material'' for residents to learn on and provides that material in the form of less powerful citizens, it is difficult to directly map these more structural observations onto the empirical data.

It would be almost impossible to document that the structural inequalities of class and/or gender *cause* a particular recommendation. It is not our intention to make such linear, causal arguments. We are suggesting, instead, a contextual, hermeneutic mode of analysis in which causality resides in a dynamic, reflexive process.

Taking micro-episodes of interaction as the starting point, Duster (1981) outlines just such a reflexive analysis. He suggests that a composite of micro-episodes can extend our understanding of social life. He proposes a picture made up of multi-levels of data as a way to bridge micro and macro. Using the metaphor of the ladder, he specifies the rungs necessary to complete a broader view of society than is usually envisioned in any one research project. His research suggestions include law, lobbying, and government; administration and organization; and interaction and community—all grounded in historical context. This is a rather large order. Collective work or the combination of studies across settings, perspectives, and methodologies are required to create a broader vision than single efforts can provide. As Duster points out, however, academia is firmly entrenched in the age of specialization—a specialization maintained by institutional stratification. Paths to publication, status in professional hierarchies, and achievement in the discipline are produced and constrained by adherence to particular individualistic ideologies and practices.

Despite these constraints, insights can be drawn from combining the work of disparate scholars to create a more complete collage than any one alone offers. The articles in this book move in the direction suggested by Duster.

PLAN OF THE BOOK

A collage is assembled one piece at a time. Our interest in this project is to further develop the piece that connects institutional authority with discourse. It is by no means a finished picture, but rather what we hope will be a contribution to a long line of scholarly debate. The book is divided into three sections, each one taking as its topic of inquiry a specific institution: medicine, education, and law. Although the articles all discuss discourse in institutional settings, they represent empirical research from several disciplines: anthropology, sociology, linguistics, philosophy, education, and medicine.

Each of the papers in the medical section addresses the relationship between discourse and institutional authority differently. The articles by Fisher and Todd, Borges, and Burgess draw from a critical perspective in sociology to argue that the institution of medicine recapitulates the hierarchical structure of society and, in so doing, provides an ideal microcosm for study.

Fisher and Todd display how the institution of medicine lends doctors power which is traditionally denied to patients. Doctors not only have technical knowledge and medical skill which patients lack, but they have the authority to use their privileged position to persuade. Fisher and Todd analyze how the institutional authority of the medical role is used to persuade women to use oral contraceptives whether it is in the patients' best interests or not.

Where for Fisher and Todd the medical interview primarily reflects institutional authority, for Borges the emphasis is on connections between the structure of a capitalist economic system and medical discourse. In her in-depth analysis of two medical interviews, one doctor emphasizes work place needs over the patient's concerns while another dismisses a housewife's malaise with a patronizing psychotropic prescription.

In a paper which unites a philosophical and a sociological perspective, Burgess illuminates how the use of institutional authority—the power to persuade—places patients at risk even in the management of routine medical matters. He argues for informed consent procedures even in such routine cases.

The next two papers extend the domain of what is conventionally considered medicine to discuss how the medical model extends to the dentist's office and a crisis hot line. Anderson argues that dentists, like doctors, have an idea about how patients ought to behave and that dentist-patient conversations are oriented toward converting patients to this belief while simultaneously convincing them that *this* dentist is the one to whom the patient should be coming for dental care.

Watson claims that crisis intervention centers, even if their staff is voluntary rather than professional, reflect psychiatric and medical conceptions. The difference in status and power between the staff at such centers and the callers is reflected in the discourse. Whereas the strength of the three former papers lies in connecting interactional episodes with more structural concerns, the strength of the last two papers lies in displaying the interactional accomplishment of the professional role.

In the section on education, McDermott and Tylbor's discussion of classroom conversations raises the issue of power explicitly. They ask how analysts can find power in talk and suggest that the locus of the search be shifted. Rather than asking *who* has power, we should ask how institutions offer *access* to various kinds of power—an offering that is reflected in discourse and which often functions to sustain an institutional stratification. Such an analysis, they argue, has the potential to illuminate the institutional constraints on communicative activities as well as to highlight what people have arranged not to talk about. This focus is continued in the next three papers.

Mehan and Hertweck, respectively, have drawn their papers from the same research project, yet their analyses are quite different. Mehan discusses decision making in committees deciding on whether to keep students in their regular classrooms or to place them into special education programs. His focus is on the role linguistic processes play in this activity. He finds a paradox within these meetings: the more professional the report and the more obscure and incomprehensible the language, the more likely recommendations are to be accepted without question rather than debated. Thus, professionals' (psychologists and nurses) contributions take precedence over teachers' and parents' contributions, establishing an inverse relationship between proximity to the student and power in the decision-making process.

Hertweck, examining the same materials, draws on attribution theory to point out the process whereby students are referred out of the classroom and placed in special sections. Her findings show a disparity between students' performance and school personnel's attributions. In the referral process, attributions take priority over performance.

In McHoul's paper the analysis shifts from an interactional analysis of discourse to a discourse analysis of policy documents. His analysis illuminates how difficult it is to create a policy which addresses sexism in schooling. McHoul shows how the very language used to transform, incorporate, and neutralize feminist discourse produces an effectively conservative document reinforcing status quo policies.

The section on law addresses the way this institution lends its dominant actors power. Those defined by the court as questioners—lawyers or judges—wield considerable power over the answerers—witnesses and defendants. Court reporters recognize distinctions in power and status as they differentially apply the rule of verbatim. Walker argues that the language of those with status gets "cleaned up" more auspiciously than does the language of those with less status. As Philips points out, courtrooms are also spatially arranged in ways that embody differences in status and power. The judge sits above the court, the jury at the side—an arrangement that influences the legal process.

The article by Shuy discusses how language itself can be used to serve legal ends. The FBI covertly collected audiotapes, an activity that would for others be considered at worst illegal, and, as Shuy points out, at best unethical. Shuy was hired by the defense to use these tapes—gathered by the FBI to make a case for the prosecution—to build a case for the defendants. At least implicitly, all involved in this trial recognized the power of language, and the strength of a discourse-based analysis.

Although all of the articles in this book contribute to the building of a link between micro and macro, language and context, discourse and institutions, they do so differently. It is these differences that provide what we hope will be a valuable source of insight for further study, moving us toward a richer mosaic of social life.

REFERENCES

Cicourel, A. V. (1981). Notes on the integration of micro- and macro-levels of analyses. In K. Knorr-Cetina & A. V. Cicourel (Eds.), *Advances in social theory and methodology: Toward an integration of micro- and macro-sociologies.* Boston: Routledge & Kegan Paul.

Collins, R. (1981). Micro-translation as a theory-building strategy. In K. Knorr-Cetina and A. V. Cicourel (Eds.), *Advances in social theory and methodology: Toward an integration of micro- and macro-sociologies.* Boston: Routledge & Kegan Paul.

Duster, T. (1981). Intermediate steps between micro- and macro-integration: The case of screening for inherited disorders. In K. Knorr-Cetina & A. V. Cicourel (Eds.), *Advances in social theory and methodology: Toward an integration of micro- and macro-sociologies.* Boston: Routledge & Kegan Paul.

Fisher, S. (1983). Doctor talk/patient talk: How treatment decisions are negotiated in doctor/patient communication. In Sue Fisher and Alexandra Todd (Eds.), *The social organization of doctor-patient communication.* Washington, DC: The Center for Applied Linguistics/Harcourt Brace Jovanovich.

Fisher, S. (forthcoming). *In the patient's best interest.* New Brunswick, NJ: Rutgers University Press.

Garfinkel, H. (1967). *Studies in ethnomethodology.* Englewood Cliffs, NJ: Prentice-Hall.

Giddens, A. (1981). Agency, Institution and Time-Space Analyses. In K. Knorr-Cetina & A. V. Cicourel (Eds.). *Advances in social theory and methodology: Toward an integration of micro- and macro-sociologies.* Boston: Routledge & Kegan Paul.

Habermas, J. (1970). Toward a theory of communicative competence. In Hans Peter Dreitzel (Ed.). *Recent sociology no. 2: Patterns of communication.* New York: Macmillan.

Habermas, J. (1981). Toward a reconstruction of historical materialism. In K. Knorr-Cetina and A. V. Cicourel (Eds.), *Advances in social theory and methodology: Toward an integration of micro- and macro-sociologies.* Boston: Routledge & Kegan Paul.

Harre, R. (1981). Philosophical aspects of the micro-macro problem. In K. Knorr-Cetina & A. V. Cicourel (Eds.), *Advances in social theory and methodology: Toward an integration of micro- and macro-sociologies* (pp. 139–160). Boston: Routledge & Kegan Paul.

Henley, N. (1977). *Body politics: Power, sex, and nonverbal communication.* Englewood Cliffs, NJ: Prentice-Hall.

Knorr-Cetina, K. (1981). The micro-sociological challenge of macro-sociology: Toward a reconstruction of theory and method. In K. Knorr-Cetina & A. V. Cicourel (Eds.), *Advances in social theory and methodology: Toward an integration of micro- and macro-sociologies.* Boston: Routledge & Kegan Paul.

Navarro, V. (1976). *Medicine under capitalism.* New York: Prodist.

Scully, D. (1980). *Men who control women's health.* Boston: Houghton Mifflin.

Todd, A. D. (1984). A diagnosis of doctor-patient discourse in the prescription of contraception. In

Sue Fisher and Alexandra Todd (Eds.), *The social organization of doctor-patient communication*. Washington, DC: The Center for Applied Linguistics/Harcourt Brace Jovanovich.

Zimmerman, D. H., & C. West, (1975). Sex roles, interruptions and silences in conversation. In Barrie Thorne & Nancy Henley (Eds.), *Language and sex: Difference and dominance*. Rowley, MA: Newbury House.

Part I
Medicine

1. Friendly Persuasion: Negotiating Decisions to Use Oral Contraceptives*

Sue Fisher
Wesleyan University
Middletown, CT

Alexandra Dundas Todd
Suffolk University, Boston

Recently Semantha, an 18-year-old, middle-class, female student told the following tale. She had just become sexually active and—not wanting to get pregnant—she decided to find out more about birth control. She made an appointment at the student health center on campus to attend a twenty-minute presentation about the available birth control methods. After carefully considering her options, she decided the diaphragm best met her needs. Her sexual activity was infrequent; therefore, she felt that the risks inherent in the other methods of birth control were not justified. With this decision reached, she made an appointment for her first gynecological examination. After her appointment, she reported the following conversation.

Semantha told the doctor that she had decided on the diaphragm, and he told her that he discourages girls from using them. He described the diaphragm as not as effective as the pill and told her that girls today find it old-fashioned. She was not convinced and said that she was afraid of the pill, having heard so many stories about its negative side effects. The doctor claimed that the media has given the pill a bad press and proceeded to persuade her. He said that the majority of users find the pill a very satisfactory method of contraception and suffer no side effects. Semantha was still not convinced. She told the doctor that she didn't feel she needed such a constant method of birth control. He responded by telling her it is better to be safe at all times. She capitulated and left the clinic with a three-month supply of low-estrogen birth control pills.

Semantha's experience is one example of the numerous tales we have heard and interactions we have observed. Our research suggests that persuasion is more the rule than the exception in the delivery of health care. For doctors, persuasion is often seen as part of the job they have to do. It is their responsibility to insure medical care that is in the patient's best interest. Since patients live in the same

* We would like to thank William Corsaro, Donna Eder, and Hugh Mehan, for their helpful comments on this paper.

3

social world and frequently share a reciprocal view of the appropriate roles for doctors and patients, it is not too surprising that patients often concur.

This is the functional relationship described by Parsons (1951) as benefitting both doctor and patient. The reciprocal benefit of the doctor-patient relationship has been challenged, however, by patients as well as by those studying the delivery of health care (Waitzken & Waterman, 1974; Freidson, 1970). More specifically, those in the women's health movement have argued that doctors' use of persuasion, while friendly, may not be in women's best interests.

THE CONTEXT OF PERSUASION

The moral, political, and economic context for the prescription of contraception can best be understood when placed against the background history of the development of the medical profession. The growth of a predominantly male medical profession during the nineteenth century was closely tied to a redefinition of women's reproduction (Barker-Benfield, 1976; Gordon, 1976). Prior to the nineteenth century, reproduction was seen as a natural process. Women midwives attended and supported but rarely intervened in the birth process. The regular doctors of that time were urban-based members of the upper classes who were competing for legitimacy and financial resources. To gain income and status, physicians redefined themselves as male midwives, promulgated a view of female midwives as dirty and ignorant, birth as dangerous and in need of medical intervention and management, and women as sickly, irrational individuals always at the mercy of their reproductive organs and in need of medical ministrations (Wertz and Wertz, 1981; Ehrenreich & English, 1978; Gordon, 1976). As Conrad and Kern (1981) point out, this view of women served a dual function—it made women incapable of providing medical care or getting a medical education while at the same time converting them into an ideal population of patients.

The consolidation of a predominantly male medical profession was more the result of power and privilege than the development of medical expertise.[1] The professional monopoly of regular doctors was enriched by its ties to the monies of the newly formed foundations (e.g., Carnegie) as well as to state and government bodies—ties cemented in class and gender interests (Ehrenreich & English, 1978; Stevens, 1971). These ties—when combined with an erroneous and demeaning conception of women and a mood of social reform—shaped the medical

---

[1] The neophyte medical profession would have been hard-pressed to demonstrate its skill. Medical knowledge and technique at the time was limited and often dangerous. While today the medical profession is heralded with having improved the health of the population and especially with controlling infectious disease, others (see Dubos, 1959) argue that these improvements preceded medical advances and were the result of social reforms—for example, better sanitation and nutrition as well as a rising standard of living. Nevertheless such discoveries as smallpox and polio vaccines do give modern medicine a basis for asserting its skills—skills that nineteenth century doctors did not have.

profession. As Friedson (1970) suggests, one of the organizing features of the profession of medicine is its autonomy. Autonomy combines with a professional monopoly and state support to give physicians top position in the medical hierarchy. Physicians have state-supported control over every aspect of their training and practice. They monitor the education, licensure, and conduct of their fellow practitioners. By so doing they have nearly total control in determining health care practices and policies. The consumer often has little voice. In more recent years the power of the American Medical Association (AMA) has been replaced by what Ehrenreich and Ehrenreich (1970) call the "medical industrial complex"—the tremendously profitable corporations that produce drugs and medical supplies, the hospitals, insurance and nursing home industries, as well as the medical profession.

This health care system is oriented toward technological cure for acute disease. The medical model is organized to treat dysfunctional body parts. Women seeking reproductive control do not fit easily into this model. Contraception is a preventive measure, not an acute or chronic disease. Once in the medical system, a biomedical framework is laid on. Women are encouraged to manage a situation that is psychosocial and biological in nature within a technological model. This technical fix for a social problem engenders a conflict, one which has the potential to have an enormous impact on women's lives, for contraception use can be closely tied to women's sexuality and family relationships, as well as other moral, political, and economic issues (Todd, 1982; Luker, 1975).

Those who are reaping the benefits from the system as it is currently organized are hesitant to see it change. Their vested interests and financial resources support powerful legislative lobbies which have been successful in resisting and limiting change while maintaining the status quo—a health care system largely under the control of a predominantly male AMA and medical corporate establishment. The male medical profession continues to function as an agent of social control using definitions of health and illness (Friedson, 1970), prescriptions for drugs and contraception (Todd 1983; Prather & Fidell, 1975), and recommendations for reproductive surgery (Fisher, 1982; Morgan, 1978) to promote and maintain the "proper" roles for women. This is not the brute control by the police enforced with guns and jail, but rather the much more subtle control by knowledge and skill, supported by institutional authority and used to persuade (Fisher, 1983). Since this control is exercised in the name of alleviating hurt and promoting health it is all the more difficult to perceive. While there have been some changes, women are still underrepresented in the medical profession, overrepresented as medical consumers, and dominated by predominantly male physicians (Fisher, 1983; Todd, 1983; Scully, 1980; Ehrenreich & English, 1978; Ruzek, 1978; Corea, 1977; Scully & Bart, 1973).

The organization of the health care system is reflected in medical interactions which are social and, borrowing a phrase (Henley, 1977; Waitzkin & Stoeckle,

1976), micropolitical. They reflect and sustain larger cultural, structural, and institutional factors and, in turn, are shaped by them. While medical decisions are interactional accomplishments, the interactants—medical practitioners and patients—are not equal partners in the decision-making process. Doctors have medical knowledge and technical skill which patients lack. By virtue of their institutional authority they have the ability to act as gatekeepers controlling patients' access to and understanding of contraceptive information.

In this paper we examine doctor-patient communication during the medical interactions through which decisions about contraception are reached, and we discuss how these interactions are characterized by a style we call friendly persuasion. We analyze how this style is social and micropolitical—how it is accomplished through communication during face-to-face interaction and how the authority of the doctor's role and gender stereotyping combine, contributing to the decision to prescribe birth control pills even when they may not be in patients' best interests. Since it is our purpose to display the intricacies of how contraceptive decisions are accomplished, we use a case study method analyzing three cases in depth.[2] Based on our research, women persuaded to use birth control pills fall into three categories: new users, continuing users claiming side effects described in the medical literature as "nuisance" problems, and continuing users with medical problems acknowledged as potential contraindications for continued use.[3] We chose an illustrative case from each of the categories in which persuasion was likely to occur.

THE RESEARCH CONTEXT

The data for this paper were gathered in five settings in two disparate geographical regions across a combined period of six years. While we did not work collectively, our observations and data-gathering techniques were grounded in the commitment to study a language event systematically, in this case medical interviews. In addition, our research had a similar focus. We were both interested in women's health care. While there is much written about the politics of health care for women (see, for example, Scully, 1980; Ehrenreich & English, 1978; Ruzek, 1978; Corea, 1977; Dreifus, 1977), the actual discourse which expresses and maintains the doctor's authority has received much less attention

---

[2] We neither provide nor seek statistical relevance in this paper. We present and analyze discourse between medical practitioners and patients. It is our contention that the kind of data, analyses, and findings in this paper contribute toward a preliminary examination of connections between macro-systems and micro-communication (see also Knorr-Cetina and Cicourel, 1981, for a more complete discussion of this point).

[3] Logically, there is a fourth category: continuing users showing no adverse side effects. While it is obvious that such patients exist, their medical interactions were not the topic under discussion in this paper. Such interactions were not characterized by a continued discussion of birth control methods. A choice had been made at an earlier time and if it involved persuasion, we were not in the examining room to observe it.

(see Fisher, 1982, 1983; Todd, 1982, 1983; West, 1982; Silverman, 1981; Strong, 1979).

Doctor-patient discourse was recorded on audio and video tapes and transcribed for later analysis. We analyzed eighty-four transcripts of medical interviews, blending taped discourse with more impressionistic ethnographic data. It seems reasonable that neither practitioners nor patients say aloud all that contributes to the medical interview process. For example, patients rarely say aloud that they do not trust their medical practitioners or that they feel unheard, manipulated, and dissatisfied with the medical care they have received. Similarly, neither private physicians, staff doctors, nor residents say aloud that patients look like poor women or talk like uneducated women. They do not say that the way patients talk, act, or dress leads them to believe that patients are not responsible and influences treatment recommendations. Practitioners do not usually say aloud to a patient that she is not smart enough to use a diaphragm. Yet while not said aloud, our observations and interviews with doctors and patients suggest that these factors, and a host of similar ones, contribute to the diagnostic-treatment process (see Fisher, forthcoming; Todd, 1982).

One of the main benefits of ethnographic research is derived from the time spent in the field. While we were sociologists in medical settings to gather data, we neither began to gather data immediately nor occupied all of our time taping. We spent time talking informally with various staff members asking questions about values, attitudes, and practices. We spent time watching interactions and overhearing conversations, as well as consultations. We spent time participating in the functioning of a clinic and a residency training program. This time provided a sense of the social world and made us privy to the beliefs and practices of the participants. But perhaps most importantly it provided a richer background from which to interpret the data.[4]

We observed highly trained specialists—a physician in the private practice of obstetrics and gynecology, staff physicians and residents in the department of reproductive medicine and the specialty of gynecologic oncology (cancer of the reproductive system), and residents in a model family practice clinic. We observed residents in teaching hospitals—where they were under the supervision of attending staff physicians—and in a community health clinic—where they were hired by the hour from nearby hospitals to staff the women's clinic. The medical providers were gynecologists, oncologists (cancer specialists), and family practice providers who were prescribing birth control. They told their patients and reported to us that they considered the birth control pill the most efficient method

---

[4] While our interpretation is perhaps only one of the many that are possible, it is nevertheless grounded in a way that others cannot be. It is grounded in our experience in the settings under study, backed by audio and video tapes available for study. Corsaro (1982) does an excellent job of reviewing the pros and cons of AV recording, stressing the need for additional ethnographic data to provide a broad enough picture for sociological inquiry.

of contraception available. Their opinions are consistent with general prescription patterns in the United States. Next to sterilization the birth control pill is the major interventionary form of contraception used in the United States today.

In our data—regardless of the setting, who the practitioners were, what they were doing, or how they were paid—the diagnostic-treatment process was characterized by friendly persuasion. We have identified three interrelated persuasive patterns that cut across our data and are exemplified in the cases to be presented. These patterns include the selective use of science, the selective presentation of information, and the selective use of authority. They are the interactional mechanisms which function to produce decisions about birth control.

Scientific information provides medical practitioners with a double-edged sword. On the one hand, it supports the institutional authority of medical providers and legitimizes their presentation of contraceptive information. On the other hand, scientific findings can be ignored to make a case for one method over another. Scientific information is used selectively in another way as well. When used in the service of the doctor, it reinforces authority. When used by the patient, it is overwhelmingly dismissed as a media scare tactic.

In the cases to be discussed, the selective presentation of information takes several forms: a systematic downplaying of the negative side effects of the pill, deleting contraceptive options from some discussions while coloring the presentation of contraceptive options in other discussions.

The selective use of authority is harder to see. Patients rely on medical practitioners as authorities and medical providers act like authorities. Since none of these patients came to the clinic certain that they wanted a prescription for the birth control pill, the reliance on and use of authority functions to persuade.

It becomes apparent in the analysis which follows how these strategies interweave across the flow of the medical event producing contraceptive decisions and placing patients in a double bind. While medical literature documents many potential health hazards with both the pill and the IUD (intrauterine device), doctors in our data systematically pushed for the pill and against the IUD, while ignoring or downplaying all other contraceptive methods. If doctors give information using their directive power to persuade or withhold vital information, the consequences for patients are often similar. Patients are systematically denied the information they need to participate actively in the contraceptive decision, yet this decision making has the potential to affect their lives. This process can be seen in the first case.

THE NEW USER

Ms. S is a quiet-spoken, shy Anglo woman dressed in a conservative, middle-class style. She is 23, unmarried, and has only recently become sexually active. While her stated reason for coming to the family practice clinic is for a Pap smear and a pelvic examination (her first), it quickly becomes apparent that her motivation for coming to the clinic includes a prescription for birth control. During the opening phase of the medical interview the patient brings up the topic of birth control and toward the end of the medical history phase she returns to it.

Patient: Would you be able to prescribe an oral contraceptive for me, since you don't know my family history?

Doctor: Well, I was going to talk to you about that. See, you want a birth control pill for birth control?

Patient: Uh huh.

Doctor: Alright, well we ought to talk a little bit about all the different types of birth control and I could tell you about some of the side effects and what are the good effects. First of all, do you want children?

Patient: Yes.

The doctor begins with a discussion of the birth control pill.

Doctor: OK, well, let's go through them all. There is birth control pills which is a little bit over 99 percent effective. Which is pretty good odds. If you take them right and don't miss your pills you are going to be in pretty good shape. Uhm, and of course everybody, everybody uses birth control pills. But as you know, anybody that reads the paper knows, that there are some side effects from them. The short-term side effects, the biggest one that everybody worries about is the likelihood of blood clots. It's very uncommon, l haven't myself seen one. I haven't had a patient to have it but, of course, everybody knows somebody who's had a patient who's had a blood clot while they were on it and it usually forms in the legs and the reason it's bad is 'cause sometimes it can get into your lungs, cause that kind of problem we see in girls that smoke.

Patient: Uh uh (shakes head no).

After establishing that the patient does not smoke and is not overweight, the resident continues by discussing the side effects of the pill.

Doctor: . . . The short-term studies look pretty good but//[5]

Patient: //what are the short-term studies? How long does it run? five years?

Doctor: Five- or ten-year studies. You know, uh, the, I think the cancer that everybody worries is the endometrial cancer. Not necessarily cervical cancer . . . it doesn't appear to be related. Now if you told me your mama had cancer of the womb and my aunt had breast cancer, and my grandmother died of female cancer, then maybe we should talk a little bit more. But that sounds like cancer runs in the family. It doesn't sound like uh, you have any, you know, predisposing uh factors with cancer, so you know I think we can feel safe on birth control pills. So they're, they're 99 percent effective and all side effects short term, but there are a lot of little nuisance problems, some ladies have that we

---

[5] Double slash marks (//) are used to indicate simultaneous speech overlaps or interruptions.

can blame on birth control pills. Some ladies seems to have headaches, uh, that never had headaches before. Uh, but I'm talking about this as what has been recorded and this is not you, not just going on birth control pills and gets headaches.// (*Patient:* //uh huh.) Uh, that's happened that some ladies get skin rashes. Uh, some ladies complain that they feel different on these, you're in a worse mood. Uh, I guess that's probably the three biggest complaints that there are.

Patient: Are those short-term, are you just suggesting to me what they are?

Doctor: Yeah, usually if you just ride it out in that short term, that means that some ladies get . . . short term headaches, . . . headaches are so common and so many people have them, it is hard to say whether or not birth control pills uh, cause, I mean, if you never had a headache and two weeks after you started taking the pill, you get a horrible headache, we got some (headaches) that the birth control pills start and I think if you uh, hang in there a little bit they will go away, and sometimes we can adjust the medication in the pills, try a new one and it doesn't cause them. And we can do the same thing with the other little problems ladies get// (*Patient:* //Um hum.) and I think every complaint that has ever come up has been blamed, at one time or another on the birth control pills, so we just hang in there, but most ladies that I prescribe birth control pills for, they, they take them and they go away and they never have problems/(*Patient:* Uh hum.) One thing I will tell you is really not a long-term problem, it's sometimes a short-term problem. When you decide, I want a child, I think its good to get off of them six months before you wanna start trying because there's such a thing called post-pill amenorrhea. Which means after you quit the pill there will be several months interval in some ladies where they don't have a period.

At this point the doctor goes into quite a lengthy explanation about how birth control pills work and what happens physiologically when the patient goes off of them. He then moves on to the next type of birth control, the IUD (intrauterine device):

Doctor: The other type of birth control is the IUD. Now what that is is a little coil that we put inside of the uterus and . . . uh, we're not sure exactly how they work . . . but they are pretty effective, about 99 percent effective. Now, but, I don't recommend them for anybody that's never had a baby. Their side effect is that they occasionally cause a pelvic infection which can get into your tubes and cause scarring and infertility. So I never recommend it for someone who definitely wants children, too much risk, and I won't use it. Some doctors may use it, but I don't not on// (*Patient:* //when) not on you, someone who wants babies. Now if you had three children and don't want two more, I think it is pretty well worth the risk.

The doctor moves on to a discussion of barrier methods of birth control (the diaphragm and condom).

Doctor: OK, now you are down to diaphragms. Diaphragms are reported to be anywhere from 85 percent to 95 percent effective and what it is, it's a rubber shield that you put over your cervix. You slip it in before intercourse. It's kinda like a guy wearing a condom. Here what you're doing is blocking the pathway of the sperm way to the cervix. You're keeping it on the outside and keeping the egg and the womb on the inside and also you put a little jelly on it that's fairly effective. When somebody is intelligent and that would take time in putting it in. A lot of people won't take the time to put it in, so if it's not in, it's in the drawer next to the bed, it doesn't work, so that's a reasonable form of birth control. Now the birth control pill is safer uhm, and of course you've got condoms, which are very effective as long as they are intact. They are effective, there's no way, uh, just according to your feelings are toward them// (*Patient:* //Uh hum.) If it's, intercourse, is just as pleasuarable for you and your mate well there's no reason not to use it. It's safe as long as you're sure there's not a hole in it.// (*Patient:* //Uh hum.)

And finally he discusses over-the-counter birth control remedies.

Doctor: OK, and then there's foams and jellies and uh they are anywhere from 70 to 85 percent maybe. I don't think they are as high as 85 and there are a lot of failure rate on foams and jellies. So I don't recommend them to anybody// (*Patient:* //uh hum.) I mean if your playing with fire, you might get pregnant before long, but eventually I think, I think it will catch up with you. Uh, o.k., so that's it.

Patient: OK, let me ask you this, it's kind a personal question, if your wife had to use a form of birth control what would you give her? What would you recommend?

Doctor: Well my wife, we uh, have used birth control pills in the past, but she doesn't use them now. We have a child, and we want some more. We use a diaphragm. It has been very effective for us// (*Patient:* //Um hum.) and its no side effects, and if she got pregnant accidentally it wouldn't be any great problem, because we want some more children// (*Patient:* //Um hum.) but then I have one couple uh, whose wife has caesarians and the physician feels that there's no way that she should have another child . . . and she has used a diaphragm for 30 years and she is still fertile . . . and I feel safe using that. You know I never had a lady get pregnant on the diaphragm, course I don't have 1000 patients with a diaphragm// (*Patient:* //Um hum.) but as far as I know no one's come back pregnant// (*Patient:* //Um hum.) But you know, for a short period, I don't see anything wrong with the birth control pills. I don't like them but I don't hate them. Uh, its a hard decision to make. You know that there are a lot of birth control methods around, but they all have their drawbacks. There's not a perfect birth control yet. Well when you decide not to have any more children you are, yours could have your tubes cut, either a vasectomy or have a tubal ligation for you// (*Patient:* //Um hum.) that's nice// (*Patient:* //Would take care of it.) it sure does, but you're really gonna have to be the one to make your decision on that// (*Patient:* //Um hum.) You plan to get married soon, or . . .[6]

Patient: Uh huh// (*Doctor:* //OK) it wouldn't be until I get out of school which should be next summer.

Doctor: Well, what would be perfectly acceptable for me, if I wuz in your shoes, is to be on the birth control pill until next summer for sure, and, uh, that time see how you did on them and if you don't like them you know you can always switch over to a diaphragm or he can switch over to a condom.

Ms. S wants information about birth control. Early in the medical interview she brings up the topic and while the resident is taking her medical history, she returns to it. In response to her questions the resident provides quite a detailed description of the available contraceptive methods. Since she exhibits none of the medically accepted cautions for avoiding the birth control pill—she is under age 35, there is no family history of cancer, she does not smoke, and she is not obese—she leaves with a prescription for oral contraception (the pill.)

Ms. S's interest in contraception coupled with her desire to avoid an unwanted pregnancy is evident in the transcript. Thus, at first glance, the decision reached has qualities of an interactional accomplishment jointly produced by doctor and patient. But while Ms. S, and patients in general, do have some input into the decision-making process, it is the doctor who has the authority to persuade. We have included large segments of this transcript to display the persuasive way language is used to influence the patient to choose this method of contraception—persuasive strategies which we have observed frequently in our research. Information is presented selectively. The IUD is efficient but risky—infection and infertility are possible outcomes. A diaphragm is all right if you are intelligent and it is inserted properly, the condom is okay if it is intact, and foams and jellies are not recommended. The doctor explains that foams and jellies are not as safe (in preventing pregnancy) as the birth control pill.

Scientific information is used selectively. Despite several noted risks the birth control pill is advised. When the birth control pill is pushed, the more negative aspects of its use are systematically downplayed. Blood clots and endometrial and breast cancer are all called "short-term side effects" and their dangers are qualified. Blood clots are declared uncommon. And, while the evidence is not in yet, endometrial cancer and breast cancer are said not to appear to be related to pill use.[7]

---

[6] A series of dots (. . .) are used to indicate that the speakers voice is trailing off, providing juncture into which the next speaker may insert an utterance.

[7] If the doctor had favored the IUD, we believe we would have observed reverse persuasion

The selective use of authority, while running through the transcripts, becomes more evident as the resident qualifies the major contraindications for taking the birth control pill, and dismisses the minor ones as "nuisance problems." These problems include headaches, mood changes, and skin rashes. He tells the patient that if these nuisances appear, all she has to do is "hang in there a little bit, they will go away." He further implies that women often blame problems on the birth control pill when other sources are the culprit. However, studies have shown that these "nuisance problems" can be serious contraindications for taking the pill (see Seaman & Seaman, 1977). Further, when patients come back to doctors with problems they associate with the pill, medical providers can blame the patients, not the pill, for the problems.

Toward the end of the presentation of information about birth control methods, Ms. S asks for a recommendation. It is here that the selective use of authority is clearest. She asks: "If your wife had to use a form of birth control, what would you give her?" In response, the resident recommends birth control pills and grounds that recommendation in the patient's status as an unmarried woman who cannot risk pregnancy. This recommendation provides an example of how the doctor, while providing information, also expresses more subtle assumptions about women, family arrangements, childbearing, and birth control.

THE CONTINUED USER: NUISANCE PROBLEMS

In the second case, as in the first, the doctor's presentation of information about birth control methods moves the patient toward birth control pills. However, this patient is somewhat different than the last. She is not a first-time user of contraception coming to the doctor to learn about the available methods. Rather she has taken birth control pills for five consecutive years, has vague complaints but no strong medically accepted indications for discontinuing them, and has come to the clinic to investigate alternative contraceptive methods.

A gynecological resident hired by a community clinic is talking with the patient, Ms. D, in the examining room. She is a low-income, 22-year-old, Anglo woman who is dressed in a skirt and blouse. She has never married, never been pregnant, and has given no information in this interview as to how she envisions her future reproductive life. While her birth control pill history has been uneventful, she presently feels a growing dissatisfaction with this method. Recently she has been vaguely uncomfortable. She has occasional headaches and feels "bloated" much of the time. Her concern is that oral contraceptives can have a cumulative effect on the body. She thinks a break from this method would be advisable and is potentially interested in the IUD but knows little about it. In her first question to the doctor she asks:

---

concerning the pill and the IUD. Our point here is that doctors selectively use scienific information to persuade.

Patient: What about the IUD? I'm really interested in um changing . . .

Doctor: I, I have a very negative opinion of the IUD, particularly for young women who haven't had their family yet, because if//

Patient: //Um, they give it to girls who have abortions and miscarriages. Why, why is that?

Doctor: I think that's just because it's, the, the women don't feel that they could take the pill, and it's some, it's some form of birth control, at least. For women who just can't remember to take the pill or won't, that need protection, then the IUD is some you know, is second best. But you're really taking a big chance of infection. We're seeing at least I'd say five in a hundred IUDs that we put in are coming back with some, some sort of infection, often not serious, but it can be very serious. It can mean hospitalization and antibiotics into your veins, and some of them even have their organs operated on or removed because they get so infected, it can even result in death, then, you know, so it's, again, a remote possibility the same as blood clots are with birth control pills, although it's not as remote as that. It happens, it really, you know, much more frequently. Uhm, I think the scariest thing, even if, you know, you don't get an overwhelming infection, with the IUD is that we don't know what we, what your future fertility would be like. The IUD works by causing a little infection inside your uterus and it can climb up inside the tubes and it may destroy the normal structure of the tubes enough so that the egg, which is very small, and the tube, which is also very small, don't fit, and they can get hung up. There's a// (*Patient:* //I see.) higher incidence of ectopic pregnancy, tubal pregnancies, when the egg stops in the tube and then tries to grow into a baby there, with women who've had IUDs. So I, I really think, unless you're really adamant and you, you're willing to take all those chances, I really wouldn't tend, wouldn't recommend it.// (*Patient:* //Oh, I see.) So it sounds like maybe the pill really is the right thing.

Patient: (laugh) Okay, that answers . . .

Doctor: Do, do your legs swell, is that part of your problem or do you just feel kinda bloated?

Patient: My, I don't know, my stomach just feels really, like it's out here, you know, very//

Doctor: //uh hum. Sometimes things get blamed on the pills that aren't always the pills' fault so, like// (*Patient:* // What?) women who say they gained weight because they're taking the pills when ordinarily they're expecting to gain weight, so maybe they eat a little bit more, and, uh, then they gain weight, and say, oh, look at the pill made me gain weight.

Patient: But it makes me hungry. When I'm not on the pill, I don't feel hungry.

Doctor: I've never heard that one before (laughs).

Ms. D, like Ms. S, wants information about her contraceptive options. Her question about the IUD triggers a response from the doctor which stresses a concern for her reproductive capacity while also reflecting how interactional mechanisms function to persuade. First, scientific information is used selectively. While the resident expresses concern about the IUD, there does not seem to be an equal concern about the birth control pill or the physical complaints the patient associates with taking them. Then information is presented selectively. After discussing the problems associated with the IUD, the pill is recommended with no discussion of the diaphragm, condom, foam, or jelly—all methods which are available in the clinic. Finally the selective use of authority is evidenced as the doctor's presentation makes it seem that Ms. D has two contraceptive choices—the IUD or the pill. Whatever the doctor's motives (a possible belief that it is in the patient's interest to continue using the birth control pill), medical authority has been used to persuade. Scientific information has been provided selectively—infections, hospitalization, surgery, and death are all possible effects of the IUD. While blood clots are presented as a remote problem with the pill, they are not dealt with in the same depth as were the side effects of the IUD. Further, the resident declares that while infection and death from the IUD are serious, the "scariest" outcome is infertility. By stressing infertility as the most serious possibility, the doctor[8] uses medical authority to reinforce a traditional assumption: young women center their life priorities around motherhood. By omitting detailed discussion of contraceptive options, by excusing the pill and blaming the patient, the case for the pill is made. The patient leaves with another prescription for birth control pills and a conviction that the problems she is experiencing with hunger and bloating are hers. If she could only diet more effectively, her problems would be relieved (see Todd, 1984).[9]

THE CONTINUED USER: MORE MAJOR PROBLEMS

In the third case, as in the first two, the doctor does not take an active role against the pill. This patient is different than the last two. She is neither a first-time user seeking contraceptive information nor does she have vague "nuisance problems" which she associates with birth control use. Rather, she is representative of the category of patients who have medically acknowledged risk factors which raise serious questions for remaining on the pill.

The patient, Ms. A, is a young, unmarried, sexually active VISTA worker. She is a gregarious Anglo woman dressed in jeans and an embroidered Mexican shirt. Her stated reason for coming to the model family practice clinic is that she needs a prescription for birth control pills. However, throughout the medical

---

[8] We have data on both doctors and residents interacting with patients. To minimize confusion in this section we use the term "resident" and "doctor" interchangeably.

[9] There is an interesting continuum between this case and the last. When discussing the side effects associated with the pill, contraindications are dismissed as "nuisance problems. . . ." In so doing the doctors displayed their attitudes about pill users and the pill.

interview she expresses her ambivalence about being on the pill, her knowledge of the scientific information about their side effects, and her concern over what she sees as potential contraindications for continuing to use them. In response to the doctor's opening question, the patient states her reason for coming to the clinic and voices her ambivalence about the birth control pill.

Doctor: Nice to meet you. What are you doing here?

Patient: . . . I'd like maybe to get a prescription for the pill. I'm on it now and I'm just about at the end of the month and ah I'm not sure I want to continue taking it but I do want a prescription for it.

Doctor: Ok, what alternatives do you have in mind if you don't continue taking the pill?

Patient: I don't know yet, that's why I'm probably going to take it.

Doctor: Do you think that//

Patient: //But I want to get a prescription, but I'm not sure if I want to keep taking it or not. I don't like taking 'em you know.

Doctor: Have you had any problems with it before?

Patient: No, I haven't had any problems.

While the patient claims not to have had any problems on the birth control pill, she discloses a concern—a possible contraindication for continuing on the pill.

Doctor: Well, are you having any other problems or things we need to direct our attention to today?

Patient: OK, there is another thing that has been weird. I don't know what's causing it. I've been getting these cramps in my legs. Once in a blue moon I'll get em, just out of the clear blue sky, and I always thought that on the pill there's a sort of relation, you need to know about that and smoking too, you know. But I was on the pill, I've only been on the pill for about five months.

Doctor: Never before that?

Patient: Yeah, I was off it. I was on it, I was off the pill for over two years.

Doctor: When did you start taking the pill?

Patient: I don't remember the year. I was on the pill for two years or so, I went off it a little more than two years and I just started again. Now I am usually in perfect and never feel a cramp in my body whatsoever, but I was about four weeks ago, or something like that I was in N, and I got the strangest, it won't go away, it was all the way up along in here and in my leg and it lasted all day, hurt like anything. It wouldn't do like this. It felt really tight. I didn't know if it was my circulation or my muscle and then last week the same thing happened on this leg. But it wasn't near so bad. It didn't last as long and like I worry so I don't like, but that's all there was just that weird cramping sensation in my leg.

Doctor: I worry too, ah cramps, muscle cramps are a reason or a caution like in birth control pills. Uhm, it's, ah, one thing that makes doctors think that maybe it shouldn't be taking birth control pills.

Patient: Um hum, well that's why I'm here, to check into that.

Doctor: And the fact that you smoke and take birth control pills increases your risk of cardiovascular disease// (*Patient:* //Um hum, I know that.) about ten times and you're skirting several risk factors. There you really have a backing on that. You're young and have a lot of reserve and all that sort of stuff. The longer you take oral contraception the more chance// (*Patient:* //uh hum) of some of the side effects and that happen to you ah, if there is a reasonable alternative to birth control pills for you, I would urge you to give it serious consideration.

Patient: I do really get bad cramps (menstrual) when I don't take the pill.

Doctor: When you don't take the pill?

Patient: When I don't take the pill. When I am on the pill everything is under control. No cramps whatsoever, a very light flow. It's nice and comfortable. When I'm off the pills it's like unusual cycles// (*Doctor:* //um hum) terrible cramps (menstrual).

Doctor: Which string of pills are you taking now?

Patient: Norlestrin or something, they call them.

Doctor: Norlestrin, right.

Patient: Is that mild?

Doctor: Uh hum.

Patient: That's what they told me.

Doctor: So you haven't had any problems you can relate to the pill?

Patient: They do, when I was off for two years I never had one cramp in my legs, you know or whatever, cause (unintelligible) I'm really, you see, I know facts about some of the pills that's why I kind of ask for this mild one and they said//

Doctor: //What facts about the pill were you . . .

Patient: Just the facts that you read on that I know there could be a chance of a problem, you know, side effects with them// (*Doctor:* //yes) I don't care to get a blood clot or you know// (*Doctor:*//yes) stuff like that, but then again I don't want a baby. But there's other birth control methods, I'm sure. But like I was saying, I get very sick when I am on my period and ah my cycle is always irregular, you know so I//

Doctor: //You kind of have to weigh the benefits and bad things about it and come to a decision about whether the good outweighs the bad// (*Patient:* //I know.) Uh, your risk factors are *annual*. The longer you take the pill, the more you start, and if you have leg cramps it's kinda worse.

Patient: Well like with that leg cramp, now as soon as it went away, nothing ever happened to my leg, and it scared me, you know and I said well, I want to stay on the pill, but if I get a lot of cramps, I mean that's I don't think I will.

As the medical history continues, the patient disclosed a history of hypertension in her family. In fact her mother has high blood pressure—another possible contraindication for staying on birth control pills. At the close of the medical history portion of the examination the doctor asks:

Doctor: Can you think of anything else that I haven't asked you?
Patient: Trying to think, just cramps at the bottom of my legs that is a concern of mine.
Doctor: I think we all occasionally have leg cramps// (*Patient:* //um hum) occasionally is not anything to worry about if it gets to be a pattern then we start to worry.
Patient: Then I'll have to stop taking the pill like I said I probably would sometimes, but . . .
Doctor: I would be thinking about stopping birth control pills or stopping smoking within the next couple of periods, give a little, OK?
Patient: un huh.
Doctor: That's, that's, I'm beating my wife in the head trying to get her to stop one or the other.
Patient: She doing both of them too?
Doctor: Yeah.
Patient: I noticed that with two it's really bad. One is bad enough, you know. I know that.
Doctor: Both of them are atrocious, really increase your risk of having problems.

At this point the doctor gets a nurse and the physical examination is performed.

While this medical interview sounds different on the surface, the results are much the same. Ms. A, like Ms. D, comes to the clinic concerned about continuing to use the birth control pill. Unlike Ms. D her complaints are not vague, "nuisance problems" which can be easily dismissed by the medical provider. She has at least three medically accepted risk factors—risk factors that at least signal caution for her remaining on oral contraception. She smokes, has a family history of hypertension, and recently has experienced leg cramps which may indicate cardiovascular problems. Doctor and patient acknowledge these to be serious problems with grave potential consequences, yet, when all is said and done, the patient leaves on the birth control pill.

Why, then, does the patient remain on birth control pills and how is her continued use of them an interactional accomplishment? The transcript gives us several clues. First, Ms. A tells the doctor more than once that when she is not on birth control pills her periods are irregular and she has severe menstrual cramps. Second, Ms. A indicates at various intervals that she has come to the doctor for advice, perhaps even for direction. When telling the doctor about the leg cramps and about smoking she says, "You need to know." When the doctor tells her that muscle cramps are a reason to be worried and that such symptoms make doctors think about taking patients off the birth control pills, Ms. A responds, ". . . that's why I'm here, to check into that." Yet, by the end of the interview, the resident selectively uses his authority to suggest that she stop smoking or stop taking the pill within the next couple of periods. He selectively presents scientific information by telling her, ". . . we all occasionally have leg cramps", and even more subtly, by acknowledging that his own wife is a smoker and a birth control pill user. By so doing he encourages the patient to stay on the birth control pill. More obviously, the doctor selectively presents information. He does not give Ms. A the facts she needs to reach an informed decision. He does not discuss with her the seriousness of continued use of the birth control pill nor does he give her information about other forms of contraception. He uses the authority of his role to withhold information in another way as well. He does not share his medical knowledge about ways to manage menstrual distress other than the birth control pill.[10] While there is no completely satisfactory contraceptive on the market, the patient does have choices beyond the birth control pill or getting pregnant.

FRIENDLY PERSUASION

Each of the patients came to these doctors concerned about contraception and each left with a prescription for birth control pills. While all three patients were young unmarried Anglo women, their experience with the birth control pill and their lives were quite different. Ms. S was sexually inexperienced and inquiring about contraception for a relationship that she portrayed as premarital. Neither Ms. D nor Ms. A presented themselves with the same innocence and neither of them were first time users of birth control. Both Ms. D and Ms. A reported problems with the pill, albeit of differing magnitudes. Ms. D, who had used the pill for five years, complained of headaches, bloating, and weight gain. All of these are vague but well-documented side effects of the pill. Ms. A, used the pill for two years, rested for two years, and then returned to it, but complained of leg cramps. During the medical interview she disclosed that she also smoked and had a family history of high blood pressure. (Recent medical research has disclosed a long suspected linkage between oral contraception and cardiovascular problems.[11])

In each case doctors used the authority of their role to present information selectively about the available contraceptive methods and to influence the patient's decision. While Ms. S was given the most thorough review of contraceptive options, the presentation was colored by the doctor's preference. Information was used selectively to make it quite clear that at this time the doctor preferred the birth control pill for her. The presentation of options to Ms. D was

---

[10] There are a range of nutritional remedies such as vitamin B_6 and calcium as well as the more medically accepted aspirin-like drugs which, if taken correctly, have been found to inhibit the prostaglandins which are responsible for some types of menstrual cramps (see Seaman and Seaman, 1977). Further, there is current debate in medicine about using the birth control pill to manage menstrual disorders. It is felt that while there may be short-term improvement there is long-term damage.

[11] Sloan et al. (1981) have found in their hospital based, case-control study, that long-term use of oral contraceptives increases the possibility of myocardial infarction even after discontinuation of the pill.

more limited. She was given information on the IUD and the birth control pill; however, the information on the IUD was presented so negatively that the birth control pill seemed to be the only reasonable choice. With Ms. A, the lack of choice was even clearer. Although both resident and patient expressed concern about the continued use of birth control pills, *no* alternative methods of contraception were discussed.

These cases display three women with differing contraceptive concerns receiving health care in very different medical settings. Whether the practitioners were private practice physicians or residents, in the practice of ob/gyn or family medicine, earning a fee-for-service or on salary, in our data scientific information was presented selectively to favor the birth control pill. While this occurred in each case discussed, it is more conspicuous with Ms. S (the first case). In discussing birth control options, the resident first stressed the effectiveness of the pill and claimed that the data from the studies about the side effects of the pill were either inconclusive or not in yet. He then established that if patients try hard enough they can get used to the side effects of the pill. In so doing he displayed his attitude, and we suggest a widely shared medical assumption about pill users and the pill. This belief system provides the grounds to treat patients' complaints about the pill as neurotic, to dismiss the side effects of the pill as nuisance problems, and to keep prescribing oral contraceptives.

In the second and third cases scientific information was ignored or downplayed to make the case for the pill. Ms. D's complaints were dismissed, and she was accused of erroneously blaming the pill for her problems. If she was gaining weight, it was because she was eating more. She only thought she was hungrier while taking birth control pills. The presentation of scientific information about contraception displayed a blame-the-victim-attitude which shifted the fault away from the birth control pill and toward the patient. It also dismissed, as unimportant, problems that affect the quality of women's lives. In the third case, even when Ms. A presented medically bona fide risk factors, they were subtly downplayed, and by the end of the medical interview birth control pills were again prescribed.

Discussion about contraception was couched in terms of safety and efficacy. Again scientific information was presented selectively. Birth control pills and the IUD were presented as 99 percent effective (a fact that many would disagree with—see Seaman & Seaman, 1977). While the IUD was dismissed because it can cause infections and infertility, the problems associated with the birth control pill were deemphasized even though death has been a documented consequence of its use.[12] With birth control pills the only problem that was treated seriously was described as "short term infertility."

---

[12] It is not our intention to imply that birth control pills are never an appropriate prescription. Nor is it our intention to suggest that any of the providers were "poor" medical practitioners consciously providing "bad" medical care. Rather our goal is to use these cases to illuminate how persuasive

Again the selective use of information is clearest with Ms. S. The discussion about contraception began with the question, "First of all do you want children?" Why was a question about children first? Why not ask how much interest do you have in protecting yourself from possible iatrogenically-produced illness? This seems to us to be a critical question. Yet neither of us has ever heard it asked.

Barrier methods of contraception were only discussed with Ms. S. When information was presented about them, neither their efficacy nor their safety was stressed. When the doctor discussed the diaphragm he focused on the commitment, intelligence, and marital status of the user. The implication was that most women were neither intelligent nor committed enough to use the diaphragm effectively. With the condom, pleasure with intercourse and intactness of condom were stressed. The messages sent were subtle and potentially frightening for the patient. She had clearly stated that she wanted a safe method of birth control. If the diaphragm was presented as less safe, it was unlikely that she would risk its use. And given the assumption in this society that intercourse with a condom is akin to taking a shower with a raincoat on, she was equally unlikely to risk her partner's pleasure or her reproductive security by using them.[13] In other words, in each case the selective use of science was most unscientific.

The selective use of authority in our data is evident over and over again. When prescribing the birth control pill we have each frequently heard doctors explain that even the more dangerous methods of birth control are safer than an unwanted pregnancy. In our opinion this is like comparing apples and oranges. How can the known risks of pregnancy be compared with the as yet unknown risks of the birth control pill? The pill was relatively untested before it went on the market and what testing was done was either directly or indirectly under the control of the pharmaceutical industry. Such a persuasive strategy assumes that there are only two choices for women, the pill or pregnancy, and that all the risks are known for both.[14]

---

techniques are used during medical interviews to accomplish contraceptive decision making as well as to illuminate the moral, economic, and political context in which decisions take place. The data discussed in this paper raise two questions. First, *how* doctors and patients communicate to reach common decisions about contraceptive methods, and second, *why*, despite considerable evidence to the contrary, birth control pills continue to be the most widely prescribed method of birth control.

[13] In Japan, condoms are the leading birth control method. They are sold in an array of colors and textures and presented as safe as well as sexually stimulating.

[14] There is also an important difference here in the gathering of statistics for pregnancy-related and birth control pill-related problems. When complications arise with pregnancy, the relationship between the two are generally clearly recognizable and recorded into the statistical records. The relationship between the birth control pill and potential complications, however, are much harder to identify. Blood clots, strokes, and cardiovascular problems are often recorded as just that—a stroke—rather than a birth control pill-related complication. Further, drug companies are often involved in the compiling of statistics around drug complications and their interests are in low-problem rates. This difference in record keeping distorts the data, making such comparisons all the more meaningless.

The selective use of authority is evident in another way as well. These cases highlight traditional understandings of women's roles by reflecting the twin medical concern: to preserve the reproductive capacity of these women while protecting them from unwanted pregnancy. Traditional understandings lead to the assumption that it is a higher priority to protect women who are single from pregnancy than it is to protect their married counterparts. This assumption is displayed in the resident's statement that his wife could use a diaphragm because she was married, but Ms. S would be safer with the birth control pill. Someday she will want to marry and reproduce. It is also discernable in the bias against the IUD. This bias was evident in all these cases, but was perhaps clearest in the presentation of information to Ms. D. She was told that the IUD was an inappropriate method, "particularly for young women who haven't had their families yet." While the doctor explained that death was a possible outcome of the IUD, the "scariest thing, even if, you know, you don't get an overwhelming infection . . ." is the possibility of infertility. This was all explained to a young, single woman who had not even mentioned her reproductive plans.

CONCLUSION

It is medically accepted today that no organ system of a woman's body is unaffected by the birth control pill (Seaman & Seaman, 1977). The risks associated with the pill take 10 to 20 years to mature and are too varied to enumerate here. Yet, despite this information, doctors continue to prescribe them. Several factors make this possible. First, the practice of medicine is very time-consuming, and most doctors are not able to keep up with all the latest developments in their fields. More specifically, they receive most of their information about drugs such as birth control pills from drug salespeople and medical journals. The pharmaceutical industry has reaped tremendous profits from the birth control pill. They have a history which demonstrates a greater commitment to profit than to humanitarian concerns like patient safety. They are, therefore, biased teachers. This same bias is evident in medical journals. Most journals are dependent on advertising dollars. The pharmaceutical industry is a heavy advertiser. Editorials and articles as well as advertisements reflect the journal's dependence on the pharmaceutical industry's continued good will.

Historically, the American Medical Association and the American College of Obstetrics and Gynecology have been hesitant to explain the side effects and risks of the pill to pill users. It has been argued that to do so would confuse and alarm many women patients, and to have others do so would interfere with the doctor-patient relationship. These are male-dominated, sexist assumptions based on a view of women as emotionally unstable and unable to understand complex explanations. While to a large extent the medical profession lost this battle in Senate hearings, and information about the risks and side effects of the pill are included in each packet of birth control pills, doctors still have the upper hand.

As we saw in the data, patients look to doctors as the final arbitrators of contraceptive information, and the ways in which the information is presented function to persuade. Feminists argue that to the degree that discrimination toward women is pervasive in our society, it is also deeply embedded in the field of medicine (Scully, 1980; Ruzek, 1978; Ehrenreich & English, 1978). These cultural and institutional values toward women and reproduction—patriarchal values and attitudes—play an important role in the medical treatment of women.

The persuasive communication patterns medical providers use in prescribing birth control are social as well as micropolitical phenomena. They are social in that they are produced and constrained in a social context and accomplished by the activities of the participants. They are micropolitical in that they reflect and help to sustain the status quo. The social and political factors woven into the fabric of society and mirrored in the shape of the health care delivery system are embedded in the practitioner-patient communication through which medical decision making is accomplished.

In the prescription of birth control, the selective use of scientific information legitimizes the dominance of the medical profession. Medicine is a technological approach which addresses itself to physiological or biological aspects of health and illness. Medical practitioners are separated from the social or contextual lives of patients (Todd, 1982). We did not hear medical practitioners ask women what different forms of contraception meant to their lives. We rather observed medical providers prescribing birth control pills abstracted from the social lives of their patients but embedded in their traditional assumptions about women. The technology of reproductive control developed, promoted, and found profitable by the drug companies creates a demand for its use and leads to the prescription patterns and the persuasion strategies we have discussed. Medical providers using the institutional authority of their role provide information in ways that function to persuade, and the birth control pill becomes an institutionalized, self-serving, standard medical procedure. While the persuasion may be friendly, it denies patients the information they need to be active participants in their own health care and in so doing, especially in the area of contraception, it cannot be in their best interest.

REFERENCES

Barker-Benfield, G. J. (1976). *The horrors of the half-known life*. New York: Harper Colophon Books.

Conrad, P. & Kern, R. (Eds.). (1981). *The sociology of health and illness: Critical perspectives*. New York: St. Martin's Press.

Corea, G. (1977). *The hidden malpractice: How American medicine treats women as patients and professionals*. New York: William Morrow.

Corsaro, W. A. (1982). Something old and something new: The importance of prior ethnography in the collection and analysis of audiovisual data. *Sociological Methods and Research*, 2(2), 145–166.

Dreifus, C. (Ed.). (1977). *Seizing our bodies*. New York: Vintage Books.

Dubos, R. (1959). *Mirage of health*. New York: Harper & Row.

Ehrenreich, B. & Ehrenreich, J. (1970). *The American health empire*. A Health-Pac Book. New York: Vintage Books.

Ehrenreich, B. & English, D. (1978). *For her own good*. Garden City, NY: Anchor Press/ Doubleday.

Fisher, S. (1982). The decision-making context: How doctor and patient communicate. In Robert J. Di Pietro (Ed.), *Linguistics and the professions*. Norwood, NJ: Ablex.

Fisher, S. (1983). Doctor talk/patient talk: How treatment decisions are negotiated in doctor/patient communication. In Sue Fisher & Alexandra Todd (Eds.), *The Social organization of doctor-patient communication*. Washington, DC: Center for Applied Linguistics/Harcourt Brace Jovanovich.

Fisher, S. (forthcoming). *In the patient's best interests*. New Brunswick, NJ: Rutgers University Press.

Friedson, E. (1970). *Profession of medicine*. New York: Dodd, Mead.

Gordon, L. (1974). *Woman's body, woman's right: A social history of birth control in America*. New York: Penguin Books.

Henley, N. (1977). *Body politics: Power, sex and nonverbal communication*. Englewood Cliffs, NJ: Prentice-Hall.

Knorr-Cetina, K., & Cicourel, A. V. (1981). *Advances in social theory and methodology: Toward an integration of micro- and macro-sociologies*. Boston: Routledge & Kegan Paul.

Luker, K. (1975). *Taking chances: Abortion and the decision not to contracept*. Berkeley: The University of California Press.

Morgan, S. (1978). Sexuality after hysterectomies and castration. *Women and Health*, 3 (Jan/Feb): 5–10.

Parsons, T. (1951). *The social system*. New York: Free Press.

Prather, J. & Fidell, L. (1975). Sex differences in the content and style of medical advertisements. *Social Science and Medicine*, 9 (January): 23–6.

Ruzek, S. B. (1978). *The women's health movement*. New York: Praeger.

Scully, D. (1980). *Men who control women's health*. Boston: Houghton-Mifflin.

Scully, D., & Bart, P. (1973). A funny thing happened on the way to the orifice: Women in gynecological textbooks. *American Journal of Sociology*, 78: 1045–50.

Seaman, B., & Seaman, G. (1977). *Women and the crisis in sex hormones*. New York: Bantam Books.

Silverman, D. (1981). The child as a social object: Down's Syndrome children in a paediatric cardiology clinic. *Sociology of Health and Illness*, 3 (3), 254–274.

Sloan, D., Shapiro, S., Kaufman, D., Rosenberg, L., Miettinen, & Stolley, P. (1981). Risk of myocardial infarction in relation to current and discontinued use of oral contraceptives. *The New England Journal of Medicine*, 302 (August 20). pgs. 420–424.

Stevens, R. (1971). *American medicine and the public interest*. New Haven: Yale University Press.

Strong, P. M. (1979). *The ceremonial order of the clinic*. London: Routledge & Kegan Paul.

Todd, A. D. (1982). The medicalization of reproduction: Scientific medicine and the diseasing of healthy women. Unpublished doctoral dissertation. University of California, San Diego.

Todd, A. D. (1983). A diagnosis of doctor-patient discourse in the prescription of contraception. In Sue Fisher & Alexandra Todd (Eds.), *The social organization of doctor-patient communication*. Washington, DC: Center for Applied Linguistics Press.

Todd, A. D. (1983). Women's bodies as diseased and deviant: Historical and contemporary issues. In Steven Spitzer (Eds.), *Research in law deviance and social control*. Greenwich, CT: JAI Press.

Todd, A. D. (1984). The prescription of contraception: Negotiations between doctors and patients. *Discourse Processes*, 7, 171–200.

Waitzkin, H., & Stoeckle, J. D. (1976). Information control and the micropolitics of health care: Summary of an ongoing research subject. *Social Science and Medicine,* 10: 263–76.

Waitzkin, H. B., & Waterman, B. (1974). *The exploitation of illness in capitalist society.* Indianpolis: Bobbs-Merrill.

Wertz, R. W., & Wertz, D. C. (1981). Notes on the decline of midwives and the rise of medical obstetricians. In Peter Conrad & Rochelle Kern (Eds.), *The sociology of health and illness.* New York: St. Martin's Press.

West, C. (1982). When the doctor is a lady: Power, status and gender in physician-patient conversations. In Ann Stromberg (Ed.), *Women, health and medicine.* Palo Alto: Mayfield.

2. A Feminist Critique of Scientific Ideology: An Analysis of Two Doctor–Patient Encounters*

Stephany Borges

Santa Ana, California
University of California, Irvine

In capitalist countries with advanced technologies, it would not be an exaggeration to say that people are uneasy. They feel insecure. And what are the reasons? A casual survey of major social problems indicates that we are insecure about our health, our relationships, our jobs, and the future of the planet. It appears there is not one front to which we can turn for solace, for the assurance that we are not, in fact, an endangered species. Yet, ironically enough, most people still cling to some semblance of the myth of salvation through science and even more specifically the illusion of medical salvation.

There is a prophetic voice to the Frankfurt School's critique of science. Thirty years ago they saw the problems of alienation and diminishing autonomy of the individual that stemmed from pitting the power of reason against the forces of the natural world. "Men pay for their increase of power with alienation from that over which they exercise their power (Horkheimer & Adorno, 1982, p. 9). With the rise of science and technology has come one of the striking features in our lives today: alienation. The gratification of one of our most fundamental needs goes unmet—the need for intimacy.

Life under present-day capitalism is, in many ways, a life of deprivation. Even the peasants in the fields, working shoulder to shoulder with the worker next to them, have more opportunity to satisfy this basic need for intimacy than does the average office worker. We flock to experts for help, who often charge unbelieveable fees, because we take personal responsibility for what are often social and political problems. We blame ourselves and our individual psyches.

The consequences of alienation are familiar to all of us. They are most visible in our overflowing prisons and mental hospitals. People find it hard to trust one another. "It is not merely that domination is paid for by the alienation of the spirit, the very relations of men—even those of the individual to himself—are bewitched" (Horkheimer & Adorno, 1982, p. 25). Families fall apart. The individual's options are limited. Both science—and with science I include tech-

---

* I would like to acknowledge my husband, Dr. Howard Waitzkin. He provided the transcripts analyzed in this paper. The transcripts came from a research project sponsored by the National Center for Health Services Research (HS 02100).

nology—and religion provide possible solutions for the individual's plight. Pain, loss, personal responsibility for decisions—these struggles can be diluted by technology's capacity to seduce us by delaying the problem of actual interpretation and choice. Science, as well as religion, helps to mask the underlying social causes of suffering.

Habermas argues in *Toward a Rational Society* that our beliefs in the power and the promise of science and technology produce a subtle ideology with far-reaching social and political consequences. He argues against the lie of the neutrality of science. It is in the Frankfurt School's critique of The Age of Reason and the critique of science that the scientific method, the bedrock of science, is reexamined. In scientific principles can be seen an archetype of domination because of its fundamental relationship with the natural world: nature is viewed as object, something to be controlled. With the domination of nature follows the domination of man and more especially women. "Technology is the essence of this knowledge. It does not work by concepts and images, by the fortunate insight, but refers to method, the exploitation of others' work and capital (Horkheimer & Adorno, 1982, p. 4).

An investigation of the way in which the scientific method is a tool of domination (man against nature) leads members of the Frankfurt School, like Horkheimer and Adorno, to come to conclusions that modern day feminists support. Science and philosophy are steeped in sexist assertions that rest upon a devaluation of the feminine principle, be it nature, the irrational, or woman herself. "As a representative of nature, woman in bourgeois society has become the enigmatic image of irresistibility and powerlessness. In this way she reflects the pure lie that posits the subjection instead of the redemption of nature (Horkheimer & Adorno, 1982, p. 72). This force of nature, the feminine, is elemental. It is something that has been dimly realized all along; however, it has usually been classified as the irrational. Dangerously unintegrated, repressed, it lurks in the consciousness of the world, shadowlike and sinister: it is our paranoia, our dis-ease. It appears that the result of absolute domination is destruction.

Horkheimer and Adorno express little sympathy for people under capitalism. They see human beings at odds with themselves and everyone else. They even view them as "virtual Nazis." The bourgeoisie has regressed in this Age of Reason for "the curse of irresistible progress is irresistible regression" (Horkheimer & Adorno, 1982, p. 36). It takes little imagination, given the historical period, to understand what they are talking about. This regression stems from the intellect's domination over the senses (mind over body). Furthermore—and even more disasterously—because of the complex social and scientific advances, experiences themselves are impoverished. People are morally, physically, and spiritually disabled by the machines and institutions that dominate them.

One of the most succinct one-liners in the body of the Frankfurt School literature is: "Protection is the archetype of domination" (Horkheimer, 1982, p. 35). And surely we can see this in the dominant ideology of technological optimism that sees our salvation coming through science. It is at this point that the tie between religion and science becomes obvious. Our notion of salvation has become mechanical rather than one of meaning and caring. Because science, and particularly medicine, has the invincible ideology of "service" and protection as its justification, its potential for exploitation is enormous. The cost is high: we are losing our ability to dream, to love, and to rejoice collectively.

We live in an age when bureaucratic domination can be justified by the fact that bureaucrats and politicians act upon scientific recommendations. Science, at least the fetishism of science, has become an impenetrable veil of social control in modern life. "In this universe, technology also provides the great rationalization of the unfreedom of man and demonstrates the technical impossibility of being autonomous, of determining one's own life" (Habermas, 1972, p. 85). Because technology questions science's role in the determination of reality, the Frankfurt School not only questions method but the institutions of science as well, though these questions remain largely on a theoretical level.

In their quest to discover the forces of domination at their roots and, with the intent of abolishing them, the Frankfurt School attempts to dispel the illusion of the autonomy of reason—hence the autonomy of science, technology, healthcare, and so on. Members of the Frankfurt School see the Enlightenment as an essentially totalitarian force (all of reality in its perview). The School tries to penetrate the ideology of reason and science to uncover the elements of social control that pervade modern society.

Ardono does not so much hold out a new version of "the truth" but rather prescribes a method whereby truth that is conceived of as constant (i.e., as those truths proven by the scientific method) is challenged. He asserts there are no absolute foundations—that truth is open, always partially not there.

Let us move from the general and the theoretical to the particular and the concrete and examine a particular institution of science and look at the way it perpetuates the dominant ideology of salvation through science. Medicine, and more particularly the doctor–patient relationship, allows us to look at an institution exemplar. Medicine, like science, permits the rational control of the individual under the rubric of caring and protection.

Like science, medicine involves a body of advanced knowledge that is dispensed by a group of specialists. Therefore, ordinary people are dependent on professionals to translate this knowledge for them. In effect, the health care system serves to reproduce those patterns of domination inherent in the Enlightenment. Of course it is the ideology of excellence that further justifies this type of domination as well as stated end: to serve and protect the people. The development of "people's medicine" during certain stages in the People's Republic of China was a direct response to this type of domination inherent in the ideology of excellence.

One of Marcuse's basic theses was that technology and science take on the function of legitimizing political power. That in fact they are not apolitical but political and serve to reproduce the ideology of the ruling group. Therefore, it is in the interest of dominant ideologies to adopt an uncritical acceptance toward the institutions of science—private medicine being one.

In examining the way in which dominant ideologies are reproduced, I am going to focus on two specific encounters between doctors and their patients. In this way we can try to find out to what extent micro-level encounters between individuals reproduce macro-level structures of oppression. "The critique of medicalization holds that medicine has become an institution of social control and that the health-care system helps promulgate the dominant ideologies of society" (Waitzkin, 1983, p. 138). The medicalization of social problems is the way in which many areas of the patient's personal and social life come under the auspices of medical control.

In presenting two medical encounters and doing a contextual analysis of each encounter, I want to show how the medicalization of nonmedical problems occurs and the way in which the doctor–patient relationship helps to legitimate and reproduce structures of oppression. Because both of the encounters are with women, there will be special attention paid to the way in which our patriarchal society reproduces itself.

The complete transcripts of the verbal interactions can be found at the end of this chapter. It might be helpful to turn to them and read Encounter A (pp. 36–45) before reading the analysis. The same applies for Encounter B (pp. 46–48).

In Encounter A the doctor is a 39-year-old, Caucasian male. A moderately religious man from working-class origins, he states that his father, a traveling salesman, never went beyond a high school education. This doctor has been out of medical school for 13 years and his specialty is in internal medicine. He is in private practice and says his decision to study medicine was based largely on "the chance to help people and do work of special interest." Economic incentives do not figure importantly on his list of reasons for entering the profession.

The patient is also Caucasian. Thirty-seven years old, with a college education, she is currently going through a divorce. She is diagnosed as suffering from "situational depression." She has been seeing this doctor for seven years and has come in for a routine checkup. She is the mother of three children.

The doctor begins by asking the patient about her work situation. From her response it is easily inferred that she is not happy at Xerox. A brief reference is made to her thwarted attempts to teach Italian. Yet, they quickly get back on the track as the doctor says, "You're at least still . . ." Her ability to work is the first issue addressed for the patient's role in economic production is a primary concern: the ability to work signifies health.

They then discuss old medical problems. This leads to a primary issue in medical encounters when the patient is a female: birth control. In this discussion she reveals her lack of sexual contact at this time, her depression, and the fact that she has begun taking the pill. She has begun the pill not so much to stop conception as to control her moods. "I find the pill calms me down. It's a very strange thing."

The doctor, a bit surprised, reminds her she stopped taking the pill because of side effects—headaches. He then asks her what kind of pill she is on. She doesn't seem to know. When he asks for a description, she answers, "It's a tiny white pill." She, like most patients, has suspended all critical judgement and does not even know the name of the medicine she has chosen.

Then he discusses what he considers to be the related problem, not yet having clearly stated what "the problem" is. He explores with her the status of her marriage and discovers she will file for a divorce that fall. This leads to a discussion of her husband's employment. The husband has left his old job and is looking for another. The patient then describes that her husbands wants her back but that it would be "suicide" to let him into her life again.

The familiar story emerges. He drinks. She still has frequent contact with him, even having meals with him because she sees it as "very good for the children" . . . "very difficult for me." Never once does she acknowledge that her own well-being and mental health would be good for the children in and of itself. It appears she has a lot of guilt about breaking up this marriage and feels she must suffer her husband's presence for the sake of her children.

The doctor explores the issue of custody. It is apparently a sensitive issue. He immediately drops it and begins to update the family history and her own medical history. "No major illnesses?" When he comes to her weight he is surprised to see she has lost 15 pounds. When he asks her how she has managed this, she replies, "Not eating."

The doctor probes. The patient confides, "I feel so good when I'm a decent weight. I really do." And later she says, "It's great." It is the only enthusiasm she expresses during the entire visit. It reflects woman's preoccupation with the body. It shows the degree to which women have been socialized into believing that to be thin is to be free of problems. It turns out that when she doesn't eat she smokes more and drinks more. They both laugh when she says, "Maybe when I get to 130, I'll stop smoking."

As a responsible professional, the doctor checks to see just how serious a problem alcohol is in her life. After a few questions, he seems satisfied that she is not in immediate danger and jumps back to her depression which he calls "problems at home." She tried to put the blame on her body—"It's something physical." It is as if she can't face the social implications of her situation. She brings it back to the specifically feminine—"the period"—as the likely culprit.

The doctor in a caring manner explores the area of outside help and finds out she and her husband were in therapy for awhile. She goes on to say, "But it didn't seem to help the marriage. It could have helped me, as a person, but, uh, it's too expensive." It is after this brief stint of therapy that she decided to put herself on the pill.

He also checks to see if she is suicidal. He is reassured by her that she wouldn't do it now because of the children. After the children are grown . . . perhaps . . . if there is nothing of value in her life to replace them. It comes out she lives in comparative isolation with an "enormous family back home."

Because of her husband, she is unable to relocate nearer to her family. When the doctor asks if she has someone to talk to, she says, "No, but I know I should do something about that." It seems he has touched upon one of the major problems in the structure of her daily life: she has no one to talk to in a period of stress and crisis. She seems to clearly know that she should do something about it, but she thinks she can't because of economic imperatives. Therapy is too expensive.

It becomes clear that because of her economic position, a single parent with three children, she feels economically tied to her husband. Her mobility is also hampered because she must live in the area her husband lives so that her children can maintain contact with their father, something she sees as desirable. In effect, she sees herself as living for her children until they are grown. Ironically, it is the children who give her life meaning and yet also place her in a position where her options are severely limited: they require a constant sacrifice on her part, not the least of which is allowing her husband to stay in her life. It is because of the children (at least in her own eyes) that she doesn't travel to her much cherished Italy, change jobs, move, or make any other major change that might alleviate the symptoms of her "situational depression." She opts for starving herself to become fashionably thin, taking a little white pill, smoking, and drinking alcohol.

The doctor suggests various alternatives to expensive therapy: "through family service and such . . . there are some alternatives to, uh, going to the poor house." He immediately breaks that train of thought with—"the uh, questions of animal fat in the diet here." The transcripts reveal the extraordinary way in which medical and nonmedical issues are discussed with an almost impossible interpenetration of the two areas, clearly a case of the medicalization of social problems. He then says that she can call him and talk if necessary before she starts to plan to do herself in. Obviously, the doctor is a caring professional. He does all the right things. But what purpose has it served? Her response is to affirm that she knows what she needs but can't afford it, another basic myth of the capitalist system—if I just had the money, I could solve this problem.

He concludes the appointment by setting up a new one for four months down the road, "just to sort of touch base and see how things are going." He then goes on to say, "If you're feeling perfectly well and things are rosey, simply call and cancel it." If things are not going well at that time he alludes to "intervening with some medication or something." She leaves with the assurance that he knows her situation, cares what happens to her, and that she can see him again after a set period of time if things haven't improved. But is this medical help? I wonder. In theory a clergyman, a social worker, or even a friend could have provided this function.

Looking back on this encounter one striking element is the extent to which the medical encounter deals with the private issues of this woman's life and the lack of any sort of critique of the social relationships that seem to be the cause of her depression. There is a remarkable absence of a critical analysis of the distressing social patterns within her family and little mention of strategies for structural change (except therapeutic intervention). It is as if the health professional may ask all these questions about family life and may make limited suggestions— "call me if you need to"—"get professional help"—"talk to someone"—but major structural alternatives are lacking. For instance, it seems the mother is responsible for all the child care; however, she tolerates her husband's presence at dinner because she feels her children need him. The question of her resentment because of her woman's role is not even addressed.

The patient leaves the doctor's office and little has changed. Yet, she regards the encounter as completely satisfactory: she got what she came for. It is not hard to see that "one of medicine's most profound effects may be the defusing of socially caused distress."[9] In this way, the medical encounter can be seen as a conservative social force; this is the subtle and often unrealized ideologic impact. From this brief encounter, we can see that medicine, as an institution of science, is not objective and value-neutral; it is an effective tool of social control. Because social control in medicine is often an unintended process, health professionals assume control of many areas of social and personal life without realizing their role in legitimizing and reproducing class structure.

In Encounter B the doctor is a 47-year-old, white male, who denies a religious preference and states that his ethnic background is Russian. He specializes in general internal medicine. He has been this patient's doctor for seven months. The patient's diagnosis, according to this doctor, is "acute and chronic (anxiety) depression." The encounter occurs in a private suburban practice.

The patient is a 30-year-old woman who has gone to college, but she states that her profession is "housewife." She is Jewish and the mother of two young children, ages three and five. She says the reasons for this visit are her "tiredness and nervousness." She also responds that she has been completely satisfied with this medical encounter.

The patient begins by describing her symptoms: she states she is "just not feeling well." She seems to believe it is caused by lots of "social butterfly stuff." She has busied herself with various, unspecified volunteer activities. She blames her fatigue and general sense of malaise on overwork outside of the home. No mention of her housekeeping or child care activities is made throughout the interview. The patient gives a list of vague, general symptoms—loss of appetite being one.

The doctor, commenting on the way she describes her symptoms (as if she's had them before) suggests that she knows herself well. This brings out an almost defensive reaction: "I'm not really terribly depressed . . . just irritable a little bit." From the way she qualifies and softens her assertions it's not hard to perceive that this patient has a hard time justifying her own feelings to herself.

The fact that she knows that staying at home is a factor in her depression (a worse factor apparently than exhausting herself on meaningless types of social activities . . . "The Welcome Wagon and that sort of thing") is never explored. The why of her depression from staying home and possible solutions (a part-time job, further education) are never discussed. Instead the doctor makes a verbal diagnosis. She has the "suburban syndrome." He then compliments the patient on her ability to diagnosis herself: "You know damn well what you're doing." His advice is to learn to say no.

It also comes out that she has recently moved. This event is not explored. It seems to have contributed to her increased activities outside the home. Is she lonely? Does she find the constant company of preschoolers less than sufficient companionship? What are her alternatives? None of these things are discussed. After the doctor has given her "a diagnosis" she remains dissatisfied. In short, she feels tired *now* and wants action *now*. She is most worried and troubled by her general achiness. It turns out she has been treating herself with stady doses of Bufferin.

The doctor then suggests a tranquilizer. "You use it four times a day. If you don't need it, you use it once a day." Then he tells her that if that doesn't fix things she might need a complete physical, which includes blood work. As we don't know when she had her last physical or much else about her medical history, it might be unfair to be critical of the doctor for not doing the blood work before giving out medication. Yet the patient seems to think the blood work would be a good idea.

She asserts herself and asks if the blood tests might be done that day. She wonders if perhaps she is anemic. The doctor becomes condescending. "Don't choose a diagnosis out of the blue. Buy a medical book and get a real nice diagnosis. He dismisses her desire for lab work and goes back to his prescription. He reassures her that it is "perfectly harmless." He continues, "If you need it, just renew it. If you don't feel good. . . ." He doesn't finish his sentence. It can be guessed that he means she can return for the physical and tests. For some reason, he doesn't want to encourage this action.

The pattern in this encounter is clear-cut: the patient has been patted on her shoulder, given a little pill to make her feel better, and sent back home with a diagnosis—"suburban syndrome." Unlike with Encounter A, there has been no exploration at possible underlying causes of the patient's symptoms, nor has there been the direct medical attention evident in the first encounter. From what little information we have here, it would not be hard to judge this type of encounter as "bad medicine."

But let's look at the facts. Though these two encounters vary rather drastically in the approaches and the attitudes of the physicians concerned, the ultimate outcomes are basically the same: nothing has changed. Both women go back into the same situations which brought them into the doctor's office seeking help. Even though the first doctor does probe to discover the underlying factors of stress in his patient's life, still there is an absence of any kind of meaningful critique of the social causes of that distress. The effects of both encounters diffuse the effects of broader social issues: they depoliticize the structural roots of the patient's suffering by making social problems medical ones.

One common, and to me striking, element in both women's attitudes was their passivity: the absence of anger. Both women are depressed, with their rage internalized and generally blamed on "the body." The women are suffering from the long-term effects of both the "woman's role" and more generally from isolation and alienation. The struggle to maintain a healthy physical and emotional life has taken its toll. Yet they do not question.

They do not question their woman's role any more than they question the comparative isolation of their lives in spite of their children's presence. Life under corporate capitalism forces people to life on the edge. "The individual constricts himself/herself. Without a dream or history, she is always aiming at some immediate, practical goal. Her life falls into a sequence of data which fit in advance the questionnaires she has to answer" (Horkheimer, 1982, p. 37). Medicine, as a tool of social control, creates dependence of the individual and thus the lessening of autonomy. Not only do these women shift the responsibility for understanding themselves upon their doctor's (belief in scientific salvation); but because of the false expectations they nurture, they in turn create a growing market for technical experts and their products (tranquilizers, birth control pills, etc.). The human needs for intimacy—family, friendship, and community—are transfered onto the mystique of the physician, a technical expert. Not surprisingly, fiction writers like Kafka draw upon society's pseudo-reliance on the doctor. In his short story "The Country Doctor," we find the doctor bemoaning the fact that "they misuse me for sacred ends." This may be the paradox at the heart of the doctor–patient relationship in developed countries: though the patient's have lost their ancient beliefs, they still turn to the doctor as healer in a rather ritualistic fashion to escape from the burden of personal responsibility and suffering in our most dehumanizing age.

Habermas believes our new technocratic consciousness, though less obviously ideological than previous ideologies, is much more totalitarian than older ideologies. "Today's dominant, rather glossy background ideology, which makes a fetish of science, is more irresistible and far-reaching than ideologies of the old type. For with the veiling of practical problems it not only justifies a particular class's interest in domination and represses another class's partial need for emancipation, but affects the human race's emancipatory interest as such" (Habermas, 1972, p. 111). As seen in the two doctor–patient encounters, the general tendency to rely on technical solutions (at least quasi ones) for personal problems that would otherwise involve matters of individual responsibility and choice leads to a depolitization of the individual and society.

In the United States of America, as in other advanced capitalistic countries, the burden of physical and psychological health tends to be placed on the individual's life style. The life style of the individual is usually regarded as the most likely culprit: "She eats too much . . . worries too much . . . smokes too much . . . doesn't get exercise." Because the emphasis on life style tends to be conservative, modern medicine tends to obscure the relationship between health and broader social conditions.

Obviously, for certain groups, such as women and people with low incomes, the emphasis on personal life style is especially oppressive. It does not allow for the consideration of the greater health risks these individuals are exposed to on the job or the effects of inadequate food and housing. Nor does it take into consideration the toll of the thousand daily little stresses in their daily lives, not to mention the stress of job insecurity.

This is not to say that an analysis of the individual's life style is unnecessary. Actually, in some ways, though the burden of health rests with the individual, wholistic health care has gained momentum as an alternative to mainstream health care because the "technical" solutions of modern medicine do not effectively address the individual's life style. While wholistic medicine has pointed out some of the inadequate features of health care practice, it, too, remains a conservative social force: the responsibility for wellness still rests with the individual rather than being tied to broader social issues.

Medicine, because of its conservative social force, should not escape our notice as it hides behind the value-neutral ideology of science. "As an overall strategy, activism should expose, highlight, and in some cases exacerbate the social contradictions which are sources of health problems. These efforts also should address the structures of oppression that the social organization of medicine both reflects and helps maintain (Waitzkin, 1983, p. 231). The demystification of modern medicine's technical solutions calls for action. Critical analysis of the institutions of domination is the first step; the second is organized resistance.

One type of organized resistance can be found within the women's movement. It didn't require the analysis of the two doctor–patient encounters in this paper to illustrate some of the problems women have obtaining adequate health care in such a patriarchal institution as medicine. It does not escape the women's movement that illness is often linked to economics or that stress is vitally tied to job security. Organizing against sexism means demands for improved living conditions–be it in the doctor's office, in the home, or on the job.

Because of medicine's role in fostering structures of oppression it is important for the physician to realize the role of health care workers and their mediating role in the perpetuation of medicalization. A good beginning would be for the physician to be aware of what is medical and what is not. This sounds simple, but it would require a different type of medical education than is now available. This kind of self-critical posture on the part of the physician would help to debunk the myth of technical solutions for social problems. Physicians have a key role in making this kind of demedicalization possible.

We live in a difficult period in history. As citizens of one of the most potentially destructive nations that has ever existed upon the face of the earth, our collective responsibility for our country's actions has never been greater. The political machinery that has led to the present moment in history is inextricably bound to our scientific and technical "advances." To attack one is to attack the other. As long as the ideology of science and reason go unchallenged, political structures that derive their justification through them will continue. "Scientific management of instinctual needs has long since become a vital factor in the reproduction of the system: merchandise which has to be bought and used is made into objects of the libido; and the national Enemy who has to be fought and hated is distorted and inflated to such an extent that he can activate and satisfy the aggressiveness in the depth dimension of the unconscious (Marcuse, 1966, p. xii). It is time to question and to challenge not only our political system but the science and technology which so effectively legitimizes our system. It is time to become aware of the way in which the political content of encounters such as the doctor–patient relationship perpetuate the status quo and serve the interests of the corporate state.

ENCOUNTER A

D: OK, so this year you're 37

P: Right.

D: an::d are you still with, uh, Xerox, uh,

P: Yes, hm hm.

D: Uh, that's the educational division-

P: -Right, uh huh-

D: is it not, yeah.

P: Yeah, /I'm going/

D: /Are you / using your Italian in that, uh?

P: A::h, no.

D: Not.

P: No. I was tempted to go back teaching Italian, because of what you just said, you know, teaching Italian /it means/ speaking the language,

D: / Yes /

P: very important for me, I don't get much of a chance, uh I haven't found (words)

D: OK, so you're at least still-

P: -Ah, Yeah, still / in Xerox /

D: / staying, / in Xerox. OK. The events of the past year, I guess the most significant probably relates to your hysterectomy. /And the decisions on that, now,/ uh, what went on? I didn't

P: /which never took place, right. /

D: hear from Dr. _____, uh, I know you had the class three Pap and he had /cauterized it and/

P: /and then, he had/cauterized it, and then came back (word) to normal and it was repeated three months later; normal, and now I've been repeating every six months regularly.

D: Uh huh, OK.

P: And it's been normal. And he said that so far it looks good, so he has changed his mind-

D: -Fine-

P: -about (word) hysterectomy, as long as the Pap smear comes back normal.

D: Okay, all right, Now, you called about a week ago and mentioned that you had some vaginal discharge. Did you contact him then?

P: Yes I did, and he did some very extensive tests, and the only thing that they're showing is uh, a yeast infection, which I've had /over the years, yes /

D: /fifteen years(?), uh huh/ And he treated that?

P: And he's treating it now, yeah-

D: treating, and no (word) problem.

P: Right.

D: OK, good. How about your menstrual cycle? When was your last menstrual period?

P: Uh, well I started yesterday.

D: Mm hmm. And have they been unusual in any way?

P: No, I would say that they're just a little bit heavier than they used to be when I was younger, but that's the /only, nothing./

D: /but otherwise, /not a big problem. OK. And contraception, what are you using?

P: U::hm, On and off I've used the pill, and, uh, I've used a diaphragm also, but I don't use it that much, because, well, for one thing, I'm single(?) right now, /uh/ there isn't that much need, but when there

D: /so/ is need, it's either the diaphragm or, I have the pill. As a matter of fact, last winter, January or February, I was very depressed, and

P: not(?) because of intercourse, because I find the pill calms me down, it's a very strang thing. But I took the pill for a month, I was upset and things. The pill does things. It makes my feelings even, /(words) / to the man's(?). I used to get very upset just before

D: /uh huh /

P: my period. Very, very upset, very nervous and very tense. I find that that helped a little bit. But then it blows me up by at least five pounds, so, .hh heh-

D: -Yeah, OK. So, so that's unsatisfactory. On the other hand, when you were on the pill, that was three or four years ago, you had an increase in your headaches. And that's why we stopped it.

P: Yes, but you know I have not a single headache since last year.

D: Uh huh. What pill have you been using when you when you've used it?

P: Well, nothing. I used just to take aspirin.

D: No, but I mean for the, what contraceptive pill has Dr. _____ given you?

P: Uh, I don't know.

D: What's it look like?

P: It's a tiny little white pill, and it's-

D: -circular?-

P: -round, circular.

D: OK. It's probably one of the Ortho-Novums, but in any case he is aware of your headache history and so /forth and has continued to give/

P: /yeah, right, I know so, yes.

D: it to you. OK. Well, uh, and at the moment at least there's no strong need to be on any permanent method of contraception.

P: No, and if I need it, I have the prescription (word) for the pill.

D: Yeah, and you have the /diaphragm/.

P: /Which, the/ reason I don't like to take the pill is because you really, it just uh, I swell up with it, I know I put on about five pounds.

D: Mm hm, OK. So that's more than you did. All right. Um, with reference to the second problem, or the related problem here, the marital stress. What's the status of that, now.

P: That, uh, well, I, ah-

D: -You still separated?

P: Yes, right. /And / there should be a divorce in the fall.

D: /Any:/   You're filing, or he?

P: I'm filing.

D: Mm hm. And he's still with, uh, MIT Press?

P: Well, no. He's, ah, he's gone from MIT Press.

D: Mm hmm. What's he doing now?

P: Um, presently he's doing consulting and he's looking for another job.

D: Mm hm. Do you have any significant stressful contact or nonstressful contact with him, now?

P: Ah, it's dormant stressful contact, in the sense that he desperately wants to get back, and I just, uh, it would be just suicide for me to get back with him, because it would just be repeating the whole thing all over again, and-

D: -Is he still drinking fairly heavily?

P: No, much less. That has improved.

D: No, the kids are, what age?

P: They are twelve, ten, and seven.

D: And, how have they reacted to this, separation?

P: Ah, not bad at all, because (words) get along with their father. Their father comes over all the time. So,-

D: -Yeah. Where's he live?

P: In Cambridge.

D: In Cambridge, uh huh.

P: So, and I have not excluded him from the house, so better—for worse for me, but for better for the children. He comes (words) and he has supper with us, and all that. Which makes it very difficult for me, but it's been very good for the children.

D: Mm hm. Yeah, so OK, but they're aware of the divorce plans and so forth, or?

P: No, well, I never really openly spoken to them about it, or when or why (words).

D: Do you, you would anticipate that you would have custody of the children?

P: I anticipate that, yes, definitely.

D: Yeah, OK.

P: Uh, I have temporary custody of the children /unless/ there was a

D: /Yeah, so/

P: court battle, unless—you know, I don't know.

D: You don't—do you expect that he will?

P: No, I don't-

D: -contest it?

P: Oh, yes. Definitely. He'll protest everything, but uh, /he has no reasons/

D: /But, at least he /

P: right now.

D: OK. Now, um. All right. Lets just go over your list here for a minute. The other areas that we have looked at in the past, there was the concern about, although they were all benign tumors, that the, your father had the benign brain tumor, your mother had the benign breast tumor, cystic fibroids; anything more in terms of changes in family history in the past year?

P: Not at this point. Not at this time, you know.

D: And your two sisters still hypertensive?

P: Yeah, right. /Otherwise, no major illness, no worsening of any situation, no./

D: /But there was no illness that you really (words)   / OK. Your weight today is 135? Is that yours?

P: Yes.

D: It didn't say, oh, so you've gotten lost. OK. most people check it (words). And you've lost 15 pounds. What do you account for that?

P: Not eating.

D: Really starving yourself /or on a special/ diet, or what?

P: /Well, you know,/   I suffer cramps the first two days, but after that I'm not hungry any more. And with me that has to be style of life, I decided. I put on weight, just much too easily. When I eat, I put on weight. I don't burn it off, I guess, so I, I just, I, I hope to go down to 130, and I hope to stay always between 130 and 135. Because I feel so good when I'm a decent weight, I really do.

D: Yes, uh huh.

P: It's great.

D: OK

P: But the only way to do it is not eating. I tried every diet possible, even that crazy Dr. Atkins, I was so sick from it-

D: .hh heh heh heh

P: .hh I was so sick five days after, that, oh, I was terribly constipated, and I had terrible cramps in my stomach, and I said to hell with these stupid diets, not eating was the only thing.

D: Yeah, yeah, yeah. OK. But you're not talking about absolute starvation, or-

P: No, no, no. I eat salads, and I, I drink my glass of wine, and uh, /I eat strawberries and, but very very very little of what I eat, you know/

D: /OK, OK, but it's fairly strict restrictions and being very cautious, OK/

P: almonds, I treat myself to mushrooms and whatnot.

D: Yeah, OK, but you don't indulge yourself in all the things you'd like to. OK.

P: No.

D: Um, OK, no change in eyesight, your eyesight, or any problem there. Do you wear glasses at all?

P: No.

D: Not at all. OK. And tobacco, how much are you smoking now?

P: Oh, half a pack a day.

D: You made any effort at uh /stopping completely? /

P: /I wasn't smoking at all/ for about eight or nine months,
and it's always when I stop dining I start smoking.

D: Yeah, that's the, you know the bad/trade off/, uh, when,/yeah, well/ /(words)

P: /words /

D: I guess what you can, you know, get down to 130 and stop smoking. .hh heh ha

P: .hh heh heh ha.

D: OK. Ah, there's certainly no magic, and uhm,

P: I drink more, I should say this, and I should be very honest about it. When I don't eat, I drink more. And by that I mean I find myself drinking just a little more wine, and I don't usually drink hard alcohol, like whiskey or gin, but I find myself saying yes if it's offered to me, where I ordinarily would just drink the wine.

D: Yeah, yeah.

P: OK?

D: OK. Of course, you know, there /there's still a fair number of calories there, in alcohol as well.

P: Yeah, but its, its, I don't know, maybe (words)-

D: Do you find that in terms of your drinking, that you're concerned that you're using it for more than the social occasion?

P: No, no

D: No, it's just that somebody offers /it's not that you're/

P: /No, uh uh   /

D: /coming home and pouring yourself a double before you go to bed or anything/

P: /No, I never drink alone, I, ah, I never drink alone, no./

D: OK. And the urination at night. You would attribute that to just-

P: Well that's always been, I just put it down because-

D: Yeah, but it's no change, it's not burning

P: No

D: stinging, or?

P: No.

D: OK. Now, the questions of depression and uh, problems at home, those are really the topics we've—do you think, now, when you were depressed, and you mentioned that you started on the pill in February, was that related to the marital situation at that time, or do you think it was you know, no real change, that you could put your finger on, that you were just, you know / (words)   /

P: /Well, it was a combination of,/ of, uh, yes, of home and (word) being alone a lot. Which is natural.

D: Yeah. Have you been able to date or-

P: It's something physical, I think it's something a little bit physical, too, because it's preperiod depression, it's really bad. I've noticed it this year very strongly.

D: Uh huh. Have you really, you know, gone to the depths of depression, that you thought, you know, I've got to either do something dramatic or get some help-

P: -Yeah, I have-

D: -in the past year?

P: Yes I have.

D: Now, you were seeing Dr. B _____, or your / husband, I guess / was, and you

P: /yes I did, we both/
   /we both did. /

D: /say him jointly/, yeah, and what happened with that?

P: Well, it was tough, because the reason for going, I thought I could save the marriage. I thought there could be a dialogue between myself and my husband, and (word) some of the problems, but it didn't seem to happen about the marriage. It could have helped me, as a person but, uh, it's too expensive, I can't afford it.

D: Mm hm, mm hm. Did you, now, other than simply going on the pill,-

P: -But he did point out that I was the kind of person that would get depressed, and I would get worse with age, that I should try to snap out of it now, so (words)

D: Did you talk to anyone or see anyone in February?

P: No, nobody, no.

D: OK, and you just, on your own, then, started the pill, because you'd observed that you felt pretty well, or you, uh huh,

P: Yeah, it calmed me down, somehow, it just, but it could have been that I was just desperate at that time, I guess, I would have tried anything, you see, uh, and that was a time when I wasn't smoking and I wasn't drinking. I only drink a little and I smoke when I'm a little happier. It's very strange with me, I have to be happy and I have to be with people to do this, in other words it is nothing that pulls me out of this, it is not that I can go into drinking, or something like that.

D: Yeah, OK. And have you ever been so depressed that you thought that, you know, well, the only out is suicide or something like that?

P: Yes, but not having, I, I, I have. (words) probably I have, but not that strongly, I mean, but there are times when I thought that after all the children are growing up, and they really won't need me that much more, and unless there is some cheerfulness in my life, unless there is warmth and love, you see, its, I miss my family a lot now, /I don't have anybody around./

D: /Yeah, they're all, yeah your/ are dead, and your sisters, where?

P: Well, you see, I have an enormous family back home, but uh, _____ won't let me go.

D: Mm hm, mm hm.

P: And, which is something I have to work out, I don't know. And I, I don't find being with other men is the right thing. At least in terms of-

D: Hm hm, no. Can you find that you can date, or that there'r either coworkers, or other /associates that you,/

P: /Well, it's difficult/, it's just a very touchy situation because a lot of people I know are married, and they (words) keep men, and I work and I'm at home with the children so much, I don't get a chance to see anybody, and its just one of those vicious circles.

D: Yeah, OK.

P: I mean, there are a lot of men around, but not that I can call really dating, or anything like that-

D: -Yeah, or that /you can think of establishing a relationship/ with, yeah.

P: /at least (words) yeah,   yeah/
Well, not so far, and yeah.

D: Mm hm, yeah. OK. Is there anyone that you feel you can turn to, at you know, those times when you really feel very depressed, either a clergyman, or a friend, or anybody that you can really talk things out?

P: I haven't this winter, but I should perhaps, find someone, I don't know how (words) find that. I haven't, really. I have not done it. I know I should do something like that.

D: Yeah, cause, there, you know there are alternatives, and certainly everybody is going to have cycles in their mood, and uh, and certainly I would expect that withdrawal, and there's the question of divorce, and so forth, becomes more a reality, you know, things are going to be a little bit tougher, but uh-

P: -Yeah, I think next winter will be a very difficult winter, too. I'm, and I should plan to do some good things for myself, I don't know what.

D: Yeah, yeah.

P: I don't know what.

D: OK, but you feel financially dependent on your husband enough that, you know, the question of going to Italy and, uh, such, you couldn't sw-

P: Well, I do depend on him financially, I wish I didn't. A little bit I do depend. Half and half. Half mine, half his, But uh,

D: But you think you need his permission for you to,-

P: -Yeah-

D: -go back?-

P: -because of the children. You see, and uh, /because of the children/

D: /Oh, I see, because, /
because you have legal custody, you mean? That you-

P: -Yeah, well, I'd take the children with me off, /I'd not leave them behind/

D: /Oh, I see, I see./

P: OK?

D: OK, yeah.

P: Now, I couldn't leave them now, /not until they're college age/

D: /gotta stow away, /stow away on a freighter.

P: Until they get to be 18 or 19.

D: OK. All right, um yeah. That's naughty (?). I would think that you know, certainly, there are a number of alternatives that uh, that can be at least explored. You know, some are counselors, and there are available counselors that uh, and psychiatrists, that through people that at least I'm familiar with here, also sometimes medication does help, it's not going to, you know, magically solve your marriage.

P: Yeah

D: But at least it may help you to deal with it, and I would think. you know, before you get so overwrought that you really start thinking of doing something very dramatically, or start to plan ways to do yourself in, it would probably be worth, uh, worth a phone call anyway to say, you know, how farther down could you go before you go up? So uh-

P: You mean, like uh, I should have a name, somebody's name here /(words)/

D: /Or at / least, I
guess what, what I'm saying is at least I think it's reasonable to have my name or at least to /feel that you can/ you know that you can

P: /Oh, yeah, well I—/

D: uh, and certainly through family service, or —Clinic, there's some very capable psychiatric social workers and such, who, you know, appreciate the financial commitment that's necessary if you want to get into private psychiatry, there are some extremely capable people there, too, that have, at least helped /a lot of people see their way through

P: /I'm, I'm sure would
benefit
from it enormously, but, financially we are in a very bad situation right now, and I have to find a new job and all sorts of very bad things went on last year (words) certain business in the hole, it's, ah, so I have to just limit / (word) /

D: /Well, through/ _____, _____ Clinic, they will scale it according to income and ability and so forth, and nobody's going to (word), so uh,-

P: -all right-

D: -it might be worth knowing that /there is that opportunity there/

P: /and at (word) clinic, I would get/ what, eh, like, uh, counseling?

D: Yeah, well, there are a variety of activities-

P: -oh,
I see-

D: -to some degree, you know, there, basically what it involves is an initial appointment and an intake interview with someone who sort of gets a feeling, you know, what are your problems, and uh, and then tries to make some decisions. Sometimes its a group, a group session, you know, a group of women with similar problems, /and you can/

P: /Oh, I see./

D: you know, with a, with a counselor. Sometimes its a one-on-one, sometimes it's with a trained non-M.D. professional, and sometimes it's with one of the M.D., and the, just depending on where your problems lie, or how you jointly sort of decide you need help as. So, again, it's not the, it's not the whole panacea, but it, uh, it may help, and uh-

P: -I'll keep it in mind.-

D: -At least knowing that opportunity is there, and uh, and through family service and such and uh, there/ we're for/tunate at least

P: /I'll keep it in mind/

D: that there are some alternatives to, uh, going to the poor house. OK, the uh, questions of animal fat in the diet here are of, ah, you're obviously aware of the dieting factors and we've talked about the chloresterol and such in the past, less urgent in a woman than a man, but your chloresterol's always been good, and uh worth knowing about. And the vaginal discount (?) we've talked about too. So, let's see if you're still ticking. (5) When were you last back in Italy?

P: Last summer.

D: Last summer.

P: (words) stayed (words) credit card.

D: How long were you there?

P: The children loved it. I took all three for three months.

D: Do they speak Italian?

P: Yes.

D: They do.

P: Ah, they were doing very well.

D: Yeah (sound of blood pressure being taken)

P: Great. (20)

D: OK, your pressure's good. Still about 130 over 80, that's the same general range that it has stayed.

P: Has it always been 130? Or was /that high/

D: /I think 1, oh, 120 over 80 a year ago.
I think, you know, basically 120 over 70. As long as the upper number, the systolic level stays below 140 and the lower number below 90. From minute to minute I would imagine I could check it again after we uh finish here and your pressure would probably be 120 or something. So in either case, it's normal. (15) OK, look right straight ahead. (30) All right. (8) How about dental problems, is there anything wrong?

P: No.

D: No. Nothing at all? OK. (5) All right. (5) All right. Can you swallow for me please? You once had some question of thyroid trouble but nothing significant, right?

P: No (words)

D: Yeah, deep breath. OK. Had you had any significant colds in the past year.

P: I've had (words) couple colds-

D: -Excuse me?

P: I've had a couple /(word)/ colds.

D: /couple/   Yeah. Deep breath. (5) OK, they're clear,
   without any wheezing.

P: Yep.

D: Can you lie down. Were you admitted to the hospital at all for, with the cauterization
   or conization?

P: No.

D: So you've not had a chest x-ray since last year.

P: Uh uh. (45)

D: OK. Are you aware of any lumps in your breasts at all?

P: No, the doc-doctors told me that, you know-

D: He examined you, /and you   /know how to examine yourself.

P: /yeah, oh yeah/   Uh huh.

D: It's always a good idea to do it about the same phase in your menstrual cycle so that
   the /uh there/ if there is some pattern of engorgement or

P: /yeah? /

D: such that uh, (word) but basically they're normal with no problem. (5) OK, would
   you breath deeply? Once again. All right. And the pulses all seem good too. OK
   Fine. (sound of chairs covers words) see if there's anything else you need, so we'll
   send you down for a chest x-ray and uh, some lab tests for general screening
   purposes.

P: OK

D: And you had a normal chest, or a normal EKG a year ago and I don't think there's
   any need to repeat that again this year.

P: OK

D: So, uh,-

P: -(word)-

D: -I think /what we might/ do, yeah, as far as I can see, there's no

P: /might help /

D: problem. I'm delighted to see the weight loss and uh, I think what we might do is just
   schedule a follow-up in say about four months or so, maybe in October, just to sort of
   touch base and see how things are going. If uhm, if there's a concern, uh, if you're
   feeling perfectly well and things are rosey, simply call and cancel it, but I think just
   to /at/ least have that, uh, uh, it may be that at that

P: /OK/

D: time that either, intervening with some medication or something is appropriate.

P: OK.

D: If so, we'll do it. OK, so I'll write the slip for the lab and the, uh x-ray and uhm, you
   can go down.

P: Thank you very much.

D: OK, right.

ENCOUNTER B

Patient: I'm here because I'm just not feeling well. I uhm, I feel exhausted lately, I've been running around doing lots of things entertaining and lots of social butterfly stuff and I'm just exhausted. Everything hurts me. I don't know whether I have a cold in my body, my back, muscles. My shoulders hurt, my arms, my fingers, my wrists. When I wake up my legs hurt and my feet hurt, and I haven't been walking during the night. And uhm, going along with it I just feel sort of nervous on and off. Loss of appetite at times, frequent urination, oh, tired. I and uhm, oh. Occasionally I get this very itchy feeling on my skin when I take my clothes off. Whether that's due to some kind of nerves or not, I don't know. And even last week I felt I was hyperventilating a little bit, which uh, /stopped after/ a few minutes, but I felt that I was doing.

Doctor: /you know enou—/
         You know enough about that I take it, you've done that before.

Patient: I'm not really terribly depressed or anything, I'm just sort of tired and uptight about things, irritable a little bit.

Doctor: You have a pretty good insight, huh? Haven't you?

Patient: Well,

Doctor: Hmm?

Patient: Insight into what?

Doctor: Your story that you give me almost gives the answer with it, doesn't it?

Patient: What I'm going through.

Doctor: Well, I don't know if madly would express it. With the story that you give me certainly, uh, you're telling me that you're doing too much and you ache and you push yourself and you keep going. And you keep going and then you feel more tired and then you keep going—

Patient: Well, at first I didn't think, I think it's better for me to keep going than to just be very docile in the house, because then I get depressed doing that. But uhm, it just started with this achiness and I thought at first that I had a cold and that's why I wanted to come to you initially, but all these other things /[inaudible]/

Doctor: /How long/
         has it been going on?

Patient: About a week. And uhm,

Doctor: Is this a very sudden change or pretty gradual?

Patient: What? /The nervousness or?/

Doctor: /This sudden feeling/ No, no. This whole sort of complex that seems to have come on you. Did it come on you real quick in the last week, or / [inaudible]

Patient: /No, no no.

Doctor: Gradual onset. But it's been worse in the last week.

Patient: Yep.

Doctor: Can you pin it down to anything specific?

Patient: No, I've, I've been out a lot during the day, visiting and meetings at night.

Doctor: What do you do at them?

Patient: Well we just [inaudible].

Doctor: But you don't want to pay the price. Huh?

Patient: We're, you know, we're fairly new to the area, too, and I've become involved in certain things. Trying to limit it, not to, you know, join everything and be in everything. But it just happens that I guess the springtime lots of things are going on and they climax around this time of year, and sort of taper off during the summer.

Doctor: Well, and you're learning something very interesting. It's not the housewife syndrome, it's called the suburban syndrome. And what you have to learn is something that you learned many years ago, that is how to say no. Because once there's a willing worker, you then, starting from Welcome Wagon on,

Patient: Hm hmm.

Doctor: all sorts of religious, religious, political, and social groups are just going to be knocking on your door. And uhm, I think you're, you're just going to go through cycles like this. It's perhaps a little horrendous what people go through, and I think that uhm, your insight, this is what I'm talking about about, it's right. You know damn well what you're doing.

Patient: Right. But I just need something now to [laughs]. And if it's you know, it's not something that's gonna last forever, uhm, it's just that it's got me so tired now that I just feel listless and can't do very much.

Doctor: Then why don't you stop?

Patient: Okay, so I stop, but I still feel tired now. You know what I mean?

Doctor: No.

Patient: And even if I take somethin, like a Valila, Valium, [inaudible] You know, if I feel nervous for a day or two, uh, and take one of those, there just [words, mumble] I've just been living on Bufferin, I think, for the past week, just because of the achiness that I have. And that's more, I'm worried about that more than anything else.

     . . .

     [later]

Doctor: Would you like something called meprobamate? /[inaudible]

Patient: /I don't know/ what it is.

Doctor: Fine, I'll call the pharmacy and [inaudible]. And you can mix that with aspirin. That's perfectly fine.

Patient: And what, how does it work?

Doctor: It's /a tranquilizer/

Patient: /And what does it/

Doctor: It's a tranquilizer.

Patient: Is it, does it work quickly, or does it over a long period of time?

Doctor: I don't know.

Patient: Uhm,

Doctor: What I mean by that is your reaction to it.
Patient: In other words?
Doctor: Can't predict. Each person is different. You use it four times a day. If you don't
          need it you use it once a day.
Patient: Okay.
Doctor: And if you feel lousy, you have a complete physical so you have a blood work,
          and . . . . .
Patient: That's what I though maybe you would give me a blood test today, see /if I was
          anemic./
Doctor: /For what?/ Nah, /[inaudible]/
Patient: /I sometimes/ feel like that.
Doctor: I know.
Patient: And my mother, and my mother tends to be anemic.
Doctor: Don't choose a diagnosis out of the blue. Buy a medical book and get a real
          nice diagnosis. Well, and you, I'll order them. Which drug store do you use?
Patient: Uhm, I think the gal behind the counter/
Doctor: /—It's perfectly harmless, you can,
          don't worry about it, it's you've been feeling overtired and this makes you feel
          slightly more relaxed.
Patient: Uhm, okay, I use the uhm, _____ Apothecary.
Doctor: Good, I'll give them a call.
Patient: Now, okay.
Doctor: That was definitely nothing valuable. [laughs] But look it's renewable. If you
          need it, just renew it. If you don't feel good. . . .
Patient: Okay.
Doctor: Bye bye.
Patient: Bye bye. Thank you.

Source: see text.

REFERENCES

Horkheimer, Max, & Adorno, Theodor W. (1982). *Dialectic of Enlightment*. New York: Continuum. p. 9.
Habermas, J. (1972). *Toward a rational society*. Boston: Beacon Press.
Horkheimer, M. (1982). The end of reason. In *The essential Frankfurt School reader*. New York: Continuum.
Waitzkin, H. (1983). *The second sickness: Contradictions of capitalist health care*. New York: Free Press.

3. An Empirically Grounded Approach to Ethical Analysis and Social Change*

Michael Burgess

University of Calgary, Canada

Medical ethics, as applied philosophy, analyzes concrete situations and makes recommendations to improve these situations. Many of these recommendations rest on social generalizations which sociology can support or critique, enriching the ethical discussion and resulting in more appropriate recommendations. Furthermore, an empirically based analysis can contribute to the determination of whether ethical requirements are fulfilled (e.g., informed patients; voluntariness of behavior) and reveal the social-political nature of the practice of medicine as well as the recommendations designed to alter the social interaction between medical professionals and patients. This combination offers a potent mixture of empirical method, social analysis, normative ethics, and concrete, verifiable recommendations.

What follows is a discussion of medical ethics as it is currently practiced and a theoretical discussion of some shortcomings to which sociology and an empirically based methodology can be corrective. The second section is an application of the theory to the ethical problem of informed consent as studied through videotaped interactions.

MEDICAL ETHICS AND SOCIAL GENERALIZATIONS

As applied philosophy, medical ethics seeks not only to analyze ethical situations but to make practical suggestions which resolve or at least clarify ethical problems in concrete medical situations. Ethical analysis and both forms of recommendations utilize social generalizations which are usually unsupported but apparently noncontroversial. Consider, for example, the claim that compassionate and ethical physicians are the best means of assuring ethical health care in patients' best interests (Veatch, 1981). It is easy to imagine social factors which could prevent even the most compassionate and ethical physician from delivering ethically sensitive health care in the patient's best interest. Lack of time for proper deliberation, lack of funds for tests and treatment, limited cultural ex-

* In this paper, the medical information used was obtained as part of a larger study conducted by Sue Fisher in a family practice residency. The research was partially funded by a Research and Development Award from the University of Tennessee in Knoxville. The data and analysis presented in this paper are based on research presented in my Masters' Thesis, ''Informed Consent in Routine Contexts'' (The University of Tennessee, Knoxville, 1983).

posure and understanding, failure to understand patients' complaints, and fear of malpractice may all limit the "ideal" physician's ability to act in the most ethical and sensitive manner.

Were Veatch's generalization accurate, then the most fruitful approach to medical ethics would be the sensitization of physicians to ethical issues. Social analysis of the actual system within which medicine is practiced is needed in order to either verify the accuracy of the generalization or to correct it and redirect the efforts and recommendations of ethicists.

In the more subtle process of drawing a distinction, the analytic method of philosophers who are medical ethicists may result in "clarification" and recommendations which omit ethically relevant social factors. Beauchamp and Childress (1979: 81–82) contrast "coercion and undue influence" with "mere influence or pressure to make a decision." The authors emphasize a distinction between "generally coercive environments" and "individual acts of coercion." The former are contexts in which informed consent may be valid while the latter are not. What must be shown is that the influence and pressure or generally coercive environments still permit voluntary decisions. If this is highly unlikely, then their distinction collapses: the influence and pressure of a generally coercive environment may actually be undue influence in individual cases, rendering consent invalid. (Beauchamp and Childress are not unaware of this; see their p. 81.)

In the process of making policy recommendations, social generalizations play a critical role. Paul Ramsey's medical indications policy (1978) is in part an attempt to establish a means whereby ethical decisions could be arrived at regarding involuntary treatment of patients (1978: 159). He argues that physicians are best qualified to determine what treatments in particular cases are "medically indicated" or will aid the patient's health without unnecessarily prolonging imminent death. This appraisal of physicians' qualifications and decision-making abilities is based on the assumption that any such evaluation is "an objective medical determination" and that any disagreement "may be a *real* disagreement over an objective medical situation and what should be done in a particular case." The empirical support that Ramsey's argument requires is that medical judgments and disagreements are based on physiological facts as opposed to nonmedical or "non-objective" components. Examples of nonmedical or non-objective factors would include personal or social biases, considerations of social-psychological aspects of patients and patient care, and concern over the convenience and expense of treatments for staff and family. Ramsey might counter by claiming that such considerations ought not enter into physicians' deliberations over medical indications. The empirical question then becomes whether it is possible for such "purified" deliberation to occur in the social context within which medicine is practiced.

Finally, at the case level, social generalizations or assumptions can result in recommendations which ignore ethically significant social factors. Ackerman

(1982) suggests that if the physician knows what the patient would choose among the treatment options if informed and agrees with that choice, then no harm is done in not informing and involving the patient in the process since there would be no difference in treatment decision. Others suggest that informing a patient who expresses the desire for the physician to act in the patient's behalf and does not want to be informed is unethical (Freedman, 1975: 269–272; Ingelfinger, 1972: 465–466), violating both the patients' autonomy and the trust relationship between the physician and the patient. Such assertions are based on a particular picture of the doctor–patient relationship and the context in which medical care is provided. Assumed in this picture is the absence of influences (such as physicians' belief systems) on determination of what the patient would choose if informed, and the absence of any social or psychological factors which would render blind trust on the part of the patient inadvisable. Although such considerations are not purely empirical, empirical generalizations are importantly involved. Research into these assumptions would either strengthen or counter the arguments and is therefore ethically relevant.

Empirical generalizations are found in all recommendations of applied ethics. Where the generalizations are false or inaccurate, the recommendations are likely either to be ineffective or to create more ethical difficulties. It is therefore important to find a basis from which these generalizations can be researched. Such research can sensitize medical ethicists to the social generalizations inherent in their analyses and suggestions; it can either verify the assumptions or serve as a basis from which to critique current discussions and move in more fruitful directions. Such an understanding may benefit ethical analysis and recommendations by isolating empirically verifiable criteria for the fulfillment of particular ethical requirements. This potential is explored in the next section.

VERIFIABLE FULFILLMENT OF ETHICAL CONDITIONS

One of the major obstacles to formulating practical recommendations from ethical analysis is ascertaining whether specific ethical requirements are fulfilled. Much discussion is centered around questions of concrete criteria for determining such ethically relevant conditions as death, personhood, voluntariness, competence, rationality, and whether one is "informed." Usually medical ethicists point to the vagueness of such terms and set out to give them more precise definitions. For purposes of continuity with the later analysis, the ethical issue of informed consent will be the primary example.

Informed Consent as an Ethical Issue

Within the context of medical ethics, consent is the agreement of patients or subjects to allow professionals to treat them therapeutically or as research subjects. Legal and ethical discussions emphasize that consent is valid only if the patient is informed (Capron, 1974–1975: 340–438). This concept and its application have several implications. First, consent is valid only if the consenting persons are free agents; what use would information be if one were not free to use it? Second, the qualification entails educable agents; they must be able to receive and comprehend the information (Inglefinger, 1972: 465–466). Third, the procedure consented to is such that some specific patient or subject must comprehend and consent. Fourth, since the requirement of informed consent is based on the recognition that individuals bear responsibility for their persons, the information imparted should be sufficient to allow the person the greatest possible amount of freedom and control over the decisions being made (Capron, 1974–1975: 340–346; Faden & Beauchamp, 1980). Considerations of "therapeutic privilege" suggest an exception when the physician considers the information harmful to the patient (Beauchamp & Childress, 1979).

The basic concerns which constitute the issue of informed consent can be summarized in terms of voluntariness, comprehension, sufficient information, and consent. Concrete criteria for voluntariness, comprehension, and adequacy of information are problematic. In discussions of implicit consent the criteria for actual agreement can be just as elusive, with a few easily recognizable exceptions (Graber, 1978: 233–244; Burgess, 1983). Most discussions in the current medical ethics literature focus on standards of disclosure in an attempt to determine criteria for "sufficient information" (Inglefinger, 1972; Alfidi, 1971; Veatch, 1978; Fried, 1974; Capron, 1974; Freedman, 1975; Jonas, 1969; Faden, 1977). These discussions consider content and method of disclosure since disclosure without comprehension does not fulfill the ethical requirement of informed consent (Munsen, 1979: 121–122). Little progress has been made in establishing criteria for verifying comprehension. This hinders application of the doctrine of informed consent.

If empirically verifiable criteria of comprehension could be found, they could serve as a practical measure of the fulfillment of the ethical requirement. Sociolinguistic studies of practitioner–patient interviews help by describing and analyzing the exchange of information and the contributions which each participant makes to the interview and its outcome (Fisher, 1983: 135–157; Todd, 1983: 105–133; Robillard, White, & Maretzki, 1983: 159–187). In such studies specific elements of talk and action can serve as criteria of the comprehension and contributions of the patient to the treatment decisions and informed consent. This is not to say that such descriptive and analytic tools determine what ought to be the case. Rather they can describe what is the case in sufficient detail to ground judgments as to whether the ethical requirements for informed consent (etc.) have been fulfilled, and thus aid in making ethical recommendations. Ethicists can utilize such analyses as an index to how active a role patients take or physicians allow the patient, how much understanding is displayed, and the like. This could result in recommendations whose effectiveness could be checked by further study, which would also suggest ways of revising them.

Ethical analysis and recommendations based on such empirical studies as have been suggested would require further social analysis. Consideration of the kind of recommendations that would arise from such a methodology is the task of the next section.

MEDICAL ETHICS AND SOCIAL-POLITICAL IMPLICATIONS

Sociolinguistic analysis of interactions proceed on what has been construed as different levels of analysis (Fisher, 1979; Fisher & Todd, 1983). The interactional level concerns factors that are closest to the data. This approach concentrates on how participants organize the medical interview, increasing our understanding of the everyday reality of medical practice as it is experienced by both doctor and patient (Davis, 1963; Roth, 1963; Millman, 1977, Bosk, 1981). Frankel (1983: 45) describes the value of such an approach:

> The value of an interpretive view in medicine is that it radically transforms the nature of the physician's participation in the health care encounter from an objective, dispassionate giver of advice to an interactional partner who actively participates in the social construction of illness, its treatment and outcome.

Through subtle interactional nuances practitioners emphasize and deemphasize patients' fears and conceptualizations (Paget, 1983: 55–74). Ethical concerns regarding accurate and sufficient comprehension must be placed in this context. The practitioner's responsibility or role might more productively be characterized in terms of using touch, gaze, and talk (Frankel's focus) to solicit questions and focus patients' attention, constructing with each patient a social context more likely to result in effective information exchange. Adopting this level of analysis to ethical deliberation, the medical ethicist might emphasize the overall character of the interaction, rather than particular forms and content for disclosure. The implication of such an analysis is that disclosure of information may occur in a context that defeats comprehension and may minimize rather than respond to patients' concerns. The requirement of informing the patient then implies that the medical interview needs to be made more conducive to comprehension and sensitive to patients' concerns. Only through a detailed understanding of the social organization of medical interviews can concrete recommendations be formulated.

The "organizational" level of analysis is one step removed from the data gathering (Fisher, 1979; Fisher & Todd, 1983). It is represented by such sociologists of medicine as Eliot Friedson and David Mechanic and incorporated in analysis by some discourse analysts (Fisher, 1979, 1982, 1983; Todd, 1982; Fisher & Todd, 1983) bearing further implications for ethical analysis and recommendations. More specifically, by considering the entire "event" (i.e., medical interview) discourse analysts have discovered that the conversation is not entirely locally produced but occurs in, and is constrained by, an institutional order (Fisher, 1979, 1982; Fisher & Todd, 1983; Mehan et al., in press). The discourse in medical interviews is arranged to facilitate the accomplshment of institutional goals (Fisher, 1979, 1982; Fisher & Todd, 1983). These analysts are demonstrating that the institutional authority of the doctor structures the discourse, shapes the flow of information, and influences the process of medical decision making. Not only do the professional and institutional affiliations of professionals vest them with authority, but since practitioner and patient share a common social world, the view of the practitioner–patient relationship is shared. Consequently patients are often easily persuaded that their best interests are served by the physician's recommendations. The emphasis on institutionally situated language events enables discourse analysts to consider the influence of such nonlocal factors on interactions, the production of meaning, and consequent practical outcomes.

Such insights into practitioner–patient interactions suggest that simple case-by-case approaches which treat each ethical difficulty as unique to the particular case (except for relevant abstract ethical factors) are short-sighted. Consider again the instance of informed consent. In response to a patient's signing a consent form for an invasive procedure without any disclosure taking place, the case study model would recommend a procedure of informing the patient prior to requesting a signature on the consent form. This ignores the issues raised earlier regarding practitioner control of the direction and outcome of the process of getting informed consent (Frankel, 1983: 19–54; Paget, 1983: 35–74; West, 1983: 75–106; Robillard, White, & Maretzki, 1983: 107–153). Sensitivity to these factors might result in recommendations to change interview techniques (Shuy, 1983: 189–202) or to develop interactional strategies more conducive to accurate information exchange and sensitive to patients' concerns (Frankel, 1983; Paget, 1983; West, 1983). Specific disclosure standards might at least introduce into the interview an unbiased account of the relevant general medical information. Yet practitioners utilize interactional "strategies" to emphasize and deemphasize elements of this information, influencing patients decisions. (Robillard, White, & Maretzki, 1983).

Some discourse analysts (Fisher, 1979; Fisher & Todd, 1983) suggest that the institutional authority of physicians and the reciprocal conception of the doctor–patient relationship causes patients to give undue credence to practitioners' recommendations. Without going into detailed examination of discourse analysis (for which see Fisher, 1979, 1982; Fisher & Todd, 1983) the implications for medical ethics are clear. The problem, for instance, of informed consent is not simply a problem of a lack of disclosure or patient comprehension. Rather it is a problem rooted in the shared assumption that "doctor knows best and is working in the patient's best interests" together with the authority of the physician. This simplistic assumption creates unreasonable expectations of physicians and patients. The institutional authority reflects and reinforces the assumption through professional privileges and autonomy and promoting patients' dependency. This asymmetric relationship is established before the physician–patient interaction begins.

Suggestions by medical ethicists which promote increased patient responsibility and control through informed consent (e.g., Capron, 1974–1975; Beauchamp & Childress, 1979; Veatch, 1978, 1981) represent an implicit recognition that the presupposition is unrealistic and misleading. Assuming the ethical legitimacy of increasing informed patient participation in health care, this analysis finds two interrelated obstacles; the assumption that "doctor knows best and is working in the patient's best interest" and the asymmetry in power resulting in practitioner-directed or controlled interviews and decisions. These are problems rooted in the manner in which medical professions and the delivery of health care are organized (Fisher, 1979, 1982, 1983; Todd, 1982; Strong, 1979; Freidson, 1970). In the light of this analysis, the ethical judgment that patients ought to be more involved in all aspects of their health care carries implications of social change. If analyses of the organization of medicine as reflecting and being based on societal interests are accepted (Fisher, 1979, 1982, 1983; Todd, 1982; Parsons, 1951, 1968; Waitzkin & Waterman, 1976; Stevens, 1971; Navarro, 1973; Ehrenreich & Ehrenreich, 1970; Ehrenreich & English, 1978) then similar implications follow at the level of social-political concerns.

CASES AND ANALYSIS

The cases presented are not ones in which common medical practice would require informed consent. Informed consent is usually an attempt to assure that the patients themselves choose to take the risks involved in a procedure. When the risk is substantial, as in major surgery, the need for informed consent is well recognized. In routine medical procedures the degree or type of risk is usually considered negligible or minimal; thus informed consent is deemed unnecessary. Physicians' and patients' conceptions of their reciprocal roles allow the physicians to take responsibility for the decision. Whether or not the information is given, patients usually simply take physicians' advice. That this is acceptable to both parties is based on the assumption that the nature of the decision is routine as well as on the shared expectations of the participants.

The purpose of the following research is not to evaluate either the individual physician or the profession as a whole. Rather, it is an attempt to illustrate how varying levels of risk and influence are managed in everyday medical practice by physicians and patients. The cases are not chosen because they are exceptions to the rule, but rather as illustrations of the rule; ordinary medical practitioners do not usually concern themselves with informed consent for routine cases. The analysis is not meant to be a case-by-case argument. The issues emerged as a pattern after recording, transcribing, and analyzing 43 doctor–patient interactions.

Ethnographic Description

The data for this study were collected over a three-month period in a model family practice clinic in a teaching hospital that serves a largely rural area. I participated in the project from its inception through data-gathering and analysis.

The model family practice clinic is simultaneously a setting for the training of residents and a facility delivering health care. First-, second-, and third-year residents work in an arrangement that simulates a group practice. Patients may call or walk in for an appointment. Unless they request a particular physician when calling for an appointment, each new patient is assigned to a particular physician. When a resident is unable to see his or her patient another resident will substitute as would occur in a group practice. This simulates the delivery of health care that a family practice is organized to produce.

Three staff physicians and some members of the local medical community are either in attendance or on call to the practice for the residents to consult. Nurses in the model family practice are assigned to a particular resident for one month at a time. This gives the kind of continuous working relationship with a nurse that the resident will experience in private practice. There are also professional support personnel on staff. A nutritionist, a health psychologist, and a social worker are available for consultation with residents and patients.

The patient population is set by the model family practice charter and purports to represent a population similar to that which the resident will have in private practice. The charter is set up by the American Board of Family Practice and requires that any accredited residency have no more than one-half indigent patients (including Medicaid but not Medicare). The model family practice unit also stimulates the fee-for-service character of group practice.

When new patients are booked they are given an appointment time half an hour prior to the time they are scheduled to see the physician. In this half hour the patients are individually called into an office off the waiting room where a questionnaire is given by a medical worker. The questionnaire asks about social and medical factors in patients' lives as well as means of payment (Medicare, Medicaid, insurance, personal payment). The patient information sheet is placed with a note regarding the presenting complaint in a holder on the examining room door. Before meeting the patient, the resident reads the note which lists the presenting complaint and has access to social and financial data.

Generally, the residents interview patients regarding presenting complaint and medical history and leave the room for the patients to change if the examination requires that the patient be undressed. Nurses are sent in ahead of the residents to prepare some patients (such as women scheduled for pelvic exams) and for lab tests (drawing blood, urine tests, etc.). Following the examination patients are asked to dress before the resident returns to close the interaction. During the natural breaks the residents may consult with each other or with a staff physician. Staff may also be asked to examine the patient for a second opinion. Sometime during the day the residents dictate the patient records. Typed reports are placed in patients' files and at a later date are reviewed by staff physicians.

Research was conducted with new women patients coming to the family practice clinic for the first time. After bringing a new woman patient to an examining room the nurse would notify the primary researcher or myself. One of us would then approach the appropriate resident and ask for permission to tape the medical interview. Then we would approach the patient and ask her to sign a written consent form (see Appendix). When audio tape was used one of us would sit in on the interaction to take notes on nonverbal and impressionistic aspects of the exchange. In situations where the interaction was video taped one of us would monitor the taping from a separate room.

The tapes were transcribed and they served as a basis for analysis. These typed verbal accounts were augmented by our knowledge of the setting, casual discussions, field notes, and patient files. It was in the process of reviewing the transcripts that interactional patterns regarding informed consent emerged as a topic of interest. These routine medical interactions were found to ential both patient risk and inconvenience and as such may be interactions which should be covered by an informed consent procedure. The basis presented here are attempts to reconstruct for the reader typical interactions which illustrate this pattern and to empirically ground ethical claims.

The Cases
In the first case the patient, Sheila, is a young Anglo woman who is from out of town. The physician is a third-year male Anglo resident. Sheila has been staying in her husband's hospital room for three weeks while he is being treated for injuries resulting from a motorcycle accident. Her presenting complaint is a sore throat. The resident orders a strept screen and prescribes penicillin for five days, to be increased if the screen is positive.

On physician examination the resident notes that one of Sheila's ears is "a little retracted but not red." After examining her throat he says:

D. Okay, you may have a little strept throat, I, I'll tell you what we will do. We'll go ahead and get a throat culture// (double slash lines—//—indicate an interruption)

P.   // Uh huh.

D.   and I'll go ahead and start you on some antibiotics. If the culture, the culture could still be (unintelligible) //

P.   //Uh huh.

D.   if it's uh, if it is _____ then you won't need to take a full course of antibiotics but it, it's strept well we'll have you go ahead and take a course. You're not allergic to penicillin are you?

P. No I'm not.

D. Take a deep breath. Okay. Again. Just a couple more times. All right. I'll be back momentarily. The prescription, I'll go have the nurse come do a strept screen on you.
P. Okay.
D. At that point what we'll do is give you five days worth of penicillin//
P.   //Uh huh.
D.   I want you to go ahead and take that. If your strept screen comes back negative then you can stop taking it.
P. Uh huh. After what, five days, or after?
D. Five days, after five days, what I'll do is give you five days worth, one refill. If it's positive I want you to take it for a full ten days//
P.   //Uh huh.
D.   You've taken penicillin before?
P. Yeah, uh huh. I've had to .
D. I'd like to see you again in two weeks just to make sure this is all cleared up. Hopefully you'll be all cleared up.

In the interaction the physician tells Sheila that he does not know if her sore throat is due to streptococcus (a common bacteria which can cause sore throats and is usually treated with antibiotics), that he will not know for two days, and gives her a five-day prescription for penicillin. Sheila is to take the penicillin for two days and then call to see if she should take the other three days and fill another prescription for five more days. So we can reasonably assume that Sheila is informed regarding when the strept screen can be read (48 hours), that if it is negative she does not need to continue the antibiotic, that she needs to take 10 days of antibiotics if the screen is positive, and that she should be better within two weeks.

The attending physician has attempted to cover two aspects of this type of presenting complaint in his treatment plan. First of all, he starts the patient on penicillin immediately. The usual reason for this is to prevent the somewhat rare occurrence of rheumatic fever and reduce the risk of complications. Secondly, he takes a culture and arranges for an opportunity to terminate treatment if the screen is negative. The unnecessary use of antibiotics is usually discouraged due to the slight chance of various allergic reactions, increasing sensitization to a valuable drug which reduces its later efficacy, depressing the growth of normal bacteria and contributing to the development of resistant strains of bacteria in the population at large. So this physician has treated Sheila in a manner that shows his sensitivity to the attendant problems in the treatment of sore throats with antibiotics.

Are there any factors that Sheila is ignorant of? Clearly the medical criteria specified above are not disclosed. Consequently there is good reason to believe that Sheila is not aware of why she has been given the particular treatment plan.

The next patient, Maria, is a 24-year-old Mexican-American woman. She is a heavy-set, outgoing woman who during the interview discloses that she came to this area with her boyfriend and is currently living in his house. Her presenting complaint is persistent pain in her leg following a motorcycle accident. The motorcycle she was driving slid on gravel and she fell off injuring her leg. The physician is a third-year male Anglo resident of conservative religious persuasion.[1] During the medical history she reveals that she has had three abortions and one miscarriage and thinks that she may be pregnant again. If she is pregnant, she states, she plans to have an abortion and asks the physician if they do abortions at the teaching hospital or if he knows of anywhere she can get one without having to pay cash for it up front. He tells her that hospital abortions are very expensive and that he does not know about other places in town.[2] He then has her leg x-rayed. The x-ray does not reveal any fractures or breaks. The following dialogue begins just as the resident re-enters the examining room. He is reading the package insert on the pain medication he has brought for her:

D. Well, I'm real hesitant about medication//

P.   //Yeah.

D.   You're not sure, even though, you know, you think you may want to have an abortion//

P.   //Definitely. I could make the mistake but it's not mine.

D. You may, it looks like uh, well the medication I want to use it's not recommended during pregnancy for treating nursing mothers or during pregnancy, tell you what to do. What kind of work do you do?

P. I'm a cook.

D. A cook. Uh, where do you work at?

P. I work at Hefty's Truck Plaza on Dixon Road. (names have been changed)

D. Uh huh. Are they pretty good to you?

P. Yeah, but they won't pay me (laughs).

D. They won't pay you//

P.   //Except peach pie.

D.   Okay, I bet within another day or two you'll be able to get up and stand on it without a whole lot of pain, and right now I would just use extra-strength Tylenol//

P.   //Okay.

---

[1] This resident's conservative religious beliefs were common knowledge in the clinic.

[2] There is a practice in the university hospital of referring abortions to the only licensed clinic in town—a women's reproductive health clinic. The center, in order to be licensed, had two physicians on call. In casual conversation in the family practice clinic I have heard the reproductive clinic referred to as practicing "ethically." Furthermore, abortion was frequently discussed in the family practice clinic conference room. In the discussions that we were privy to, the general attitude toward abortion was negative. This particular resident at one time said that no doctor "worth his salt" would get "messed up" with abortions.

D.
                                        and stay with that. The x-ray is negative, if the pain persists you need to get back in touch with me.//

P.   //Okay.

D.   but I don't see anything there that//

P.   //I just wanted to make sure that it wasn't fractured.

After emphasizing that Maria ought to consider birth control and denying knowledge of abortion clinics around town, the resident closes the interview:

D. Alrighty. I'd like to see you back if you've got time to come back in and see me//

P.   //Okay.

D.   otherwise if you still haven't had a period in 10 days you probably ought to consider yourself pregnant and probably come back in and get a pregnancy test or//

P.   //Or start praying hard and heavy.

D. Yeah, or start going to Mass two or three times a day.

P. (laughs) For sure. I appreciate your time.

D. Yes maam, it was nice meeting you.

P. Same to you. I'll come back whenever I need to see a doctor cause I'll never have a doctor here.

D. Hopefully 24-year-old ladies don't need many doctors.

P. Yeah, okay. Thanks a lot, bye bye.

In this second interaction the physician recognizes Maria's need for pain medication yet does not provide it. The pregnancy is considered as a contraindication for such medication, notwithstanding the patient's declared intent to abort if she is pregnant and a history of three earlier abortions. Maria is informed of the fact that her x-ray does not reveal any fractures, that the physician decided not to give her a prescription for pain medication because it is contraindicated for pregnant women. She knows that, in her doctor's opinion, the leg should feel better in a few days and that she can take extra-strength Tylenol™ for the pain. Maria is also told that if she does not have her period in ten days, she is probably pregnant.

The drug which the physician was going to prescribe and dispense presents a threat to the health of the fetus, not to Maria's health. The physician has said that the drug was contraindicated for pregnant and nursing women. The physician has not presented information regarding abortion which Maria requested. He has suggested that Maria consider birth control and explained that if in ten days she does not have her period she is probably pregnant and could get a test done at the family practice clinic.

So Maria is not informed on where to go for an abortion and that the pain medication is contraindicated for the possible fetus' health, not her own.

The third patient, Vicki, is a 26-year-old Anglo woman. Vicki works in a university library while her husband attends graduate school as an art student. The physician is a third-year Anglo male resident also in his late twenties. Vicki has several presenting complaints; a cyst on her tailbone, a skin rash, and several moles. The moles are brought into the discussion by Vicki after the physician has examined her rash:

D. What other problems or questions do you have?
P. Okay. Um I was wondering if you could take some moles off for me?
D. Okay. Where abouts?
P. (unintelligible) There's one on my forehead. Right there. _____ (unintelligible).
D. Any others?
P. Um, how many can you do at once?
D. Half dozen. Well, the problem is that, ah, on ah, young attractive females I don't usually take them off the face. But I can do it and probably everything will go well, but those are best done by either a dermatologist or a plastic surgeon. But I'll be glad to do it. We can do one in another location and see how it goes, and if you feel comfortable with it and I feel comfortable with it we'll do the one on your forehead.
P. I would not be afraid to have you do it at all. First of all I can't afford anybody else.
D. Okay.
P. But it's like (unintelligible) I would not be ashamed to have a scar.
D. Okay. Well it shouldn't leave a scar//
P.   //Okay.
D.   unless they infect or something like that. Okay? So what else would you like?

After discussing Vicki's presenting complaint, taking a medical history, and doing a physical, the physician explains what he is going to do about the cyst:
D. Okay. Uh, if it's all right with you I want to have one of our *old doctors* come look at this mole on your forehead and get his opinion on it. I was telling him about it, you know, describing it and uh, you know, as I was saying family practitioners normally don't take moles off faces, faces just because of, uh, mal, you know, they have to go up on your malpractice insurance and things like that, that we normally handle by people who do it all the time, however, I have removed them off people's faces without any problems before. It's just that we are being conservative and protecting ourselves when we do so. But I wouldn't hesitate at all to take that one off.
P. Okay.
D. But I'll get him to look at it and get his opinion on it, okay?
P. Okay.

The staff physician enters the room, lists Vicki's three complaints, and examines the moles:
SD. Okay, uh, if you remove it you're gonna will have a little scar but it probably won't be but about an inch or more, you'd have a scar that'll match this little line right here//

P.   //(laughs)
SD.   parallel, that way it'd be easy to hide it. Now see what you got here. Has that been there for a long time you say?
P.   Uh huh. Can you get rid of that? But I was never sure what it was . . . (interval)
SD.   We're reluctant to cut on women's faces.
P.   Well I'm not very vain on my face.
SD.   Well, we are (laughs).

The family practice resident works through his lunch hour and a noon conference to remove the mole on Vicki's face. After removing the one mole, he explains that he would like to remove the others later:

D. You know what? It may be, uh, best if we do these others in a, at a different time?
P. Why is that?
D. Well, uhm, we're already run way over this morning, for one thing.
P. Okay.

A few minutes later the resident refers to the difficulty the nurse had in getting the proper instruments set up:

D. Next time I'd like to use, make sure that I have the exactly instruments I want, too.

Finally, as he closes the interaction, the physician makes special arrangements to check on the incision and remove the stitches on his day off:

D. But I'll tell you what. I may just, I may just come in Monday since I'll be in town. What appointment will be best for you Monday?
P. Anytime before four.
D. Why don't we make it early in the morning. I'm actually on vacation but I'll come in just to make sure that this is okay.
P. All right.
D. And don't be grossed out by the fact that the incision is a little longer than you might have expected but I opened it a bit like that so that it would be, leave less of a scar.
P. I won't be.
D. You're not too particular are you?
P. No I'm not. I was planning on taking the stitches out myself. I//
D.   //Well, on this one I'd like to see it, on the others I might go along with that idea, okay?
P. Uh huh.
D. This one is on your face. I can't have that, you know. Turn around. _____ (unintelligible).

Vicki has come in for, among other things, the removal of moles. The resident has introduced himself as a doctor, indicated his discomfort with removing moles from women's faces, and his preference to at least do a less conspicuous one first. He has said that it is better to go to a dermatologist or surgeon but that he is capable and willing to do it. In fact he has taken moles off other people's faces at prior times. He explains that family physicians do not routinely do such removals because it would increase their malpractice insurance. He also informs the patient that he would like to have an "old doctor" give a second opinion before proceeding. The surgical room does not have the proper instruments, the operation takes longer, and the surgical scar is longer than the resident apparently thought they would be. He makes special arrangements to come in and remove the stitches and examine the incision even though he is on vacation.

Vicki asked the family practice resident to remove her moles—all of them. The reasons she gave were that she could not afford to have anyone else (a higher level specialist is implied) do it and that she was not concerned about having a scar. She is told that this particular physician has done such removals before and is not hesitant to do hers, though he might prefer to do a less conspicuous one first. She has been told by the resident that the removal should not leave a scar and by the staff ("older") physician that the scar will not be more than an inch long. Vicki is also informed that the physician can do about six removals at a time. After the removal she is told that the physician has "run way over time," that the instruments were not exactly the ones he wanted, that she should return to get the stitches removed and to have the other moles removed.

This third-year resident expressed hesitancy about removing the mole from Vicki's face, consulted with a staff physician, and worked through lunch hour to remove it. He has, despite his suggestions to the contrary, removed the most conspicous mole first. After noting that dermatologists and plastic surgeons are best qualified to remove facial moles, he explained to the patient that he was capable and experienced if she really wanted him to perform the removal.

What factors are there of which Vicki is not informed? She was never explicitly told that her attending physician was a resident and that the "older" physician was a supervising staff physician. She was incorrectly informed that all of her moles could be removed on that day. It appears as if neither she nor the resident knew that the equipment would be below the standards the resident expected, nor that the removal would take as long as it did. She also apparently was under the assumption that she could remove the stitches herself. Finally, she is also assuming that the removal performed by a family physician is less expensive than when performed by a dermatologist or a plastic surgeon.[3]

In all three cases, treatment decisions are arrived at by the physicians without patients ever having sufficient information to make an informed choice. In Sheila's and Maria's cases, the decision is simply expressed and they comply. In Vicki's case the decision is in harmony with her request and presenting com-

---

[3] The fee scale at the family practice would allow for fees for the removal of three moles in two or three visits to vary from $30 to $153. Local dermatologists varied from $25 or $30 to $175 for the removal of three moles. Most dermatologists claimed that they would complete the removals in one 30- to 45-minute appointment.

plaint. What is not clear is what influences the resident to comply with Vicki's request despite what he expresses as the usual practice to refer, and despite such adverse factors as running through the resident's lunch hour and a noon conference, lack of desired surgical equipment, and the expressed desire to do a less conspicuous one first. I first look at each case to explore the consequences of these treatment decisions for the patients. The main issue at this point is whether the treatment is *clearly* in the patient's best interest.

Analysis

Sheila received five days of antibiotics with a chance of refilling the prescription for another five days or of discontinuing if the strep screen was negative after two days. Consequently Sheila is subject to all of the risks and benefits of antibiotic treatment. Positively, she is protected from the rare occurrence of rheumatic fever and is less likely to be contagious, both of these risks being present only if she has a strep infection. Negatively, Sheila is subject to the infrequent occurrence of allergic reactions, a possible reduction of the drug's later efficacy due to sensitization, depression of normal bacterial growth (sometimes related to various yeast infections), and a societal impact of contributing to the development of resistant strains of bacteria. Whether the risks are worth the potential benefits is a controversial question in medical literature (Lasagna, 1971).

On the practical side, the treatment method has several consequences for Sheila. If the screen is positive she will need to make another trip to the pharmacy to refill the prescription. But she will not have to come back to the clinic or call the physician to get a prescription; something she would have had to do if he had either not prescribed at all or had not given her a refill. If the strep screen is negative, then Sheila is left with extra pills that she has purchased. If the physician had not prescribed before reading the screen, Sheila would not have purchased the unneeded five days' worth of pills. So, given the medical and practical costs and benefits, was the decision made in Sheila's best interest? (see Table 3.1.)

As was indicated, the medical indications are controversial. There are small chances of major risks with either treating or not treating. So on this level the treatment decision is largely a choice between consequences—it is not a *clear* medical decision. Practically, the decision influences time and money expenditures for the patient. In this case the decision to accept the risks and particular expenses/inconveniences is made for Sheila by the physician when he prescribes five days of penicillin with one refill. She is neither asked for her preference nor given the options of buying two days worth or of waiting for the screen to be read. Neither is she informed as to the basis for the physician's decision.

Maria has not been given medication for her pain. The consequences of treatment and nontreatment in this case are reasonably straightforward. Medically, treatment of the pain with the particular drug that the physician was considering carries with it the risk of damage to the fetus Maria might be carrying

Table 3.1. Costs and Benefits of Treating

Costs	Benefits
Medical	
1. Anaphylactic rections	1. Avoid rheumatic fever and complications
2. Reduction in later efficacy of drug	2. Less contagious
3. Depression of normal bacterial growth	3. May recover earlier
4. Social influence—contributing to resistant strains of bacteria	
Practical	
5. Expense—either	4. Will not need to visit doctor's office again
(a) purchase 5 days of unneeded pills, or	5. Saved expense of second five days worth of pills if screen negative
(b) need to make another trip for more pills	

but plans to abort. The benefit of treatment is reduction of pain. We could further imagine that reduction of pain might carry with it the practical implication of more comfortable use of the leg. This in turn may create a situation in which the leg injury could be made worse or prevented from healing. Practically, Maria, if treated, would be more likely to be able to work normally and not lose income. If she is not treated, Maria may need to take time off work and lose earnings, though it is possible that her leg might be saved further injury and heal faster. Given these factors, was the decision not to treat in Maria's best interest? (See Table 3.2.)

The medical cost/benefit comparison is between relief of pain and threat to the fetus. The treatment decision, within the parameters of this interaction, is whether or not to treat the pain.[4] The consequences of the physician's decision not to treat are the protection of fetal health, continued pain for Maria (unless the over-the-counter medication suggested works), and either an uncomfortable working situation or lost time at work resulting in loss of income. If Maria does take time off work, it may be that her leg will heal faster and avoid further damage. The physician makes the treatment decision without ever asking Maria for her preference. Neither did Maria state her preference unsolicited. Maria is told that the pain medication is not recommended for pregnant and nursing mothers but is not told that it is the health of the fetus she might be carrying that would be at risk. Maria does explain that she will not get paid, presumably for time off work. None of the other consequences are explicitly addressed.

The physician does tell Maria that she could take extra-strength Tylenol,™ an over-the-counter medication. So while he decides not to treat Maria with a

---

[4] There are other drugs which do not threaten the health of the fetus or the mother.

Table 3.2.   Costs and Benefits of Treating

Costs	Benefits
Medical	
1. Threat to fetal health	1. Reduction of pain
2. Threat to healing and chance of further injury with use	
Practical	
3. If further injury, may need to take time off work	2. More comfort at work
	3. No loss of time at work and in earnings

prescription pain medication, he does instruct her as to how she can get some relief. This medication is not contraindicated for pregnant women. And perhaps if Maria is doing further damage to her leg while working, the over-the-counter medication would not prevent her from feeling the pain.

Vicki has had a facial mole removed at her request. The consequences in this case are a little less obvious than in Maria's case. Part of the reason for this is because the consequences include determination of risk; the likelihood of Vicki's suffering a particular consequence. The treatment is not obviously medically indicated but is performed at the patient's request. This further contributes to the difficulty in assessing the consequences of the treatment decision.

The consequences of removing Vicki's facial mole include the usual risk of infection that always accompanies this type of operation (as Vicki was informed by the resident). In this case the risk of a more noticeable facial scar is greater than in other circumstances.[5] The risk is increased by the fact that the physician is a family practitioner with less experience than a dermatologist or a plastic surgeon. Furthermore, the physician is a third-year resident who is likely to have less experience than a family physician who has been in practice for several years. Finally, the surgery room is less than ideally equipped for the removal. Practically, the removal of this and the other moles is likely to cost Vicki more in time than if she went to a specialist or perhaps even a more experienced family physician. Financial expense may or may not exceed that of some specialists in the community. Finally, treatment does rid Vicki of her moles. A referral which results in a removal by a specialist such as a dermatologist or a plastic surgeon would entail the usual risk of infection and disfigurement but not those associated with inexperience and ill-equipped surgical rooms. (See Table 3.3.)

Vicki asked the physician if he would remove her moles and he decided, after some hesitation, to do so. Vicki expressed as her reason for coming to this particular physician instead of a dermatologist or plastic surgeon that she could

---

[5] Different circumstances would include a specialist with more experience and training and a better equipped surgery room.

Table 3.3   Costs and Benefits of Treatment

Costs	Benefits
Medical	
1. Usual risk of infection and disfigurement	1. Removal of moles
2. Risk due to non-specialist performing surgery	2. Fulfill patient request
3. Risk due to resident performing surgery	
4. Risk due to lack of proper equipment	
Practical	
5. Loss of time and money (?)	3. Save money (?)

not afford anyone else. The resident explains that his hesitation is due to the conservative practice of referral to which most family practice physicians adhere in order to avoid higher malpractice premiums.[6] Experience, or lack thereof, is never explictly mentioned except when the resident reassures the patient that he has removed moles from people's faces before. Vicki presents her particular problem which requires medical attention and the physician deliberates and chooses to treat Vicki as she has requested. Whether Vicki's estimates or expectations regarding costs are accurate are never addressed. Vicki's mole is removed, and the others at a later time, and she is subject to all the consequences of that treatment. Only the obvious risk of infection and disfigurement that accompanies this surgery when done by the best of surgeons is explicitly mentioned. Vicki is not asked whether she knows of or is willing to be exposed to the other risks and inconvenience.

All three patients probably received care that met, to varying extents, their medical needs. If only clear medical decisions were to be considered, it might reasonably be said that the treatments were all in the patients' interests. The existence of other aspects of patients' interests which are entailed in the treatment decisions enlarges the issue so that it is not so easily evaluated. Where patients have explicitly described their preference concerning these aspects, we have some basis to attempt a judgement. Where the issues are not explicitly addressed we can only describe the alternatives. Unless the advantages of one option heavily outweigh that of the other, we have no basis on which to judge patient preference. The same is true for physicians seeing patients. Unless the patient has expressed preferences, the presumption of a particular preference is generally not at all founded.

The existence of nonmedical cost/benefit factors in all three cases illustrates this issue. There are also medical factors that seem to lie within the patients' realm of responsibility since they concern them and do not require medical

---

[6] Family practice insurance, including that carried in the clinic, does cover such "office surgery" as mole removal.

expertise to judge. Choices between closely matched options are made by physicians on not entirely medical grounds such as cost analysis. A patient might rather pay the extra cost to increase convenience or for other personal reasons. Expense of time and money, accompanying benefits which might merit such expenses, and general convenience arise in Sheila's case. Maria's nontreatment involves the rejection of prescribed pain relief to protect a fetus with the possible loss of time at work and earnings and the possible benefit of being more sensitive to doing further damage to her leg. Vicki's treatment includes risking minor disfiguring and inconvenience due to inexperience on the presupposition that she will save money. Further costs which she might want to consider include additional risk due to a lack of ideal equipment and the inconvenience of needing to return for stitch and mole removals. It is my contention that these management strategies with their potential risks are outside the realm of the physician's responsibility and need to be presented to the patient for a decision.

Since patients were not asked to make a decision given the "facts," the question arises as to why the physicians made the particular decisions they did. Obviously, we cannot get at the intention that motivated a particular physician's decision. What we can do, since these are routine cases, is consider what factors might have influenced its formation. Such an analysis accounts for the factors which influence the formation of particular medical practices which result in treatment decisions. These decisions either presuppose or ignore aspects of the treatment which are legitimately within the realm of the patient's expertise and responsibility.

The ethical issue that is here examined is whether there are any influences in the delivery of routine medical care the ignorance of which could prevent or discourage patients from being involved in decisions that are their responsibility or could lead to care not in their interests. Factors inherent in the routine practice of medicine may manifest themselves as a tendency of the medical setting to guide the physician toward particular decisions and habits. The particular cases are illustrations of how these factors are manifested in the treatment of patients.

In all three cases the women lost time, money, or both. Some degree of risk was present in Sheila's and Vicki's cases. Yet these factors seem to have had little effect on the physicians' actions. The physicians suggested particular modes of treatment or nontreatment which they judged medically sound and the women agreed—as most patients do in the face of the authority of the medical role (Scully, 1980; Fisher, 1979, 1982; Todd, 1982; Fisher and Todd, 1983; Rothman, 1982). If consent to following such medical advice is implied in entering a therapeutic relationship, then the basis of consent is inadequate information. It cannot be claimed that these are decisions that require medical expertise since the common element is personal loss of time and money.

The shared presupposition that medicine is practiced in the interest of the patient helps explain why the women did not protest the physician's decisions. Other factors may also be influential. When patients do not understand the reasons for treatment they may assume that it is the imbalance of medical knowl-edge—physicians are the experts and patients the uneducated—that results in this lack of comprehension. Assuming that the particular treatment plan is in their best interest, patients do not consider whether other factors or interests might influence physicians' decisions. Patients go to physicians to have their primary or presenting complaints addressed. Both parties share the assumption that the physician will also take care of patients' general health by providing medically adequate care. This assumption is what traditionally makes informed consent for routine procedures apparently unnecessary. This is one of the ways in which knowledge is power—the physician can make decisions for whatever reasons and under various influences and the patient often does not have the information to question (Freidson, 1970; Fisher, 1982). If the physicians' treat-ment decisions are influenced by interests other than the patients', they may not have met the assumption of medical adequacy or general health.

The question now arises as to what factors that may not be in patients' interests may have influenced the physicians' decisions. As I have indicated before, I will argue that physicians tend to treat as they do because of organiza-tional and structural factors which, if not known by the patient, render informed consent invalid.

Sheila's case may be a manifestation of a profession-wide routine treatment. If we accept that the prescription of antibiotics prior to the reading of the culture is common practice (Lasagna, 1980) then we can ask what influenced the forma-tion of such a practice. Circulars and information supplied by pharmaceutical companies in the *Physician's Desk Reference* (1979: 1874) recommend the pre-scription of antibiotics *after* the presence of bacteria has been verified and sen-sitivity of the bacteria to the antibiotic has been verified. The obvious argument for prescription of antibiotics prior to reading the culture is to check the spread of the infection before it gets any worse. It may be that medical professionals feel that the risks to patients and society are minimal in comparison to the risks involved in a spreading infection. But might there be other factors involved in this practice?

For one thing, prescription of antibiotics before reading the screen means that the physician does not have to see the patient again to dispense a prescription. All that the patient needs to do is fill the prescription and the physician is saved the possible inconvenience of prescribing over the phone and explaining to the patient what the treatment is. Furthermore, the patient is less likely to get sicker and so the physician will not need to deal with a sicker patient. In Sheila's case the physician is finished with her when she leaves the office. If she calls in and the screen is positive, she already has a refill. If the screen is negative, she simply stops taking the prescription.

Structural factors may also enter into the explanation of the routine prescrip-tion of antibiotics prior to reading screens. In discussions with pharmaceutical representatives I have asked what they thought of the growing involvement of persons with doctorates in pharmacy (Pharm. D.'s). The response is usually one of discomfort. The problem with Pharm, D.'s, from the pharmaceutical representative's point of view, is that they do not want to use drugs except as the clinical trials have proven them effective and safe while any physician knows that drugs have numerous other good uses not described in the *PDR* or circulars. Except in cases where a physician is unusually well educated in pharmaceutical matters or consults a Pharm. D., most information regarding such matters is acquired through the pharmaceutical representatives or advertisements in medical journals (Silverman and Lee, 1974). Consequently it seems reasonable to expect that information given to physicians by drug representatives influences the practice of prescribing antibiotics prior to reading the culture. This is a structural level influence because it is rooted in a social factor characteristic of a capitalistic economy; the profit motive. The effect of a practice of prescribing antibiotics before documenting a bacterial infection would be a more widespread use of antibiotics. The increase in use by the medical profession results in an increase in sales and profit for pharmaceutical companies.

Once such a practice is established in the profession it is not likely to be challenged by other professionals. And given professional dominance—the ability to regulate the practice of its members (Freidson, 1970b)—it is not likely to be challenged by patients or their advocates either. It is commonly believed by those inside and outside the profession that outsiders are not as capable of criticizing as those within the profession—they are not sufficiently informed nor are they members. Professional autonomy and dominance tends to exclude Pharm. D.'s. I have observed a hesitancy on the part of the medical profession to accept their advice or authority. Since this is a feature of the profession as a whole it can be characterized as an organizational influence. The constraints under which physicians practice—the demands on their time and energy combined with the proliferation of drugs—make it nearly impossible to be well informed on the various new drugs. This is even more so in the case of the family practitioner who deals with a heavy patient load and a wide variety of medical problems. Thus, the way medicine is organized makes it easiest and most convenient to get pharmaceutical information from the representatives and companies. And for economic reasons pharmaceutical representatives are eager to tell the medical professionals about their drugs and doctors are eager to maximize their time for more patients. Patients in general are probably not aware that prescribing practices are significantly influenced by pharmaceutical companies' salespersons and advertising. This is a detail that a reasonable patient might want to know before consenting to whatever treatment a physician prescribes.

In Maria's case, the physician does not prescribe pain medication. The drug is contraindicated for pregnant women since it could threaten the health of the fetus. Maria has, in the course of the interaction, twice indicated her desire to get an abortion and has a history of three previous abortions. It seems unlikely that she would be concerned about the health of the fetus she might be carrying. It seems likely, therefore, that the decision not to give Maria the pain medication was influenced by the resident's religiously-based moral convictions. This is not to say that he avoided treatment because he wanted to protect the fetus but only that his convictions were likely to influence his decision. Even if he did act on an intention to protect the fetus, this is neither inherently unethical nor bad medicine. The ethical problem concerns the physician's conviction influencing the treatment decision without the patient's knowledge of or consent to such an influence.

If Maria's consent is said to be implied, then a legitimate question would be whether her consent was informed. There is no way for Maria to know that her physician has conservative religious beliefs which might influence his decision whether he ought to prescribe pain medication. He is a physician and Maria probably assumes that his decision is based entirely on medical criteria. The common assumption that while caring for her presenting complaint the physician will provide generally adequate health care results in his nontreatment of Maria seeming like nothing out of the ordinary. It may be more likely that the physician's actions protect the possible fetus' life, not Maria's health.

So in Maria's case the treatment decision may be influenced by a conflict of personal values. The physician's religiously-based moral values, never quite made explicit, may have influenced the treatment decision. This influence can be analyzed in terms of organizational and structural factors which allow the physician to make the treatment decision without making this influence explicit. For example, the resident's power as a medical professional is manifested in the fact that he is Maria's only means of legitimate access to a prescription pain reliever. The medical setting and the profession as a whole have as an organizational factor the control of medical information and prescriptions. This position of power is legitimated by the state in terms of licensing, self-regulation, and a monopoly over medical practice (Friedson, 1970a).[7] Therefore most patients would not consider challenging the physician's decision.

In Vicki's case the physician performs an operation at her request. The issue in this case is why the resident performed the surgery without telling Vicki about the increased risks of having him do the surgery or the possibility that a specialist might be less expensive in the long run. While he expressed hesitation, the resident may also have been influenced by the pressure in the educational setting to gain more surgical experience. This might have influenced his decision to remove Vicki's mole on the first visit instead of having her return. He may even

---

[7] The stratification of the medical profession reflects the structure of society with physicians at the top. The higher levels of stratification in both the medical profession and society coincide with the average member who is a white male. Thus the control of prescription drugs and medical knowledge is centered in a group made up largely of upper-middle-class, white, male physicians. According to this analysis it is not surprising that the values expressed in most treatment decisions represent the values of this group of persons (Navarro, 1973). This may result in an inherent conflict of interest or perspective when the patient is a woman, nonwhite, or of the lower socioeconomic class.

have been afraid that she might have second thoughts about a family practice resident removing a mole from her face. He worked through his lunch hour and a noon conference to do the operation. This seems an unusual length to go to for a surgical office procedure unless there were some particular reason to do the removal and to do it on the same day. As he sent the nurse for certain pieces of surgical equipment, it became apparent that he was not going to have the best surgical tools for the operation—he told Vicki that he would like to have different tools next time. If Vicki had to come back at another time anyway, why was it so important to do a removal right away? And why did he remove the facial mole first when he had expressed a desire earlier to do a less conspicuous one to see if Vicki and he were comfortable with it? Perhaps the pressure to gain a particular type of experience—minor facial surgery—together with a fear that the patient might not return influenced the resident toward such a decision.

Is there any organizational support for such an analysis? Residencies are on-the-job training for physicians. It is the expressed purpose of residencies to give the graduate medical student experience in the actual practice of medicine. The opportunity for some experiences is less frequent than for others. Family practice residencies only include three months of surgery experience out of three years in residency so the rare opportunity to perform surgery is likely to be cherished. Furthermore, there has been an ongoing battle since general practitioners began trying to certify as a specialty about whether they ought to be allowed to perform surgery (Stevens, 1971: 293–317). In the dispute, the privilege of doing surgery became a sort of status symbol within the profession. Consequently a family practice physician may gain in status if he or she has additional surgery experience. So surgery experience is likely to be valued in the educational setting. The increase in frequency and kinds of procedures that a resident is involved in are also likely to be looked on favorably by those who evaluate the residents. Also, family practitioners often go into isolated areas with a population of poor patients and little or no back-up in terms of higher level specialists. The need for physicians in this kind of isolated and underserved area promoted the development of family practice in the first place and is an important ideological factor in the recruitment and training of family practice physicians. Thus there is an additional organizational pressure to learn to do a wide variety of procedures.

An analysis could also be made which includes structural factors. Ehrenreich and Ehrenreich (1970: 22, 23, Chapter 1, 2, 3) make the argument that persons in the lower socioeconomic class have long been the educational and research population in our society in exchange for lower-priced or free care. Vicki says that she has come to this physician because she cannot afford a specialist. She does in fact provide an educational opportunity for the resident. Whether she has saved money or not in the long run by not going to a specialist is a different question. The point is that due to her financial status Vicki has sought out what she thought was the least expensive care and becomes part of a class of individuals who provide educational opportunities for training physicians. This factor is structural because it reflects a dual health care system; one for the poor and another for the more affluent. It is structural in another way as well. It is argued by sociologists that the poor need more medical attention and have less access to it than do higher socioeconomic classes whose need is less (Conrad & Kern, 1981). Vicki's expression of financial reasons for not seeking out a specialist is a traditional and acceptable reason to the profession. Such professional values, grounded in societal norms, are reflected in the organization of medicine and taught inadvertently to medical students. Thus Vicki's rationale is seen as reasonable and acceptable and results in her being accepted as one who understands the consequences and desires a family practice resident to remove her facial mole.

So the organizational factor of the need for surgical experience and the structural factor of the acceptability of lower socioeconomic patients as educational material creates a conflict of interest. The resident is working in a setting and from a socioeconomic and medical educational background which makes it desirable to him that he operate on this patient (Navarro, 1973, Chapter 6). He has access to information about the risks, his limited experience, and perhaps the possibility that the cost of a specialist might be less in terms of time and money yet he performs the surgery that Vicki requests. These factors form a context of influences within which his actions seem natural, even inevitable; they present a presumption in favor of acting as he did, a presumption against which few physicians would see reason to object.

In all three cases, organizational and structural factors either provided a conflict of interest or set the stage for a personal value conflict to be both covert and influential. If these factors are not part of the conception of the role of the physician, then assumptions about how and why physicians are making decisions may be in error. I have argued that such an erroneous conception of the role of the physician constitutes a significant lack of information. Since implied consent in routine procedures can only be ethically valid if it is informed, this lack of relevant information renders the consent ethically insufficient.

CONCLUSION

The foregoing discussion has combined sociological analysis and empirical methods with normative ethical considerations. The crucial generalizations (e.g., the reciprocal view of the physician–patient relationship) are explicitly drawn and are based on empirical observations and relevant sociological literature. Evidence is provided that some instances of implied consent are not informed and are therefore not ethically valid. Contextual factors at each level of analysis (interactional, organizational, and structural) shape and also sustain the issues claimed to be ethically problematic. Consequently, based on this analysis, ethical recommendations necessitate organizational as well as social-political considerations. Furthermore, additional research along these lines ought to provide a basis to evaluate the effectiveness of both ethical deliberation and recommendations regarding the relative values of the ethical principles or consequences involved in medical interaction. Such an attempt to apply ethical theory to concrete medical situations is enhanced by the incorporation of sociology and empirical methodologies for analysis as well as for formulating recommendations for change.

REFERENCES

Ackerman, T. (1982, August). Why doctors should intervene. *The Hastings Center Report.*

Alfidi, R. J. (1971). Informed consent: A study of patient reaction. *Journal of the American Medical Association,* 216.

Beauchamp, T. L., & Childress, J. F. (1979). *Principles of biomedical ethics.* New York: Oxford University Press.

Bosk, C. L. (1981). *Forgive and remember: Managing medical failure.* Chicago: University of Chicago Press.

Burgess, M. M. (1983). Informed consent in routine contexts. Unpublished master's thesis. University of Tennessee, Knoxville, TN.

Capron, A. M. (1974–1975). Informed consent in catastrophic disease: Research and treatment. *University of Pennsylvania Law Review,* 123, 340–438.

Conrad, P. & Kern, R. (Eds.). (1981). *The sociology of health and illness: Critical perspectives.* New York: St. Martins Press.

Davis, F. (1963). *Passage through crisis.* Indianapolis: Bobbs-Merrill.

Ehrenreich, B. & Ehrenreich, J. (1970). *The American health empire.* New York: Vintage Books.

Ehrenreich, B. & English, D. (1978). *For her own good.* Garden City, NY: Anchor Press/ Doubleday.

Faden, R. R. (1977). Disclosure and informed consent: Does it matter how we tell it? *Health Education Monographs,* 5, 198–215.

Faden, R. R., & Beauchamp, T. L. (1980). Informed consent and decision: The impact of disclosed information. *Social Indicators Research,* 7, 313–336.

Fisher, S. (1979). The negotiation of treatment decisions in doctor–patient communications and their impact on identity on women patients. Unpublished doctoral dissertation. University of California, San Diego, CA.

Fisher, S. (1982). The decision-making context: How doctor and patient communicate. In Robert J. Di Pietro (Ed.), *Linguistics and the professions.* Norwood, NJ: Ablex.

Fisher, S. (1983). Doctor talk/patient talk: How treatment decisions are negotiated in doctor/patient communication. In S. Fisher & A. Todd (Eds.), *The social organization in doctor-patient communication.* Washington, DC: Center for Applied Linguistics.

Fisher, S. & Todd, A. (Eds.). (1983). *The social organization of doctor–patient communication.* Washington, DC: The Center for Applied Linguistics.

Frankel, R. M. (1983). The laying on of hands: Aspects of the organization of gaze, touch and talk in a medical encounter. In S. Fisher & A. Todd (Eds.), *The social organization of doctor–patient communication.* Washington, DC: The Center for Applied Linguistics.

Freedman, B. (1975, August). A moral theory of consent. *Hastings Center Report,* 5 Hastings-on-Hudson, New York: In Ronald Munson, *Intervention and Reflection,* Belmont, California: Wadsworth, 1979.

Freidson, E. (1970a). *The profession of medicine: A study of the sociology of applied knowledge.* New York: Dodd, Mead.

Freidson, E. (1970b). *Professional dominance: The social structure of medical care.* New York: Atherton Press.

Fried, C. (1974). *Medical experimentation: Personal integrity and social policy.* Amsterdam: North Holland Publishing Company: New York: American Elsevier.

Graber, G. C. (1978). On paternalism and health care. In J. W. Davis, B. Hoffmaster, & S. Shorten (Eds.), *Contemporary issues in biomedical ethics.* (pp. 233–244). Clifton, NJ: Humana Press.

Ingelfinger, F. J. (August 31, 1972). Informed (but uneducated) consent. *New England Journal of Medicine,* 287–9, 465–466.

Jonas, H. (1969). Ethical aspects of experimentation with human subjects. In R. Munson, *Intervention and reflection.* Belmont, CA: Wadsworth, 1979. (Originally published in *Daedelus,* the journal of the American Academy of Arts and Sciences, Boston, MA, 1969.)

Lasagna, L. (1963). Some ethical problems in clinical investigation. In E. Mendelsohn, J. P. Swazey, & I. Taviss (Eds.), *Human aspects of biomedical intervention.* Cambridge, MA: Harvard University Press, 1971.

Mechanic, D. (1968). *Medical sociology: A selective view.* New York: The Free Press.

Mechanic, D. (1974). *Politics, medicine and social science.* New York: John Wiley.

Mehan, H., Fisher, S., & Maroules, N. (in press). Students' formulating practices and instructional strategies. In the *Annals* of the New York Academy of Science.

Millman, M. (1977). *The unkindest cut: Life in the backrooms of medicine.* New York: Morrow.

Munson, R. (1979). *Intervention and reflection.* Belmont, CA: Wadsworth.

National Commission for the Protection of Human Subjects of Biomedical and Behavioral Research (1978). *The Belmont Report: Ethical principles and guidelines for the protection of human subjects for research.* Washington, DC: U.S. Government Printing Office.

Navarro, V. (1973). *Health and medical care in the U.S.: A critical analysis.* Farmingdale, NY: Baywood.

New York Regents. (1965). *Journal of a meeting of the Board of Regents of the University of the State of New York,* 787.

Paget, M. A. (1983). On the work of talk: Studies in misunderstandings. In Fisher & Todd (Eds.), *The social organization of doctor–patient communication.* Washington, DC: The Center for Applied Linguistics.

Parsons, T. (1951). *The social system.* New York: The Free Press.

Parsons, T. (1968). *The structure of social action.* (Vols. I and IV). New York: The Free Press.

Physicians' Desk Reference. (33rd ed.). (1979). New Jersey: Litton Industries.

Ramsey, P. (1978). *Ethics at the edges of life: Medical and legal intersections.* New Haven: Yale University Press.

Robillard, A. B., White, G. M. & Maretzki, T. W. (1983). Between doctor and patient: Informed consent in conversational interaction. In Fisher & Todd (Eds.), *The social organization of doctor–patient communication.* Washington, DC: The Center for Applied Linguistics.

Roth, J. A. (1963). *Timetables: Structuring the passage of time in hospital treatment and other careers.* Indianapolis: Bobbs-Merrill.

Rothman, B. K. (1982). *In labor.* New York: Norton.

Scully, D. (1980). *Men who control women's lives.* Boston: Houghton Mifflin.

Shuy, R. W. (1983). Three types of interference to an effective exchange of information in the medical interview. In Fisher & Todd, (Eds.), *The social organization of doctor–patient communication.* Washington, DC: The Center for Applied Linguistics.

Silverman, M., & Lee, P. (1974). *Pills, Profits and Politics.* Berkeley, CA: University of California Press.

Stevens, R. (1971). *American medicine and the public interest.* New Haven: Yale University Press.

Strong, P. M. (1979). *The ceremonial order of the clinic.* Boston: Routledge and Kegan-Paul.

Todd, A. (1982). The medicalization of reproduction: Scientific medicine and the diseasing of healthy women. Unpublished doctoral dissertation. University of California, San Diego, CA.

Todd, A. (1983). A diagnosis of doctor–patient discourse in the prescription of contraception. In

Fisher & Todd (Eds.). *The social organization of doctor–patient communication.* Washington, DC: The Center for Applied Linguistics.

Veatch, R. M. (1978). Three theories of informed consent: Philosophical foundations and policy implications. Publication No. (OS) 78-0014. *The Bemont Report.* Washington, D.C.: DHEW.

Veatch, R. M. (1981). *A theory of medical ethics.* New York: Basic Books.

Waitzkin, Howard, B., & Stoekle, J. D. (1976). Information control and the micropolitics of health care: Summary of an ongoing research project. *Social Sciences and Medicine,* 10, 263–76.

Waitzkin, Howard B., & Waterman, B. (1974). *The exploitation of illness in capitalist society.* Indianapolis: Bobbs-Merrill.

West, C. (1980, August). What is a medical interview? A preliminary investigation of physician–patient interaction. Paper presented at the American Sociological Association Meetings. New York.

West, C. (1982). When the doctor is a lady: Power, status and gender in physician–patient conversations. In Ann Stromberg (Ed.), *Women, health and medicine.* Palo Alto: Mayfield.

West, C. (1983). Ask me no questions. . . . An analysis of queries and replies in physician–patient dialogues. In Fisher & Todd (Eds.), *The social organization of doctor–patient communication.* Washington, DC: The Center for Applied Linguistics.

APPENDIX

The University of Tennessee

Consent to Act as Human Subject

Subject's Name: _____

Date: _____

   This study examines, for research and educational purposes, how doctors and patients communicate.

   I. I hereby authorize Sue Fisher and the assistant selected by her to gather information in the following ways:

    a) to audio-tape, video-tape, and observe interactions between me and my physician;

    b) to review my medical records;

    c) to conduct interviews with my attending physician.

   II. I hereby authorize Sue Fisher and the assistant selected by her to use these tapes and this information to teach residents about communicational skills.

   III. I understand that the information-gathering techniques described in Paragraphs I and II hold the potential to enhance doctors' and patients' abilities to communicate with each other.

   IV. I understand that my confidentiality will be protected by removing my name and all other personally identifying information from all teaching and researching materials obtained by audio-taping, video-taping, and observing the interactions between me and my physician.

   V. I understand that Sue Fisher and the assistant selected by her will answer any inquiries I may have at any time concerning the information-gathering techniques.

   VI. I understand that my participation in the study is voluntary and that I may terminate it at any time with no risk to my doctor/patient relationship or to the quality of care I am receiving.

Subject's Signature_____

Witness_____

4. The Apostolic Function of the Dentist

W. Timothy Anderson

Harvard Medical School

INTRODUCTION

The topic of this paper is the "apostolic functions of the dentist." In this context, there are three major points which will be developed. First, that Balint's (1957) notion of the apostolic function of the physician is applicable and relevant to our understanding of the typical dentist–patient encounter. Second, that through the inspection of transcribed audio and video recordings of naturally occuring dentist–patient interaction it is now possible to delineate some of the particular interactional devices in and through which dentists accomplish their "apostolic function." And, third, that this attention to the microanalytic features of the interaction allows us to begin to ground the somewhat abstract notion of "institutional authority" in some of the specific practices which create and sustain it.

The findings in this paper are the outgrowth of some two-and-a-half years of observation of the interaction between dentists and their patients. The data includes participant observation field notes, audio and video recordings of the interaction, and detailed transcripts produced from these recordings. The research approach was ethnomethodological. That is, the aim was to uncover and make explicit member's practices for accomplishing this social situation (i.e., a visit to the dentist). The sample was from a northeastern metropolitan area and varied in terms of type of practice; dentist's age, sex, and social class; sex and age of patients.

THE APOSTOLIC FUNCTION

In the course of this research, a typical and pervasive feature of the dentist–patient encounter became apparent, namely, the apostolic function of the dentist. The initial conception of the "apostolic function" was elaborated by Balint (1957) in the course of his discussion of physician's practices. According to Balint:

> Apostolic function means that every doctor has a vague, but unshakeably firm idea of how a patient ought to behave when ill. It is as if the doctor had the knowledge of what was right and wrong for the patient to endure, and, further, as if he had the duty to convert to his faith all the ignorant and unbelieving among his patients.

Balint sees this conversion of patients to the doctor's view as necessary for the "successful" encounter. That is, if the physician is not successful in this process of conversion, the patient is likely to reject the physician's definition of the situation (i.e., as "illness") and fail to enter into or continue with what the physician feels is the appropriate treatment or course of action (Friedson, 1962).

It appears that a similar phenomena is recurrently present in the dentist–patient encounter. Indeed, given certain aspects of the profession and practice of contemporary dentistry which will be elaborated in the following discussion, this paper will argue that the apostolic function of the dentist is at least as important to the practice of dentistry as it is for the practice of medicine. That is, it will be argued that a significant portion of the dentist's interaction with the patient is designed to "convert" that patient to the dentist's health belief model; to the dentist's standard of what constitutes "appropriate" behavior in the operatory; and, further, to a belief that *this* dentist, in particular, is the one to whom the patient should be coming for dental care. It is these processes of "conversion," then, which are being referenced by the notion of the apostolic function of the dentist.

THE NEED FOR CONVERSION

This section will consider some of the factors which promote the production of the apostolic function by the dentist.

First, the commonly held "folk model" of dentistry and of trips to the dentist is that it is an unpleasant, expensive, and undesirable experience. Indeed, this model of the dentist–patient encounter is so pervasive that it is often shared by dentists and their auxiliaries. An overheard conversation between a dental hygienist and a receptionist presents a typical assessment on the part of dental auxiliaries of the attitudes held by patients towards coming to the dentist and, implicitly, of their own attitudes towards the encounter:

Hygienist: Mrs. _____ hates to come here.
Receptionist: I don't blame her.

Even dentists share some aspects of this attitude, as was evidenced by one dentist when, in the course of discussing with a patient the likelihood of her keeping her appointments, he commented that:

Dr. J.:   Even I put off getting my teeth cleaned.

Interviews with dentists, dental auxiliaries, and patients readily elicited comments about the perceived potential for discomfort and the frequent sense of anxiety associated with going to the dentist. That this is a commonly held folk model in the culture is further evidenced in places as diverse as the circus (where clowns representing dentists carrying oversized drills, hammers, and so on, are a standard gag), popular magazines and newspapers (where dentists are often the butt of cartoons, most of which attend to negative connotations associated with dentistry), and even some sociological literature (O'Neil, 1972, refers to dentists as "mouth miners").

It is hardly surprising, then, that dentists incorporate an awareness of this negative image associated with dental practice into their interaction with patients. Thus, a substantial amount of the interaction initiated by dentists before, during, and after their work on the patient is designed to enhance positively the encounter for the patient. This is frequently in terms of attempts to convert the patient to a different perception or definition of what the encounter is; and thereby stands as instances of the apostolic function.

Second, the dominant form of dental practice in the United States remains private and entrepreneurial (O'Shea, 1971). Dentists thus have a vested interest in building and maintaining a private practice. In dental settings such as clinics where the maintenance of a practice is not an issue, the apostolic function is much less in evidence. In private practice, however, dentists are often in the position of having to compete with each other for patients or potential patients. In a study of the social organization of dentists in a small city, Wolock and Wellin (1971) noted:

> As to exchanges of favors among dentists . . . Spring City's dental system displayed an essential asymmetry, a lack of reciprocity.

Indeed, it appears that dentistry as a profession is characterized by minimal interaction with colleagues, either professionaly or socially. This, then, creates an atmosphere in which dentists are not only trying to convert their patients to their view of the needed treatment but, also, are actively working to convince the patient that *they* are the dentist from whom they should be receiving this treatment.

In the course of the research that served as a basis for this analysis, two features emerged which seem to sustain the view. First, it was not uncommon for dentists, upon examining a (new) patient's mouth, to assess and/or criticize prior dental work; thereby casting themselves in the role of someone who can and will do better work. Second, in the course of this study I had occasion to question many people regarding their dentists. Almost without exception, *everyone* reported that their dentist was exceptional both in technical skill and interpersonal communication—someone who I must interview and observe! Of course, most of those questioned were in no position to evaluate the technical quality of their dental work, but this makes their claims all the more interesting and raised the question of how these various dentists were accomplishing, interactionally, the inspiration of trust and positive feelings on the part of their patients. It is, of course, recognized that this is undoubtedly a collaborative enterprise, in that patients have a vested interest in knowing their dentist to be a good one, and may well proceed on the assumption their dentist is competent "until proven otherwise."

A third function promoting the apostolic function of the dentist is the widely held ethic in dentistry of preventative care and instruction. This concern with preventative care provides the dentist with a mandate and an opportunity to engage in talk with the patient regarding their dental health belief model. The ethic of preventative care relates to the apostolic function in two ways. First, a concern with preventative care provides an opportunity for the dentist to attempt to convert the patient to the dentist's view of what constitutes a "healthy mouth" and adequate oral hygiene. Once this definition is accepted by the patient, the ensuing course of treatment to create this condition of a "healthy mouth" becomes a logical and natural next action. Second, the very expression of this concern with prevention can be seen as part of the process whereby the patient is "converted" to the dentist's health belief model. That is, prevention is stressed *in terms of* the dentist's model of what needs to be prevented and how that should be done; a model which may not have been initially shared by the patient. Thus, one of the desired outgrowths of a preventative care program is what dentists refer to as a "dentally educated patient," one who accepts the "treatment of choice."

Fourth, and this is in many ways tied to the previous discussion, "emergency" visits to the dentist to alleviate acute symptoms constitute a relatively small percentage of all patient visits for the typical general dental practice. Much "needed" work (for "needed" read: that work deemed necessary *by the dentist*) does not engender, prior to going to the dentist, any unpleasant symptoms on the part of the patient. Often (especially in teeth- and/or mouth-conscious middle- and upper-class practices), a patient is asked to undertake an expensive, sometimes uncomfortable, time-consuming and frequently undesired course of treatment solely on the basis of the dentist's inspection of their mouth and/or a small strip of film, and in the absence of any overt symptoms. For example:

Dentist: "If the nerve is dead we have to make a decision, *even if it's not causing you any symptoms.* (emphasis added)

Clearly, for this to happen, the patient must come to share with the dentist similar beliefs regarding the dentist's expertise and the preferred nature of dental hygiene and treatment.

Finally, and in this same vein, most dentist–patient encounters are discretionary. Even when the patient is "dentally educated" and convinced of the eventual need for some course of dental work, this is, for many patients, an emminently "postpone-able" undertaking. For many of us, it is all too easy to be "too busy" to get to the dentist. Undoubtedly, one factor in this is that most dental problems are not perceived as being threatening to life or limb. Indeed, often it is undertaken largely for cosmetic reasons. On other occasions, this "needed" work is designed to forestall problems which could arise in the future. It is all too easy to figure that at some future time we will be braver, less busy, more affluent, or generally more ready to embark on a course of dental treatment. My observations of the dentist–patient encounter revealed that this is something to which dentists are sensitive and something to which they will utilize various strategies to effect. Consider the following summation by a dentist to a patient:

Dentist: "Right now we're only going to put in a temporary and re-evaluate what we're going to do with you, if anything. Frankly, I feel we haven't reached you yet. . . . I know there's a lot of things you'd rather do than go to the dentist's office. . . . Even I put off getting my teeth cleaned. . . . You have to be ready to walk in and sit down in the chair.

In sum, all these factors which have been elaborated work together to make the "apostolic function" an important aspect of the dentist's work. For a dentist to ensure a practice which will provide a good living, one with a stable and/or growing clientele, he/she must be able to convert, convince, or coerce most of their patients into accord and compliance with their perception of the needed course of treatment, while also establishing sufficient rapport and credibility so that they will continue to be the patient's dentist of choice.

DENTISTS AS APOSTLES

Having established the background whereby it can be projected that the apostolic function is likely to be present in many aspects of the dentist–patient encounter, it is fitting that Balint's notion be reformulated to take into account these dentistry-specific features. For the profession of dentistry, then, the *apostolic function* means that dentists have a preconceived preferred reality of the encounter between dentist and patient. In that they, at least tacitly, recognize that any given patient need not share their vision or, if you prefer, version of the encounter, it is typical for them to attempt to "convert" their patients to their health belief model and their preferred perception of the encounter. This includes: constituting what counts as a "healthy mouth," thereby providing for what the optimal treatment should be; directing the patient towards appropriate behavior, which should be neither too stoical nor too expressive; alleviating (as far as possible) patient's fears regarding trips to the dentist, thus making it more likely that the patient will continue with a course of treatment once it is begun; and creating for the patient a sense that their dentist is competent, someone to whom the patient should return.

In a global sense, it probably could be said that the "apostolic function" is an issue potentially present in each moment of the dentist–patient encounter or, that it could be an organizing feature or principle of any given moment of the encounter. However, this would be to stretch the concept so far as to make it almost impossible to investigate systematically. The aim of this discussion is to ground the analysis of the apostolic function of the dentist in the particulars of its production. The central tenet is that the *in situ practices* whereby dentists accomplish the apostolic function are of interest and, indeed, are crucial to the practice of denistry.

As should be clear from the preceding discussion, this notion of the "apostolic function" of the dentist is not merely a neutral, descriptive formulation. It is, rather, a concept with profound political implications which encompasses many of the practices in and through which dentists (and, indeed, other health professionals as well) create and sustain their credibility and authority. The "apostolic function" not only invokes institutional authority as a resource; but (following the incisive approach towards the analysis of professions taken by Dingwall, 1976—that is, not as something static or given in the world but as something which is actively *accomplished*), it also can be seen as a set of practices in and through which institutional authority is produced and/or realized in a particular setting. Thus, by promoting a version of what the dentist–patient encounter *should* be, the dentist is working to create and sustain a particular "reality" for that encounter, which includes an understannding of his role and, implicitly, characterizes the nature of the institution—dentistry, of which he is a part.

Of course, it is possible that there are dental offices in which the apostolic function is rarely, if ever, readily observable. In others it may well be that where it occurs it is not successful. That is, the patient may remain "unconverted." Neither of these possibilities, however, detracts from the fundamental import of the apostolic function to the practice of dentistry. I was told by one of the dentists whom I studied that another dentist (in the same building) that I was planning to observe was noted for being very gruff and curt, not at all interested in establishing some sort of rapport with his patients, and that as a result of this, his practice was suffering. This sounds like the type of setting in which one would not expect to uncover many instances of the apostolic function. Quite the contrary, however, in both of the tapes collected in this office; although the dentist's tone of voice and demeanor were patently "gruff," the majority of the encounter was spent laying out for the various patients just what his perception of the problem was and, therefore, what the ideal treatment should be. Indeed, these tapes stand as almost prototypical examples of the apostolic function in operation and excerpts from them will be discussed later in this paper. Thus, although differences in individual style can be anticipated from office to office, as well as differences in approaches to different patients, it may well be that the apostolic function of the dentist is a phenomenon which we can anticipate in identifying in most, if not all, dentist–patient encounters.

One further point, before we move on to an examination of the actual production of the apostolic function. A considerable amount of literature in various dental journals addresses the impact on the patient of certain structural features of dental offices and operatories. Included in this is discussion of how such features as design, shape, color, and placement of equipment, furnishing and colors of waiting rooms, the apparel of the dentist and auxiliaries, and even the music played in the background affect the patient's perception of the encounter. Quite frankly, I regard these matters as peripheral, and as beyond the scope of this study. The focus here will be on the ways in which the dentist attempts to affect the patients' perception of and behavior in the encounter *in the course* of the encounter.

CONSTRUCTING A COLLABORATIVE PRODUCTION

One of the ways in and through which dentists attempt to affect the patient's perception of the encounter is by giving the encounter the appearance of being, at least in part, collaboratively produced. That is, many of the dentist's utterances, particularly in the early stages of the encounter, give the appearance of including the patient as an active agent in the production of the encounter, rather than as someone who is merely the passive recipient of the dentist's ministrations.

An initial point, before embarking on a description and analysis of this process: any course of activity undertaken by two or more parties is an instance of collaborative activity. The concern of this section is with an activity which is produced *as* collaborative, most specifically in the sense that it is designed to give the encounter the appearance of being less asymmetrical than it actually *is* (Anderson & Helm, 1980). One of the primary strategies available to patients in order to negate or circumvent the asymmetrical advantage of the physician is noncompliance. For a variety of reasons (documented in the previous section) noncompliance is an especially likely outcome of an "unsuccessful" dentist–patient encounter. Patient satisfaction with and accord with the dentist's preferred treatment is an important aspect of the overall treatment package—thus, the interactional device or strategy of building the encounter in such a way as to minimize the likelihood of noncompliance. That is, by at least appearing to include the patient in the decision-making process and in other areas of the production of the encounter, the encounter is made less threatening and more satisfying for the patient.

Further, constructing a collaborative production can accomplish the "conversion" of the patient by fiat (i.e., by presenting the dentist's version as now "our" version). This can also work to demystify the encounter somewhat, giving it the appearance of being commonplace and spontaneously constructed. This attends to a feature of the encounter which is frequently present; that just what the treatment will be *is* flexible, *is* often open to negotiation, and is something that the dentist is often trying to convert the patient to.

How, then, is the collaborative production of the dentist–patient encounter accomplished? An initial, and quite obvious method is through the dentist's use of *pronominal collaboration*. That is, through the repeated use, in utterances which can be seen to project some course of activity, of pronouns such as "us" and "we" and other expressions such as "let's" (as opposed to "I" or "I'm" or "you"). For example:

(1) D.: Okay, *let's* take a look (.) and see what *we* see (emphasis added)
(2) D.: Tell you what uh (.) *let's* numb things up . . . (emphasis added)

It should be noted that, although some of the "we's" are undoubtedly instances of the 'Imperial We' or, more charitably, designed to include the dental assistant as an active agent in the encounter, many are quite clearly built to include the patient as a referrent, thereby invoking him/her as a collaborator in the encounter.

Another device or strategy frequently employed, which may include use of the above noted *pronominal collaboration* in its construction, is the use by the dentist of a *question format* as a way of bringing the patient into the production of the upcoming activity. Consider the following examples:

(1) D.: Oka:y, what can we do for you today?
(2) D.: Well what (.) do we have in store for you today?
(3) P.: We::ll that's for you to decide

Let us look at the second utterance by the patient in examples (1), (2), and (3), which are, quite straightforwardly, continuations of their initial answer. In a sense, then, these are not "real questions" but rather interactional devices employed by the dentist to move towards a certain course of activity while appearing to involve the patient in the construction of just what that activity will be. Or, in other words, their form is collaborative but their substance is not.

Of course, questions can affect the collaborative nature of a medical encounter in many different ways. West (1982) found that physicians use the question format as a way of maintaining their power and control in the encounter. Maynard (1982) noted how some physicians utilized questions as a way of invoking the parents as collaborators in presenting the diagnosis of a child. Mischler (1983), in his analysis of medical interviews, showed how certain questioning strategies on the part of physicians failed to attend to the patient's "story."

I'M ON YOUR SIDE . . .

One of the more subtle ways in and through which the dentists advance the apostolic function in the dentist–patient encounter is by personalizing their relationship with the patient. That is, dentists often attempt to accomplish the encounter as one with the quality of a relationship; a relationship which is more than merely practitioner–patient. Interestingly, this is also a technique available to patients, particularly middle-class, professional patients, in order to demystify the encounter and mitigate some of the status differences typically present between practitioner and patient.

The assumption on the part of the dentist *seems* to be that the more convivial and "personal" the relationship, the "easier" the encounter and, further, the greater likelihood of patient compliance. Many patients (although certainly not all) seem to share this perspective, at least insofar as it gives the encounter the form of a less stressful and more egalitarian sort of relationship.

A way in which this process of "personalizing" the encounter becomes visible to the analyst is through the topicalization, by either or both parties, of their mutual history. That is, information or interests held in common, the knowledge of which is inherently tied back to previous appointments, is frequently introduced into the talk between dentists and patients, thereby establishing this encounter as one of an ongoing set of such encounters—establishing this encounter as part of a "relationship."

Thus, in the course of my observations, I frequently heard dentists question their patients about families, jobs, recent vacations, and the like. The various dental auxiliaries would also engage in this, although to a lesser extent and, typically, before the arrival of the dentist on the scene. Further, on a number of occasions this process was initiated by the patient, he or she bringing up interests held in common with the dentist such as skiing or tennis.

These discussions, which will be classified here as "small talk," typically occurred in the form of side sequences which took place in the stages of the encounter prior to the onset of "work." The topics initiated in the course of this small talk seemed to be organized by a rule which prefers, up to a point, *as much intimacy* as possible. The basic notion here is that small talk, at least in this setting, is organized around the discussion and display of "held-in-commons." Thus, where there is a history held-in-common from some prior encounter, this is often made visible:

D.:   How's your tennis game?

D.:   Where do you ski by the way?

D.:   How's B____'s job (0.3) he just switched jobs didn't he?

Where held-in-common history is more intimate than that (or perhaps "more specific" would be better), that too will be displayed:

D.:   How's the new baby been?

P.:   You in the new house yet?

With a new patient, talk of held-in-commons is confined to more global topics such as the weather or in the exploration for more specific held-in-commons:

D.:   So, what do you do for a living?

D.:   Do you have a family?

That this small talk is organized by a preference system was most clearly displayed in the following interchange:

D.:   Yup the ninth (.2) the months rolls on (2.0) what a beautiful day out there
P.:   Where's Dad?
        (1.0)
D.:   He's in—in Boston today and then he's ah lecturing up in Vermont tomorrow. He's

gotta (.) a nice deal there (0.3) he has a house up there but they're having a lecture (0.2) . . .

P.:   Ya I know it uh:h

In this instance, this patient is the regular patient of this dentist's father. The son (D.:) initiates talk at the most global level of "in-commons," the weather. The patient interrupts, upgrading the talk to a more specific level of "in-commons" and displaying his history in this office. As the dentist replies, he is again interrupted by the patient, who affirms that what the dentist is presenting as "news" is, in fact, knowledge already held in common.

One of the features of the dentist–patient encounter which this preference system attends to is that "regulars" enjoy more status in the encounter than first-timers or occasional patients. This is similar to the phenomena found in coffee shops (and bars), where both countermen and customers can often be seen accomplishing their mutual history, thereby establishing themselves as "insiders" to this social situation.

The "coffee shop phenomena" may well explain the possible importance of "small talk" for the patient. However, the larger claim I wish to assert is that this small talk *can be,* for the dentist, an essential aspect of the apostolic function. By saying this I do not mean to imply that some dentists are not truly warm, friendly, and genuinely interested in their patients' jobs, vacations, and/or families. Rather, what I am attending to is *what may well be* an unintended consequence of their behavior. That is, that by establishing a personal (as opposed to merely professional) relationship with a patient, accomplished through the display of their mutual history, the dentist fosters a patient who is more likely to trust him or her, to see the dentist as "being on his or her side." As a consequence of this, these patients are more likely to return to this dentist and are more likely to accept the treatment of choice. Thus, the ability to make small talk may be an essential or important tool for the dentist concerned with what we are calling the apostolic function.

To go a little further in this vein, one of the primary functions of small talk in the dentist–patient encounter may well be that it allows the dentist to be better able to recipient-design his utterances for the patient. That is, by acquiring through small talk a better idea of the patient's background, interests, education, attitude towards the dentist, and so on, the dentist can then design his talk most appropriately for this specific patient. This could well begin to explain why when my dentist (and several dentists have arrived at this approach independently) tells me I need to have some work done, he presents it as an "of course" phenomenon, one we have both already accepted; while to some next patient he goes into a lengthy discussion regarding just why anyone would let somebody undertake this particular course of treatment *upon them.* Dentists are certainly sensitive to what approach is most likely to work with a given patient. One dentist reported to me, just before we entered the operatory, that: "I have *to decide* whether to scare her, intimidate her, or persuade her." Interestingly, his actual approach contained aspects of all three strategies. What was clear, however, was that he was planning an approach before he walked into the operatory, and that this approach was, at least in part, based upon his prior experiences with this patient. Thus, the establishment of an interactional history between dentist and patient may be another important factor in the aspotolic function.

SELF-ASSESSMENTS

Self-assessments are one of the more patently obvious strategies whereby dentists attempt to influence the patient's perception of the encounter. I was struck, during the course of my observations, with how often the dentist, on or near the completion of the task-at-hand, would compliment himself on the fine job he had done. On several occasions these assessments of the dentist's work were echoed or even occasionally initiated by the dental assistant. Given the inability of most patients to evaluate the dentist's professional technique, these assessments initiated by the dentist or one of his auxiliaries can serve to constitute the work just completed as "a good job."

A brief digression here may serve to underscore that self-assessments are a routine device employed by servers in client-server encounters. After becoming aware of self-assessments in the context of my data as a possible thing in the world, I discovered a setting which is particularly rich in them—hair styling salons. On the basis of several admittedly unsystematic observations, it appears that it is rare for a hair stylist and/or his assistant to fail to assess, positively, their work on or near the completion of the appointment. In this vein, both I and several of my friends have experienced leaving a hair-cutting salon after having been told that we had received a "great hair cut, looks just great," only to find that, alas its "greatness" disappeared after the first shower. What I am attending to here is not the transitory nature of hair styling but, rather, the ways in which self-assessments on the part of the server (be it barber or dentist) can affect one's perception of the "success" of the encounter. That, as noted earlier, almost every friend, acquaintance, or colleague to whom I mentioned my research reported that they had a terrific dentist who did excellent work may be evidence of the success of this device.

As was noted earlier, the notion of the apostolic function is not a neutral one. One of the consequences of the successful "conversion" is that that patient's reality is often undercut or deried. Consider, for example, the following exchange between dentist and patient:

D.:   . . . you really shouldn't be that sore there (0.5)
P.:   Maybe I'm just a little uh:
D.:   You might be

P.:   I—maybe it's a lot psychological like that
D.:   Okay
P.:   I kn—I think they hurt and they probably don't even hurt that much
D.:   Allright

In the face of the dentist's perceived authority over things in the mouth, this patient is prepared to deny or downgrade the "realness" of the sensations she had experienced, to recast them as merely "psychological." This can be seen as one example of the ways in which institutional authority is accomplished interactionally. In short, the process of converting a patient to a particular version of the encounter entailing a model of the dentist's expertise and authority can entail a consequent empowering of the dentist in the interaction.

CONCLUSION

This study has reaffirmed the relevance of Balint's notion of the "apostolic function" of the physician while expanding his original conceptualization to include another arena of patient–practitioner interaction: the dentist–patient encounter. A discussion of certain features of the profession and practice of dentistry has demonstrated that the apostolic function represents a central and important aspect of the dentist's work. Further, this analysis has gone beyond an abstract discussion of the "apostolic function" to begin to examine some of the particulars of its production. It has been argued that the notion of the "apostolic function" both invokes and can be constitutive of institutional authority as an accomplished matter. The process of "conversion" can work to promote and sustain the dominance of the practitioner over the patient. Finally, it is suggested that the "apostolic function" present for other practitioners and servers is there to be uncovered and explicated. It would be a matter of both theoretical and practical interest if the interactional devices and strategies employed by dentists to accomplish their apostolic function were there to be found in other social situations.

REFERENCES

Anderson, W. T. (1981). Behavior in painful places:Aspects of the dentist–patient encounter. Unpublished doctoral dissertation, Boston University, MA.

Anderson, W. T. (in press). Dentistry as an activity system: Sequential properties of the dentist–patient encounter. In Anderson, Helm, Meehan and Rawls (Ed.), *New directions in ethnomethodology and conversational analysis*. Irvington Press, NY.

Anderson, W. T., & Helm, D. T. (1979). The physician–patient encounter: A process of reality negotiation. In E. Gartley Jaco (Ed.), *Patients, physicians and illness* (3rd. ed.). Free Press.

Balint, M. (1957). *The doctor, his patient and the illness*. International University Press.

Dingwall, R. (1976). Accomplishing profession. *Sociological Review, 24*, 331–348.

Freidson, E. (1962). Dilemmas in the patient–doctor relationship. In A. Rose (Ed.), *Human behavior and social processes*. Boston: Houghton Mifflin.

Maynard, D. W. (1982). Delivery and reception of diagnostic news: Notes on professional–client interaction. Paper presented at the Society for the Study of Social Problems, San Francisco, CA.

McIntosh, J. (1974). Processes of communication, information seeking and control associated with cancer. In *Social Science and Medicine, 8*(4).

Miller, R. S. (1975). The social construction and reconstruction of physiological events: Acquiring the pregnancy identity. Paper given at the Midwest Sociological Society Meetings.

Mishler, E. (1984). *The discourse of medicine: Dialectics of medical interviews.* Norwood, NJ: Ablex.

O'Neil, J. (1972). *Sociology as a skin trade.* New York: Harper and Row.

O'Shea, R. M. (1971). Dentistry as an organization and institution. In R. M. O'Shea and L. K. Cohen (Eds.), *Towards a sociology of dentistry.*

O'Shea, R. M., & Cohen, L. K. (1971). *Towards a sociology of dentistry.* The Milbank Memorial Fund Quarterly, Vol. XLIX, No. 3.

Sacks, H., Schegloff, E. & Jefferson, G. (1974). A simplest systematics for the organization of turn-taking in conversation. *Language* 50 (4), 696–735. Quotations from J. Schenkein (Ed.), *Studies in the organization of conversational interaction.* New York: Academic Press, 1978, pp. 7–55.

Schenkein, J. (1978). *Studies in the organization of conversational interaction.* New York: Academic Press.

West, C. (1982). What is a medical interview? A preliminary investigation of physician–patient interaction. Paper presented at American Sociological Association Annual Meetings, San Francisco.

Wolock, I., & Wellin, E. (1971). Social organization of the dental profession in a small city. In R. M. O'Shea & L. K. Cohen, (Eds.), Towards a Sociology of Dentistry.

5.

Doing the Organization's Work: An Examination of Aspects of the Operation of a Crisis Intervention Center*

D. R. Watson
University of Manchester, England

Crisis intervention centers have attracted a great deal of attention from medical experts of various kinds. This is particularly, perhaps, the case when such centers become, or aspire to become, professionalized with full-time careered and salaried staff. For instance, Brockopp (1973) recommends that telephone counseling move toward a therapist–client relationship and away from a simple "lay conversational model" of discourse between "friends." The model of therapy that apparently represents the professional ideal towards which centers should move is that of psychiatry, which perhaps is not surprising in view of these centers' avowed concern with personal problems, anxieties, depression, mental illness, suicidal inclinations, and the like.

However, it must be noted that even voluntary organizations, with a commitment to suicide prevention and personal help of a kind which is rooted in relatively diffuse lay moral imperatives, also espouse psychiatric or broader medical conceptions, and are seen in some regards as paramedical agencies with a legitimate right to make referrals to psychiatric, medical, or welfare services. Moreover, even though these voluntary agencies may invoke a "friendship" model of telephone counseling, their work is still seen as falling under the purview of psychiatry. In an article—significantly cast in medical terms and published in *The Lancet*—Barraclough and Shea (1970) conceive of the work of one such voluntary telephone counseling agency as bringing about the kinds of personal change often associated with psychotherapy. We might, then, propose that the variations in crisis intervention agencies are best described in terms of a continuum or linear array varying from the lay "befriending" agency to the professional "psychiatry-oriented" agency.

The continuum is important in a variety of other respects, too, for it reminds us that however professionalized the crisis intervention center, it may still, to a

---

* This analysis has appeared in several prior incarnations under the title "Readings of Help" (Watson, 1973, 1975). The initial analysis owed much to an initial conversation with John Lee (Sociology Department, Manchester University) and to careful attention of John Heritage (Sociology Department, Warwick University). The extensive reanalysis resulting in the present paper owes a great deal to Maria T. Wowk's critical consideration and extension of the initial paper (Wowk, 1980). J. Michael Newton and Jonathan Theobald gave invaluable technical assistance in the earliest stages of the research.

greater or lesser degree, face similar practical concerns in the actual conduct of its business. The center whose telephone counseling work I shall be examining is a voluntary agency but probably occupies a relatively medial position on the continuum. The counselors receive some psychiatric education as part of their initial training and orientation course. While this paper is not a comparative study of crisis intervention organizations, the indications from other studies are that the problems outlined below are quite generic to telephone counseling in these organizations. Their generic nature lies, at least in part, in the fact that no matter how professionalized the agency, its counseling of clients must unavoidably be conducted in ordinary language and through mundane conceptions, concerns, and reasoning procedures; one major locus of these problems lies in the fact that it is a formal organization which is being contacted.

The data corpus under consideration comprises transcriptions of audio-recordings, taken some years ago, of telephoned communications to a crisis intervention center in Britain, here pseudonymized as "The Lifeliners."[1] These data reveal an asymmetry of knowledge, often manifested immediately following the counselor's organizational identification and standard format "Can I help you?," as we see in data Extracts A, lines 2–4, and (somewhat differently) Extract C, line 2. These examples indicate that some callers, at least, do not possess the practical knowledge of the workings of the Lifeliners which would equip them in designing their problem in terms which would at least putatively dovetail with organizational relevances. The tying of the title "Lifeliners" with the activity-descriptor "help" evidently provides the flimsiest of guidelines, as the caller in line A3[2] makes clear. It might be expected that new callers to the Lifeliners might possess only adumbrated or anecdotal (i.e., contingent) knowledge of the workings of the organization, and even previous callers may not know if a new problem falls under the rubric of the Lifeliners. We can, after all, imagine a very large set of activities that might count as "help" in some circumstance or other, for example, tracking down an alleged criminal or finding a prostitute; however, it transpires in Extracts B and C that these are not the kind of help the Lifeliners have in mind. Let us now briefly examine some of the analytic issues raised by this seemingly simple observation and some analytic

---

[1] This is indeed a pseudonym. If it transpires that there is indeed a crisis intervention center or other organization of this title, no reference to that organization is intended. I have, however, tried to preserve the nonspecific nature of the organization's title. One analytic problem here is that it is possible that prospective callers to the center might be able to infer something from the actual title (as, e.g. they could conceivably draw inferences from some title such as "The Befrienders," "The Companions"). Still, the pseudonymization of an organizational title might affect or limit this analysis in some respect, though I believe it does not substantially affect the analysis of members' explicative work. Whatever inferences callers may initially draw still have subsequently to be imparted with a practical and situated specification, as we shall see.

[2] Line A3 refers to Excerpt A, line 3. Subsequent line references will be designated in the same way.

resources which might be mobilized. Since the author is committed to the continuation of sociology by other means, these resources will largely be drawn from ethnomethodology, conversation analysis, and cognate approaches.

BEARINGS

An analytic starting point may be found in the ethnomethodological interest in the way in which scenes of action, and the courses of action and interaction through which they are produced, are rendered recognizable by society members. This in turn counts on the conception of society members as pattern-detectors and pattern-exhibitors; that is, as practical reasoners about their world. Typically, members collaboratively render visible the orderliness, stability, and rule-abiding quality of their conduct and the settings this conduct produces and is embedded in. Such transparency and perspicuity is built into the actual assembling of conduct and settings, so that the conduct and settings display themselves "for what they are." These "visibility arrangements" (Pollner, 1979) are a built-in feature of conduct and settings; their specific "here-and-now" recognizability are provided for as part and parcel of constructing conduct and settings in the first place, and this construction is done by coparticipants from within the scenes of action. The very specific orderliness and recognizability of these scenes is not imposed by means of some external standard applied *ex cathedra* from outside the scene; instead, these scenes of action are "self-organizing."

Usually, such recognizability provisions comprise a tacitly and routinely consulted "background scheme." However, as Pollner points out, under certain circumstances they may, to varying degrees, become highlighted, and instead become, for parties to the scene, an attendable matter in transacting the business at hand. Indeed, as we shall see, they may constitute a significant part of that business.

Pollner suggests that defendants in court often suffer from a shortfall of practical local knowledge regarding the way to comport themselves in court, how to competently adjudge the legal considerations which may be brought to bear on their case, and the like. Pollner shows how defendants typically monitor the court's methodic proceedings in cases prior to their own in the session so as to render the proceedings in their own case visible, sensible, observable, and reportable; in this, they are aided and abetted by judges who may go to great pains to explicate, or render visible, the methodic workings of the court during the early cases of the session, so that the local socialization of defendants may be effected. These explicative transactions are effected entirely from within the court setting. Indeed, I suggest that such local asymmetries of knowledge are likely to occur in formal-organizational settings, such as business corporations, courtrooms, welfare agencies, and the like, which are often the loci of special distributions of knowledge. Even within these organizations, the internal division of labor may confront any given office-holder with a shortfall of practical knowledge as a required guide to competent action.

I have already indicated that an asymmetry of knowledge manifested in the data at hand and a second set of resources may allow us to move towards the specification of the problem. These resources derive from some considerations concerning the logical properties of proper names for persons, which we may adapt to the study of formal organizational titles, such as "Lifeliners."[3] As Searle (1963) observes, one way of conceiving of proper names is to treat them as glossing an extensive set of (as yet unstated) ordinary-language "descriptive particulars" or "uniquely-referring identifying statements" which in principle (though seldom in practice) may be provided. In this regard, the organizational title "Lifeliners" may be seen as standing on behalf of a "family" of referring statements which together uniquely refer to the object "Lifeliners" and which stand in a logical relation to that object.

While Searle's concerns, unlike our own, are purely philosophical, they may nonetheless provide us with heuristic guidelines. Searle suggests that often such descriptive statements may be unknown, only vaguely known, or not agreed upon. In such an event, the proper name conveniently may not only gloss, but gloss over, these characteristics. In this case, the use of the name may be seen to operate in a provisional way, almost as a "mock-up" on the assumption that in principle the descriptive statements exist and could be potentially furnished. We shall see that this applies *par excellence* to the use of the organizational title "Lifeliners," particularly given the vague, yet-to-be-specified-in-this-case descriptive statements which are initially provided concerning the organization, for example, "help," or the statements in lines A5–7.[4]

Our next set of bearings derives from a foundational paper by Egon Bittner (1965). He recommends that sociologists examine the ordinary uses of the concept of formal-rational organization, the terms subsumed under its *aegis* and the specific determinations made through the applications of the terms made *in situ* by persons whose competences and entitlement to apply them are socially sanctioned. This focus on the application of terms and the making of determinations has the great analytic virtue of treating such matters as features of mundane reasoning and communication which are transacted within their natural arena— namely the real scenes of practical action and interaction out of which what we call "organizations" are composed. Orthodox sociologies have frequently tended to remove the study of formal organizations from their natural settings, as part and parcel of their "appropriation" of organizational terms, rules, and so on, utilizing them as an unexplicated background resource in the furtherance of the

---

[3] This adaptation perhaps requires a somewhat free interpretation of Searle's original analysis.

[4] In many of these conversations, the situated sense of these descriptive statements is often (though not necessarily) furnished later in the conversation. Whether such sense *is* furnished is entirely an occasioned matter.

sociologist's ends. This has characteristically involved representation of a context for these terms and rules other than their natural one, and this tactic disattends their common sense status. Bittner recommends that the terms and determinations of the organization in its natural arenas become the topics of analysis in their own right. From differing standpoints and with vastly differing analytic interests, Searle and Bittner both focus our attention on members' descriptions of the organization.

This emphasis on the use of audio- or video-recordings ("retrievable data") of naturally occurring, naturally situated data is crucial. It reflects the ethnomethodologist's and conversation analyst's refusal to proceed aprioristically on the basis of often unexplicated hypothetical-typical social scientific models of (in this case) organizational structures or operations, or of substantive stipulations concerning their purported normative or other bases.[5] As Bittner says, the invocation and representation of rational organizational schemes is unspecifiable in advance—or, as Sacks (1981a) puts it, is intuitively nonapparent. Instead of specifying a single definition of the goals of the organization in advance, we must instead examine the family of routine, common sense uses of the organization or its title—uses which although characterized by overlapping resemblances are not straightforwardly interchangeable. Bittner refers to these uses as "games of interpretation and representation" (of the organization).

To return to the utterances A5–7 and A9, we can now advance the examination of the referring statements giving the sense to the organization's title. At a lower level of abstraction, we can see that the identifying characteristics mentioned above may be taken as an explication of the organization's terms—an explication which, after hearing two examples ("people that are feeling a bit lonely, depressed or —") has to "fill in" him-/herself. Considering these matters puts us in a position to work as Bittner recommends. He points us firmly in the direction of organization-incumbent's discourse, which applied to this case, on the basis of the data, we may take to comprise the common sense resources and interactional vehicles which members mobilize in order to arrive at the disposition of a certain call (including a possible finding of "no relevance to the Lifeliners," as in Extract C) as a disposition proper to the organization. We can already see that this process does not, and could not possibly, take the form of an initial provision of some full and complete exposition of organizational terms which together serve, in recipe fashion, as a disambiguation rubric for judging in advance whether or not a given problem is relevant to the Lifeliners. In Extracts B and D not even such an initial statement beyond the standard format "Can I help you?" is offered. Where what might stand as a set of organizational terms is introduced, not only is this set far from "exhaustive" but is also manifestly open-ended ("any type of help where possible, it depends what the

---

[5] I have in mind here many ethnographic analyses of organizations as well as structural-functional and other approaches.

problem is'') but also features items establishing a guarded and provisional element to the statement (i.e. ''. . . . where possible . . . .'' and ''. . . . it all depends what the problem is. . . .''). In two earlier unpublished versions of this analysis (Watson, 1973, 1975), I termed this property ''prospective circumstantiality,'' that is, that the relevance or nonrelevance of the caller's problem to the Lifeliners is yet to be decided in the light of matters which may yet be raised. This property of the calls works in close conjunction with the provisional supposition that the Lifeliners can help, until later developments render that supposition untenable. In a sense, this property simply attests to the way in which these counseling calls operate by exclusion (of proposed activities deemed irrelevant for the organization).

These procedural assumptions represent one facet of the working of the retrospective-prospective determination of sense, which is in turn part and parcel of the working of the family of interpretative procedures known as the ''documentary method of interpretation'' (Garfinkel, 1967, Chapter 3). Cicourel (1970) gives us a general formulation of this particular property of interpretation which is highly serviceable as a framework for the features of prospective circumstantiality and provisional relevance:

> Speakers and hearers both assume that what each says to the other has, or will have at some subsequent moment, the effect of clarifying a presently ambiguous utterance or a descriptive account with promissory overtones. This property of interpretive procedures enables the speaker and hearer to maintain a sense of social structure despite deliberate or presumed vagueness on the part of participants in an exchange. Waiting for later utterances (which may never come) to clarify present descriptive accounts, or ''discovering'' that earlier remarks or incidents now clarify a present utterance, provides continuity to everyday communication.

This quotation also provides us with a framework for Pollner's (1979) observation that, in traffic courts, the recital of suspects' rights and of instructions concerning courtroom procedure did not constitute the end of all explicative work; indeed, these formal-procedural matters themselves had to be explicated by the flow of subsequent events in court before their specific situated sense could be established by defendants. However, it would be misleading to infer from Pollner's comment that the initial procedural instructions are somehow inert so far as explicative work is concerned. As Cicourel reminds us above, earlier statements can serve to clarify a present utterance, too.

These observations, then, direct our analytic attention to the explicative work which is conducted throughout the entire call; one major aspect of such explicative work refers to the proper work of the Lifeliners.[6] We shall consequently be

---

[6] Of course, explicative work is involved in performing other tasks in the call, such as explicating persons' problems; while we shall be focusing on this to some degree in the section on formulation-decision pairs (see below), limitations of space prevent us from any extensive consideration of these other aspects except insofar as they are implicated in explicating the ''proper work'' of the Lifeliners.

prepared to encounter the diverse and multifarious examples of this explicative work which pervade these conversations. I shall focus on three very different examples of explicative work: membership categorizations, formulations of gist, and some rather general comments on problem/solution construals. Despite the diversity of the set, certain areas of overlap will be apparent, as will applications to the same items of data.

The overlapping elements may broadly be defined as an analytic concern with members' descriptive work vis-à-vis the organization. Interlocutors are, in the telephone calls we are studying, unrelievedly involved in such descriptive work, describing the organization and its proper functioning, describing themselves or other relevant persons, describing their and others' activities, problems or proposed solutions, all of these being addressed to the relevances of the organization or (from the callers' perspective) its putative relevances. Since such descriptive tasks seem so pervasive in interlocutors' orientation, it is *de rigeur* that our analysis gives the issue of description, and the interactional vehicles through which it is effected, a central place. Indeed, Bittner's (1965) arguments concerning the interpretations and representations of the organization and Pollner's (1979) observations on explicative transactions in courtrooms clearly point to the centrality of members' descriptive activities as integral parts of the routine operation of organizations. These descriptions are done by members themselves within the setting, as part of the setting and of its self-organizing character. Insofar as the organization of the setting involves asymmetries of authority, these asymmetries themselves are invoked, specified, and achieved in large part through interlocutors' descriptive work. There are, of course, other more prevalent conceptions of authority; however, I feel that these conceptions of authority are less well fitted to the detailed analysis of the data here presented than is the conception I have outlined.

With more specific regard to issues of authority, we may say that the ethnomethodological analyst's refusal to account for the organized properties of (say) formal-organizational setting by reference to a standard derived from outside that setting does not mean that ethnomethodological analysis does not, or can not, study the phenomenon of organizational authority. Instead, it indicates the ethnomethodologist's conception of the proper *mode* of studying this phenomenon (*inter alia*). In other words, the ethnomethodologist would seek to treat authority as organized, through members' practices, *into* the setting and *from within* that selfsame setting—the organizational setting in this case being the telephone call. From this standpoint, the point for the analyst is not to treat authority as an element external to and constraining of the setting as a separately-conceived phenomenon. The point is, rather, to revise the *way* we refer analytically to organizational authority, to treat the substantive characterization of authority with the minimum amount of apriorism and to ensure that any analytic references to authority are firmly located in the descriptive and orientational work done and shown by members in their interaction with each other. In short, this paper seeks to analyze authority as an *in situ* accomplishment. It is in this sense that their paper is concerned with phenomena we can properly gloss as "authority," and it is this issue to which we shall return later after more groundwork has been done.

MEMBERSHIP CATEGORIES AND EXPLICATIVE WORK

Membership categories are terms which identify, describe, or make reference to persons (Sacks, 1972 and 1974). They are also part and parcel of our organized common sense knowledge of our social world, and constitute loci for the imputation of rights and obligations concerning acts, and so on, within that world. "Lifeliners" is not just an organization's title but a categorization, a way of describing a collectivity of persons. In addition to inclusion of this category in the opening utterance, we also have an activity-descriptor, "help."[7] We have, then, in the standard opening utterance, an activity that is predicated upon a category and may notionally be treated as "bound" to the category (Sacks, 1972, pp. 221–4).

However, this does not get us, or rather callers, very far, for this standard-format opening utterance ". . . . can I help you?," while certainly not inert, manifestly awaits a practical specification of sense, a "situated sense," as Pollner puts it. After all, a wide variety of persons and organizations might routinely use this introductory utterance, including assorted gatekeepers and guards whose commitment to "helping" may turn out to involve variations on the brush-off theme.

It should be noted that the "Lifeliners" title does not include a "course of action" per se.[8] The title is not one which makes generally apparent the kind of help/service offered, such as "Jones, Bail Bondsman," "Wright's Auto Repairs." Many crisis intervention and counseling centers do have such course of action particles, for example, "Gay Hotline," "Lesbian Link," "Rape Victim Counseling Center," and so on, are examples, though again the practical specification of sense waits on subsequent exchanges occurring under the aegis of the organizations so titled. For instance, the first two titles may conceivably be mistaken for dating agencies or the like. However, the titles point to the domain of activities in at least a preliminary manner; the "Lifeliners" title does so to a minimal extent.

---

[7] Note that the first person singular pronoun "I" in ". . . . can I help you?" may be unproblematically redressed in terms of the organizational incumbency of the speaker. In other words, the identification "Lifeliners" is introduced by someone competent and entitled to do so on behalf of that organization.

[8] Here again we run into the problem of pseudonyms, in that the use of a pseudonym inevitably limits the reader's access to the phenomenon itself and therefore limits the analysis. All I can say is that the same "kind" of title has been selected; beyond that I have, of course, placed the interests of confidentiality before any analytic consideration.

Nor can the term "help" be seen as tightly category-bound in quite the same way as, say, "crying" is tied to "baby," to use Sacks' well-worn example. At least, in principle, it makes less sense to ask "what sort of crying do you do?" than "what kind of help do you give?". Membership categories such as "parents," "priests," "spouse," "gas station attendant," "hostess," "telephone receptionist," "police officer," and "prostitute" may all be associated with help of a kind. We have, then, the potentiation of a kind of "category and predicate puzzle," where the activity "help" is not tied to a single category in an "always and only sense"[9]—though even here, we might see crying as not exclusively tied to the category "baby," since that activity may conventionally be ascribed to "girls" or "women," too. However, whilst one may not wish to use the term "category-boundedness," the mentioning of various categories of organization may project, however indefinitely, a somewaht differing reading of help.

For instance, in Extract A, the counselor (lines 53–4) mentions organizational categorizations such as welfare organizations, social organizations, Ireland's Own Magazine (line 77), the area center (98 and 104), and Irish Clubs (lines 109–10). Here, the counselor can count upon a domain of salient activities (however vaguely or diffusely known) organized around each category in order to begin to indicate some possible type of help for the caller. The introduction of each organizational category shifts this domain somewhat and therefore shifts the type of help projected, for example, the "area center" may well collect a different set of people from "Irish Clubs" or "Welfare Organization." However, it might be noted that the help thereby implied for each organization might be seen to fall within a certain horizon, or rather to bear overlapping and cross-cutting "family likenesses" which, *mutatis mutandis,* we might gloss as "company," various types of sociability, support, and so on, as their object. The limits of that horizon may be seen in Extract A, where some types of organization, for example, "brothels," might not be properly mentionable under the auspices of the Lifeliners, however purpose-built their help might be to the requirements of Lifeliners' clients. Thus, if we cannot specify activities tightly bound to (in this case) organizational categories, we can say that the mentioning of a given category may serve to generate a sense of generally salient activities and to exclude others. This fact may, then, comprise a considerable resource in explicating the proper work of the Lifeliners as well as organizing a search procedure for help; and in some cases, the tie between categories and relevant activities may be fairly tight, as is seen in lines B25–6.

Such issues concerning the open-endedness of "help" become even more apparent when additional membership categorizations of the interlocutors are brought into consideration. For instance, one relevant categorization is that of

---

[9] See Cuff (1980, p. 80) for some cogent reservations on the tight link between identities and activities which the notion of "category-bound activities" suggests.

"stranger." The explication of the category "stranger" is not, for members, omnirelevant to encounters where "help" is given by persons previously unknown to us. As Sacks in a lecture (1971).[10] points out, if a doctor heals our broken leg, we do not say "Thanks for doing it for a stranger." Sacks' own study of telephone calls to a suicide prevention center shows that the category "stranger" is explicitly made relevant. One caller declares:

> I'm very ashamed of myself that I bothered you. . . . Then, I thought you know it's like I know you're a stranger but. . . .

Indeed, in this foundational study, Sacks (1972) points out one set of circumstances where the category "stranger" is relevant is where the disclosure of personal troubles or some confidential or intimate matter is involved. Here, callers are concerned to show that they have envisaged turning to persons who may properly be turned to for help in these matters and, indeed, who are required to offer help by virtue of their category-incumbencies relative to those of the caller. The category "stranger" falls outside this set. These category incumbencies are not equivalent but are ordered into a set of proper availability priorities such that, for instance, a husband may properly be expected to disclose his problems first to his wife before, say, his cousins. However, if the wife is unavailable for some reason, or cannot be told (for example, if the husband has committed adultery), incumbent(s) of second-position (say, parents) and subsequent categories may not be available either, since the husband may not feel able to tell these incumbents something which his wife has a right to know, and be told first. In this respect, the husband may arrive at the conclusion "I have noone to turn to," and may therefore warrantably seek out strangers, but strangers who are incumbents of another collection of categories, those with special expertise or knowledge of and obligations concerning the handling of personal troubles. In this respect, the category "Lifeliners" at least selects out a category different from that of "stranger," though as we have seen, the latter category may be invoked.[11]

The matter of paired counterpart category-incumbencies is most important to our present study. The organization of categories into what Sacks (1972) terms standardized relational pairs such as "husband-wife," "friend-friend," and so on, are crucial for our present analysis. The pairing of categories involves interlocking rights and obligations and actions. The categories are usually derived from broader collections which Sacks terms "membership categorization devices" (Sacks, 1972, 1974) or "MCD's," for example, "family," whose categories "go together" in some way considered "natural" in the culture.

---

[10] This mimeographed lecture is one of a set of lectures analyzing in detail the "New Year's Eve" transcript of a call to a suicide prevention center in the U.S.A. See also Sacks (1972).

[11] For a more detailed exposition of Sacks' study, see Atkinson (1978, p. 191–6) and Benson and Hughes (1983).

Relational pairs of categories are highly serviceable in the performing of explicative work, particularly in view of the way in which two categories may be brought to bear on the practical specification of a tie between categories and activities. In other words, members can and do turn a "one-person problem" into a "two-person problem" (Sacks, 1968, p. 31–3). One can "fix" a person's obligations to another person by pairing them as "father" and "son" respectively. Moreover, in doing this, one can categorize alter by the categorization of ego or "work back" to ego from the categorization of alter.

An instance of the "working back" technique is to be found in Extract A, where one of the ways in which the specificity of the sense (for the counselor, at least) of the caller's statement on line 18, "I'm just simply looking for a girl (I'm afraid)" is done by searching through some of the components categories of the MCD "types of (female) sexual partner." Identifications such as "(a woman) for the night," "permanent friend" and eventually (line 91) "marriage partner" are invoked, and through this what his motives are, what type of person he is, and the like (e.g., a "prospective husband" rather than a "make-out artist").

An example of the first technique can be found in utterances 2, 3, 4 and 5 of Extract C, where an activity, "putting (the caller) in touch with. . . ." is linked to a membership category, "a prostitute." The counselor excludes this activity, and here we see how the identification of the proper work of the center is done "negatively," through exclusion. One invocable set of grounds for such an exclusion is to be found by turning a category into the first of a relational pair; *which* of a possible set of alternative pairs is given by the activity described. The activity suggested by the caller in Extract C is treatment as tied to the counterpart category "pimp," or ("pudding eater" as the British police exotically term them), where neither the category nor the activity figure in the assemblage of sanctionable categories or activities falling under the *aegis* of the Lifeliners.

Furthermore, the activity of "seeking (to get in touch with) a prostitute" might in turn be consulted for who or what kinds (categories) of person might be motivated to envisage such an activity, which might yield a counterpart category such as "customer" or "client," or less quaintly, "punter," "john," and the like. This counterpart category can then be mapped onto the "type of caller" MCD, and is usable in the disposition of the case. With regard to this disposition, the counselor is able to refuse not only to put the caller in touch with a prostitute but also to (say) give him information as to how to contact a person (such as— pimp) who could do so. In these respects, our substantive cultural knowledge of prostitutes, and those seeking them, is organized in terms of a more formal and procedural apparatus of membership categories and devices, relational pairs, and so on. It is these procedures which members jointly use to conduct explicative work on the cases we are examining—explicative work which is frequently addressed to the organizationally sanctionable nature of some activity or other.

Several features of this particular apparatus can be found in the explicative work addressed to the proper tasks of this organization. Let us for now simply note two category collections which are pressed into service to this end. First, we have a collection (A 6–7), the types of person for whom the organiztion caters are named. Here, we observe the use of a "consistency rule." Broadly put, this rule provides for the preference for seeing and treating of two or more categories as deriving from the same MCD. In this case, the categories mentioned may, by the use of a consistency rule, be seen to be components of an MCD such as "people with personal troubles," which in turn might stand as proper recipients of the organization's services. A second example has already been cited, namely the collection of organizations in conversation A, line 53.

The analysis so far has, we hope, left no room for doubt that these categorization activities are jointly transacted and monitored. It is virtually impossible to imagine how they could be unilaterally done. However, it is worthwhile considering the interactional deployment of these categorization activities. A major interactional vehicle for the joint orientation to and use of membership categories (*inter alia*) is the "adjacency pairing" of utterances, as in the pair types greetings, questions and answers, and formulation-decision pairs (see below on the last type). The procedural rules for the joint production of adjacency pairs are that on a given interlocutor's production of a first pair part (say, a question), some other interlocutor should provide a second pair part (an answer) of the same pair type, as an "immediate next action." By the orientation to each other's conformity to these rules, interlocutors can monitor each other's competent understanding of the sequence; this potential of adjacency pairs for displaying understanding (Schegloff and Sacks, 1974) is crucial to the explicative work which concerns us here.

However, understanding and the operation of "visibility arrangements" are not simply achieved at such a formal level. They are also achieved through the specification of (say) an answer as *the* answer to *just this* question at *just this point* in the colloquy. Put another way, we are concerned with the here-and-now "quiddity" or "whatness" (Garfinkel, 1973, 1979) for members of each individual instance of the question-answer class, of the unique adequacy of *this* answer to *this* question just now. The particularization of a given question-answer pair is achieved through the incorporation and preservation of specific materials across the paired utterances. These specific materials operate as threads of relevance which bind together a particular question and answer by, for example, rendering the answer not just any answer but an answer minutely designed for just this question. Such particularizations are tailored to be adquate to the "why this now?" concerns of interlocutors but are, of course, the same token equally serviceable as techniques through which to effect moves towards the specification of organizationally-relevant "help-in-this-case."

One resource for establishing the unique adequacy of an answer to a question is through the rules for the use of membership categories. The most basic technique is the preservation of a single category across a question-answer pair. An example of this is to be found in lines C2–3, where the caller's question incorporates the category "prostitute," which is preserved by the counselor as a questioning repeat[12] affiliated to an answer. A second such procedure involves the case of the consistency rule for the coselection of some second category in the answer which is derivable from the same MCD as a first category incorporated into the question. In this regard, the provision of a first category in a question may be held to contain "instructions" for the incorporation of specific materials in the designing of a reply specifically tied to the question (e.g. lines A98–103).

Furthermore, these particularization techniques are of course available for use not only within, but also between, successive question-answer pairs, or indeed any series of successive utterances. Sacks formulates a "chaining rule" for questions and answers (Sacks 1974, p. 230), where a questioner has "reserved rights" to ask another question immediately after having received a reply to a prior question, such that a Q-A-Q-A-Q-A sequence is potentiated. This rule gives us the formal lineaments of a possible overall sequential organization but again we have the issue of particularization such that a second question may be designed to incorporate specific materials from the immediately prior answer. In this respect the sequence of questioning may be seen to be a specifically *thematized* line of questioning, as "just this" line of questioning.[13] Consistency procedures in the use of membership categories may, then, be part and parcel of interlocutors' sensitivity and alignment to topic and of designing their talk to minutely focus on topic (*viz* Schegloff, 1972, pp. 102–6).

In raising these "quiddity" issues, I hope to have suggested that in addition to describing the formal features of interactional units such as adjacency pairs, we also need to pay close attention to particularizing materials which serve to identify and ratify the interaction as "just this" interaction rather than a merely interchangeable case of some formally-defined class.

In an argument relevant to these "quiddity" issues, Cuff (1980, pp. 44–49, 76–80) claims that the apparatus surrounding membership categories may be too abstract to provide for members a practically-adequate specification of identities in particular settings, and that therefore the analyst is faced with problems of applying the formal description of this apparatus. I do not doubt that this is sometimes true (as it indeed seems to be for the materials Cuff himself analyzes) but I do not see the need to take this as an invariable matter, let alone a constant problem. In some settings, the introduction of a category may well not only be adequate (as is the use of "prostitute" in Extract C) but may also be a preferred

---

[12] On questioning repeats, see G. Jefferson (1972, p. 299). She writes of the "disbelief" or "surprise" element in some types of questioning repeat, though it is to be noted that in the data we are here examining the immediately subsequent talk is not directly addressed to a remedy of the problematic nature of the product item as such.

[13] From these observations, readers may gather that I consider it unwise to regard the arguments concerning "quiddity" or "unique adequacy" as necessarily constituting a critique of conversational analysis *per se*. After all, many of the techniques mobilized in the achieving of unique adequacy have themselves been described by conversation analysts.

reference. Open-endedness or indeterminacy may be crucial resources in some contexts, as we have seen above with regard to marriage bureaus, welfare agencies, and the like.[14] Moreover, we have at least indicated that in some settings the use of membership categories may be major resources not in specifying identities of persons but in members' very specific tailoring of "just this" item of interaction.

We may now move on to the brief examination of an interactional device, an adjacency pair type whose most generic properties serve to achieve explicative work. In examining this pair type, formulation-decision pairs, we can see how the "quiddity" of these conversations, that is, their gist or upshot, is sustained or transformed through interactional negotiation.

FORMULATION-DECISION PAIRS

The formulation-decision adjacency pair type comprises an interactional vehicle for (1) the production and (2) the confirmation or disconfirmation of a specific gloss, proposed by some interlocutor, of the conversation or some segment of it thus far.

The pair type works not just to propose a gloss (i.e., a "gist" or "upshot") of the conversation but also to effect a ratification or nonratification by others of that gloss; in other words, we are looking at members' devices for negotiating a "proper gloss," as Garfinkel and Sacks (1970:350–3)[15] put it.

Formulations, then, work to achieve and manifest a practical specification of the sense of an ongoing colloquy. They are often prefaced by particles such as "So," "I mean," and so on, as is evidenced in several of the instances below. Formulations are members' interactional devices through which

> talk is continuously folded back upon itself so that the presence of "proper" talk and further talk provide both a sense of "all is well" and a basis for members to describe the arrangement successfully to each other.

as Cicourel (1970, p. 150) felicitously phrases it (though not writing of formulations *per se*).

So far as formulations are concerned, the sense of "all is well" is tied into the ways in which they manifest for members the fact that a conversation is, and has been, a "self-explicating colloquy" (to use Garfinkel and Sacks' term)—that is, an intrinsically self-describing, accountable, observable, reportable phe-

---

[14] It must be emphasized that Cuff's concerns are more or less restricted to the issues (addressed by Sacks, 1972, 1974) of members' ways of arriving at a specification of identities rather than the aspects of unique adequacy discussed here; perhaps Cuff's conclusions are a product of his restriction of the treatment of MCD uses.

[15] This section of Garfinkel and Sacks' paper also gives a broad definition of formulations. For a more extensive treatment of formulations in conversation, see Heritage and Watson (1979, 1980): it is upon these papers that the present sketch is based.

nomenon; this is the explicative work of formulations. Consequently, formulations are embedded, nonextractable features of the talk and are only recognizable *in situ*. It is part of their work that for interlocutors and analysts alike formulations occasion and require a reflexive consultation of their broader sequential environments. It is only by virtue of such a consultation that a given formulation may be assessed as a possible or "proper" gloss of the talk thus far.

Some instances of formulations, derived from our data, are as follows (F = "formulation" and D = "decision." "D+" = "confirmatory decision" and "D−" = "disconfirmatory decision").

Extract A

	116.	Co.	gest to the Sean/I mean er there's all sorts of other other kinds
	117.		of girls
	118.	Cl.	huhum huhuh
F	119.	Co.	you know, but—er sh— (these're) not the type you're wanting, you're
	120.		wanting—to meet a girl so that you might settle down one day and
	121.		married
D+	122.	Cl.	that's right sir, yes
	63.	Co.	Sean I see Sean, err:
	64.	Cl.	er
F	65.	Co.	you don't drink, and you ge— and you don't go out much
D−	66.	Cl.	er well yes I do
	67.	Co.	yes

Extract B

	19.	Cl.	now a:a blue Ford came for her and I think she phoned you before it
	20.		came, would you have any record, of it you know?
	21.	Co.	er well I'm sorry but we just can't di:vulge any information at all
F	22.	Cl.	you can't do anything
D+	23.	Co.	I'm sorry I can't no
	24.	Cl.	no:
	25.	Co.	I think your best plan would be to perhaps contact the police
	26.	Cl.	Oh I will do now yes because it's a:a criminal offence you see

Extract D

F	187.	C.	(. . .) It's a terrible cruel world, you just don't want to hear
	188.		about it
D−	189.	S.	No I haven't said that I don't want to hear at all Mrs. N.
	190.	C.	You have I can tell you have and nobody wants to know. . . .

Extract E

F	173.	S.	No, at least you know that you want = what you want to do you're
	174.		rather keen to get into the civil service
D+	175.	C.	Yeah
	176.	S.	So you know you—because you know what you want to do
	177.		you're probably as well to wait another six or twelve
	178.		months and till you've got your other "O" levels,
	179.		when do you actually take your "O" levels?
	180.	C.	I take them in June
	181.	S.	In June
	182.	C.	Yeah
F	183.	S.	Yes so you know you will get the results and you could get a job
D−	184.	C.	(Well look) you see, it's not just that get's me down it—it
	185.		you know, because my mum's, she's she's a bit (. . .)

Extract F

	19.	S.	pardon ((2 seconds)) well er . . . do you keep having depressions?
	20.	C.	pardon?
	21.	S.	do you keep having depressions?
F	22.	C.	no oh sorry it's—it's been all mixed up it must be
	23.		just a gag or something y'know
Non-D	24.	S.	Oh are you sure?
	25.	C.	must be yeah
D+	26.	S.	Okay I'm sorry about that Anthony
	27.	C.	okay then
	28.	S.	bye bye

The last three extracts are not drawn from the major transcripts (A, B and C) here under consideration, but are derived from other calls to the same center.

In the examples indicated above, interlocutors' proposed glosses of the "whatness" of the conversation are incorporated into an utterance type we have termed "(a) formulation" of gist or upshot. These proposed glosses comprise first pair parts of an adjacency pair of utterances, where the second utterance comprises a decision, namely a confirmation (D+) or disconfirmation (D−) of that proposed gloss. The relevance of the decision as an immediate next action may be seen in Extract F, where the counselor's nonprovision of a decision (non-D) is a noticeable matter and is rendered accountable in terms of the initiation of particular "insertion sequence," a question and answer pair addressed to "checking out" the formulation. Immediately this checkout is done, the decision upon the formulation is issued. In other words, the character of formulations as an adjacency pair type is attested by the fact that any insertions between formulations and decisions are of the kind one typically finds operating in other pair types such as greetings, invitations, announcements, and so on.[16]

The decisions to formulations manifest an overwhelming preference for confirmations over disconfirmations. Our data show a large predponderance of confirmations, and where these occur they are characteristically marked by agreement tokens ("yes," "that's right sir, yes," in our data). The few cases of disconfirmation show the major features of utterances which apparently do not manifest the diffusely-operative preference for agreement in conversation. In particular, disconfirmations may be momentarily delayed, prefaced by mitigators agreement tokens and the like, such as "(well look) you see. . . ." and "er well. . . ." which delay and diminish the illocutionary and prelocutionary force of the disconfirmation component. All these elements may be taken as exhibiting interlocutors' orientation to a preference for agreement (in this case confirmation) in conversation.

Since the adjacency pairing of utterances highlights the inferential richness of the social organization of talk, members may monitor disconfirmations and their accompanying reformulations for their derivative interactional effects, for example, "noncooperativeness," "disaffiliation," and so on.[17] These broader effects may be intensified where delays, agreement tokens, and the like are excised and where the disconfirmation is upgraded, as in the counselor's "No I haven't said I don't want to hear at all Mrs. N." (Extract D), where the caller's prior formulation of gist itself builds in accusatory materials. However, despite this "packaging," disconfirmations do attest to the fact that members may explicitly and in occasioned ways attend to the possibility of differing understandings or of relevances which do not fully "mesh," even though these differences are, perhaps, frequently matters of nuance rather than labyrinthine disjunctures. Flat disconfirmations, however, may proliferate disjunctive glosses as in Extract D.

Formulation-decision pair types do not simply operate at the utterance-by-utterance level, however. As thematizing devices, for instance, they can operate at the mediate level of topic organization and can work to ratify and proliferate talk to topic, as in Extract E, lines 173–175. Through their potential role in *re*formulating the talk, disconfirmations of formulations may, through the occasioning of a reformulation, occasion a shift or change of topic and re-align talk to topic. The same example, lines 183–185 yield a case in point, where the particular topic of the conversation is shifted from the young caller's qualifications for the civil service to problems concerning her mother.

---

[16] Here it must be added that some utterances encapsulating gist or upshot are not adjacency paired. Work in progress by John C. Heritage (Sociology Dept., University of Warwick, England) shows that these matters may be sensitive to issues concerning the distribution of news, information, and so on, among the conversationalists, and in particular whether or not a "news-giver" or "news-recipient" is providing the gist or upshot.

[17] For a case in point, see Heritage (forthcoming).

Finally, formulation-decision pairs can operate at the level of the conversation as an overall unit; for instance, they can be part and parcel of the closing of the entire conversation. More specifically they are frequently found in preclosing sequences, as in lines 124–5 of Extract A.[18]

So far as the explication of the organization's work is concerned, formulation-decision pairs are relevant in a variety of ways. For a start, they may be used in the assessment of the organization's/counselor's work (see again, A124–5 and D187–89). Secondly, and importantly, formulations and decisions are serviceable devices for glossing-in-so-many-words the sense of the talk so far with regard to the proper work of the organization, as in lines B22–3.[19] In this regard they are very clear examples of explicative transactions and may serve to impute the situated sense of the organization's relevances in this case. However, formulation-decision pairs are perhaps most commonly used as devices for aligning or re-aligning the talk such that it may remain attuned to, encompass, and reconcile the caller's and counselor's relevances respectively. Formulation-decision pairs are pervasively usable as devices for adjusting the sanctionable concern for the proper work of the organization, and concern for a solution to his/her problems, as collaboratively oriented—to matters. It is to these relevances that we can now turn.

PROPER HELP AND THE DISTRIBUTION OF RIGHTS IN TELEPHONE COUNSELING

The calls we have been examining are notable for the pervasiveness of ordinary conversational devices—categorization work, story formats, the asking of questions and provision of answers by both parties, the introduction of formulations and of decisions by either party, and so on.[20] This is an important point, since any analysis of this data corpus must treat these ordinary conversational devices as the generic phenomenon to be analyzed; after all, such ordinary conversational devices—"ordinary talk" rather than formal interviewing—are a considerable resource in keeping callers talking, achieving the effect of "keeping them at ease," "keeping it natural" and the rest.

Nonetheless, there are some "formal" elements in the counseling conversations, which move the "type of talk" somewhat away from ordinary conversation, with free, locally-negotiated allocation of turns and turn types and towards

[18] On preclosings, see Schegloff and Sacks (1974, p. 233–64).

[19] The necessity of a reflexive consultation of the formulation's conversational surrounds is quite evident in this case; how else can one redress the sense of "anything"? Clearly the organization must sometimes be able to do something.

[20] However, it must be said that formulation-decision pairs are particularly densely found, and seem particularly serviceable for, more formal or 'business at hand' speech exchange systems, e.g. committee meetings where, indeed, the chairperson may have specially pre-allocated obligations and rights to initiate formulations of the 'sense of the meeting', etc.

the conversation. Obverseley, the counselor may not choose to close the call although s/he may initiate a preclosing utterance, or one which may be taken as a preclosing, as again evidenced in line C7.

Unlike Pollner's defendants in traffic courts, callers to the Lifeliners can not "go to school," as golfers put it, on their own case by viewing foregoing cases in the session and, from that, work out what courses of action are organizationally allowable. However, callers can be locally socialized into the organizational relevances by consulting the corpus of problem/solution construals and reconstruals, along with the counselor's decision on each foregoing construal. The above oriented-to features provide a rubric under which this local socialization can occur.

The above, necessarily incomplete, list of features is not formulated in terms of a strict logical or temporal priority. Consequently, it can not be seen as a recursive rule-set *per se*. However, interlocutors may—through their practices—treat the relations between some of the rules in this set as standing in recursive relation to each other; this is particularly the case with regard of reconstruals. Moreover, the rule-set needs further specification as to "may" and "must" issues and such specification can only be effected by a much closer examination of members' practices with regard to the deployment of these rules than is possible here. In turn, this will also require close inspection of a more primitive order of communicative devices, such as disclosure sequences, invited stories, formulation-decision pairs (see above), and the like.

The issue of "may" and "must" is crucial since this involves various asymmetries in the distribution of rights and particularly in the pairing of rights and obligations. For instance, the caller may make a personal disclosure, but is not obliged to; the counselor, for his/her part, *must* decide on the relevance of that disclosure to the proper work of the organization.

Nonetheless, it should not be assumed that the presence of these asymmetries or in the general distribution of rights in these calls amount to a power relation in any "zero-sum" conception of that term. Instead, there are several countervailing zero-sum bases in the conversation. Each interlocutor has some basis for a margin of control over the course the call takes. For instance, one basis of the counselor's margin of control is his/her ability to decide on the relvance of a given problem/solution-construal to the organization, and to make determinations as to whether and how the Lifeliners can help.

The caller, for his/her part, has the ability to decide whether and how to disclose any personal problem. This is largely because, by definition, "personal problems" involve a particular order of knowledge, which the subject can know (or best know) and avow on his/her own behalf. This knowledge is, in other words, "experience-licensed," and not only is the counselor conventionally conceivable as having "secondhand access" to the problem, but also as possessing limited rights to the definition or construal of the problem or of the specific personal knowledge and biographical experience which might conceivably be brought to bear upon the problem. In all these respects, a caller can efficaciously "second guess" the counselor, as occurs in the caller's disconfirmation of the counselor's formulation of her problem in Extract E above.

This data extract shows how callers, from their "experience licenced" basis, can enjoin counselors to design their problem/solution construal so as to display more sensitivity to the minute specificities of the caller's declared situation or requirements. Not just *any* organizationally-proper "standard format" construal is deemed adequate by the caller; again the unique adequacy requirement is manifested. It is in this respect that problem/solution construals have to satisfy two sets of relevances, not just that of relevance to the organization.

Derivatively, the caller has a basis for the explicit assessment and evaluation of the counselor's performance, and—where telephone counseling is fully- or semi-professionalized—may be highly consequential for the organizational career of the counselor. Sacks (1971) observes that some suicides have even mentioned in their suicide note their counselors' failure to help them; especially when the note comes to be publicized in the media, the center's image and reputation may end up rather dented. In sum, clients are anything but the passive recipients of help, as is manifest in Excerpt D above, where the counselor is not only kept talking but also spurred on to greater efforts by the caller. The active participation of callers is, of course, initially apparent in the fact that they called the center in the first place. However, the use of interactional devices such as the formulation-decision adjacency pair also provide for the continuation of such active involvement (see D188–89 and A124–25).

Restrictions prevented consideration of many aspects of the calls. However, the analysis has been taken far enough to at least have indicated the promise and necessity of such a task.

REFERENCES

Atkinson, M. (1978). Discovering suicide. London: Macmillan.
Barraclough, B. M., & Shea, M. (1970). Suicide and samaritan clients. The Lancet, October 26, pp. 868–70.
Benson, D. W., & Hughes, J. A. (1983). The perspective of ethnomethodology. London: Longman.
Bittner, E. (1974). The concept of organization. Social Research, 32. (Reprinted in R. Turner (Ed.), Ethnomethodology. Harmondsworth: Penguin Books, 1974.)
Brockopp, G. W. (1973). The telephone call: Conversation or therapy? In D. Lester & G. W. Brockopp (Eds.), Crisis intervention and counselling by telephone. Springfield, Illinois: Charles C. Thomas Publishers.
Cicourel, A. V. (1970). The acquisition of social structure: Toward a developmental sociology of language and meaning. In J. D. Douglas (Ed.), Understanding everyday life: Toward a reconstruction of sociological knowledge. Chicago: Aldine Publishing Co.
Cuff, E. C. (1980). Some issues in studying the problem of versions in everyday life. Occasional papers in sociology, No. 3. Sociology Department, University of Manchester, Manchester M13 9PL, England (January).
Garfinkel, H. (1967). Studies in ethnomethodology. Englewood Cliffs, NJ, Prentice-Hall.

Garfinkel, H. (1973). Lecture series given as Simon Visiting Professor, Sociology Department, Manchester University, Manchester, England.

Garfinkel, H. (1979). Lawyers' work. Plenary session lecture presented to the British Sociological Association's National Conference on Law and Society (Easter).

Garfinkel, H. & Sacks, H. (1970). On formal structures of practical actions.' In E. A. Tiryakian & J. C. McKinney (Eds.), Theoretical sociology: Perspectives and developments. New York: Appleton-Century-Crofts.

Heritage, J. C. (in press). Analysing news interviews: Aspects of the production of talk for an overhearing audience. In T. van Dijk (Ed.), Handbook of discourse analysis (vol. 3). Genres of discourse. London: Academic Press.

Heritage, J. C., & Watson, D. R. (1979). Formulations as conversational objects. In G. Psathas (Ed.), Everyday language: Studies in ethnomethodology. New York: Irvington Publishing Associates.

Heritage, J. C. & Watson, D. R. (1980). Aspects of the properties of formulations in natural conversation: Some instances analysed. Semiotica, *30,* 314, 245–262.

Jefferson, G. (1972). Side sequences. In D. Sudnow (Ed.), Studies in social interaction. New York: The Free Press.

McHoul, A. W. (1978). The organization of turns at formal talk in the classroom. Language in Society, *7.*

Pollner, M. (1979). Explicative transactions: Making and managing meaning in traffic court. In G. Psathas (Ed.), Everyday language: Studies in ethnomethodology. New York: Irvington Publishing Associates.

Sacks, H. (1968). Statement in Session 1. In R. J. Hill & K. S. Crittenden (Eds.), Proceedings of the purdue symposium on ethnomethodology. Lafayette, Indiana: Institute for the Study of Social Change, Sociology Department, Purdue University, Monography, No. 1.

Sacks, H. (1971). Lecture (mimeo). Social Science Department, University of California at Irvine, May 21.

Sacks, H. (1972). An initial investigation of the usability of conversational data for doing sociology. In D. Sudnow (Ed.), Studies in social interaction. New York: The Free Press.

Sacks, H. (1974). On the analysability of stories by children. In R. Turner (Ed.), Ethnomethodology. Harmondsworth: Penguin Books.

Sacks, H. (1981a). Preface: Some programmatic statements by Harvey Sacks. In G. Jefferson, The abominable "Ne": A working paper exploring the post-response pursuit of response. Occasional Paper in Sociology No. 6, Sociology Department, Manchester University, Manchester, M13 9PL, England, (April).

Sacks, H. (1981b), Lecture (mimeo). Social Science Department, University of California, Irvine, April 10.

Sacks, H., Schegloff, E. A. & Jefferson, G. (1978). A simplest systematics for the organization of turn-taking for conversation. In J. Schenkein (Ed.), Studies in the organization of observational interaction. New York: Academic Press.

Schegloff, E. A., & Sacks, H. (1974). Opening up closings. In R. Turner (Ed.), Ethnomethodology. Harmondsworth: Penguin Books.

Schegloff, E. A. (1972). Notes on a conversational practice: Formulating place. In D. Sudnow (Ed.), Studies in social interaction. New York: The Free Press.

Searle, J. R. (1963). Proper names. In C. E. Caton (Ed.), Philosophy and ordinary language. Urbana: University of Illinois Press.

Watson, D. R. (1973). Readings of help. Unpublished manuscript, University of Manchester, England.

Watson, D. R. (1975). Readings of help. In D. R. Watson, Calls for help: A sociological analysis of calls to a crisis intervention center. Unpublished Ph.D. thesis. Sociology Department, University of Warwick, Coventry, England, CV4 7AL.

Wowk, M. T. (1980). Socialization and formal organizations: Counsellor-client interaction in a crisis
    intervention centre. Unpublished master's thesis. Department Economic and Social Studies,
    University of Manchester, England, M13 9PL.

EXTRACT A

Note: In the transcript, Co. = counsellor and Cl. = caller. In the interests of
confidentiality, any identifying elements have been changed.

1.	Co.	Hello Lifeliners, can I help you?
2.	Cl.	(. . .) er, well, er (2 secs.)) I-I- I just wanted to know what
3.		sort of er (I've go-) work do you er, what sort of things do you
4.		erm (of) work do you do you know, what sort of help do you give?
5.	Co.	Well we'll give any type of help we can where possible, it depends
6.		what problem is, it's mainly people that are feeling a bit lonely,
7.		depressed or —
8.	Cl.	yes (. . .) //
9.	Co.	Things like this
10.	Cl.	huhum huhum
11.	Co.	why, have you a problem?
12.	Cl.	I am afraid so yes well er well I- well I'll put it to you anyway
13.		but I don't suppose there's anything you can do, erm
14.	Co.	well if you just want to talk about it sometimes—someone just
15.		listening to you you know it helps it g- gets it off your chest and—
16.	Cl.	(well I just have difficulty . . . that's all)
17.	Co.	pardon?
18.	Cl.	I'm just simply looking for a girl (I'm afraid)
19.	Co.	Oh we can't do that for you you know it's er
20.	Cl.	(that's what I thought) well er— ((1 sec.)) erm could you put me onto
21.		any marriage bureau then or anything like that you know
22.	Co.	Onto any?
23.	Cl.	Any er you know reliable marriage bureau or anything like that (you
24.		know)
25.	Co.	marriage bureau?
26.	Cl.	yes anything like that you know
27.	Co.	er just a minute (there) ((8 secs)) oh I'll tell you what you could
28.		do, er do you get the evening paper?
29.	Cl.	well—you see er I do yes (er) what I'll tell you, I've written to a
30.		few and er er I—haven't er a—quite honestly haven't haven't had
31.		replies from them
32.	Co.	I/see
33.	Cl.	(do you know how it is)
34.	Co.	yeah
35.	Cl.	this is really the problem

36.	Co.	um
37.	Cl.	and er ((2 secs.)) then I- I did get a reply from one but it turns out
38.		(a) fantastic fee you know about-nearly- twenty pounds ten (. . .) well
39.		I'm
40.	Co.	yes
41.	Cl.	I'm afraid I just didn't have the money you know (but)
42.	Co.	I see it's just a woman you're looking for is it
43.	Cl.	well anything (see)
44.	Co.	yeah for the night?
45.	Cl.	I beg your pardon
46.	Co.	er this is just for the night/is it?
47.	Cl.	oo no no no no no no no (. . .)//
48.	Co.	you mean you want a permanent/friend
49.	Cl.	I'm quite serious ( )//
50.	Co.	yes you want a permanent friend (you want)//
51.	Cl.	(. . .)
52.	Co.	yes, well I am afraid the only thi- are you a member of any you know
53.		organisations you know these welfare organisations,/social organisations//
54.		
55.	Cl.	(. . .)// (. . .) you see the problem with me is I don't drink and
56.		I don't (go to any pub)
57.	Co.	I see// ((2. secs)) brom hom-my name is James by the way you know
58.		what
59.	Cl.	(. . . . .)
60.	Co.·	what's you first name so I can talk to you by per- first name if you
61.		like
62.	Cl.	Sean
63.	Co.	Sean I see Sean, err:
64.	Cl.	er
65.	Co.	you don't drink, and you ge- and you don't go out much
66.	Cl.	er well yes I do
67.	Co.	yes
68.	Cl.	yes I go to dances all the time
69.	Co.	you go to dances (. . .?)?//
70.	Cl.	purely to—to (. . .)
71.	Co.	yeah and don't don't you meet anybody—there you know at dances things
72.		and like this
73.	Cl.	I never meet anybody you know, no (. . .) this— this is why er you
74.		know this is why I rang you people you know just to— as a last straw
75.	Cl.	really you know
76.	Co.	well I'll tell you what y— you sound like a man from Ireland to me, have
77.		you had have you tried writing to Ireland's Own Magazine?
78.	Cl.	well, ((laugh)) I've been looking at the papers from there, they've

79.		been (. . .) over here for women to marry the old bachelors over
80.		(there so) it's the
81.	Co.	heh heh yes yeah
82.	Cl.	same thing, it's—/er taking from the poor
83.	Co.	yeah how old are you Sean?
84.	Cl.	beg your pardon?
85.	Co.	how old are you?
86.	Cl.	twenty one sir
87.	Co.	(thirty one), and have you any friends at all you know
88.	Cl.	we:ll I have friends yes I have— well you know you get the usual m— men
89.		friends (and) one thing another but I am not interested you know
90.	Co.	no—
91.	Cl.	I'd like to try and get married and settle down you know
92.	Co.	yes well er whereabouts you living (. . .) I take it I hope
93.	Cl.	well I am yes but uh quite honestly I'm a bit embarrassed I (wouldn't
94.		like to give you my address)//
95.	Co.	oo no I am not asking for you address it's just that you know y—
96.		you are in this area aren't you?
97.	Cl.	(. . .)
98.	Co.	well I'll tell you what have you tried going to the area centre on X
99.		Road
100.	Cl.	no it's a washout (. . .)
101.	Co.	It's a wash ?//
102.	Cl.	I've been there yes I have been there, I've been to the S., I've been
103.		to the z., I've been every where, you name it//
104.	Co.	no I mean the area centre//
105.	Cl.	yes yes I've
106.	Co.	you— you've been there have you?
107.	Co.	it's still the same old thing everywhere, (you know)
108.	Co.	yeah, well the only thing I can suggest is th— unless you try and
109.		join s— s— some of these clubs or— I know there's plenty of Irish
110.		clubs in the in the city you know where they have dancing/and stuff
111.		like this er— I I if
112.	Cl.	(yes yes yeah yes I know what)
113.	Co.	you know what I mean (. . .) I mean these are the only places I can
114.		sug—
115.	Cl.	you mean yes)
116.	Co.	gest to you Sean/I mean er there's all sorts of other other kinds
117.		of girls
118.	Cl.	huhum huhuh
119.	Co.	you know, but —er sh— (these're) not the type you're wanting, you're
120.		wanting— to meet a girl so that you might settle down one day and get
121.		married

122. Cl. that's right sir, yes
123. Co. well that's all that I can suggest to you (pr— / project)
124. Cl. thank you sir fair enough, well you've tried your best/(. . .)
125. Co. any how well thanks for— you know we — bye bye Sean
126. Cl. Okay bye bye now

(rings off)

EXTRACT B

1.   Co. Lifeliners, Lifeliners, can I help you?
2.   Cl. hello is there someone who-- er it's the N. Hotel across the road,
3.   Co. oh yes
4.   Cl. er no we has a lady in this morning//
5.   Co. yes
6.   Cl. who was going to the Social Security or something 'nd I'm positive
7.   she phoned you before she left here, 'nd and a a blue Ford came for
8.   'er, now she'd no money,
9.   Co. ye:s
10. Cl. she didn't tell us this—I mean she just booked in here for one
11.   night—
12. Co. Ye:s
13. Cl. now when the morning came she said I've got no money—I'm going to
14.   the Social Security for some money
15. Co. yes
16. Cl. well we didn't appreciate that very much but she said I'll come back
17.   before twelve, but she's never been back
18. Co. um
19. Cl. now a:a blue Ford came for her and I think she phoned you before it
20.   came, would you have any record, of it you know?
21. Co. er well I'm sorry but we just can't di:vulge any information at all
22. Cl. you can't do anything
23. Co. I'm sorry I can't no
24. Cl. no:
25. Co. I think your best plan would be to perhaps contact the police
26. Cl. Oh I will do now yes because it's a:a criminal offence you see
27. Co. yes
28. Cl. to er leave a hotel bill and not pay it's criminal it's not erm
29.   a civil offence
30. Co. no
31. Cl. it's a felony
32. Co. yes
33. Cl. so she could be in dead trouble then

34.	Co.	perhaps ye:::es
35.	Cl.	anyhow I've got the number of the car that she: that picked 'er
36.		up anyway
37.	Co.	yes
38.	Cl.	Thankyou
39.	Co.	bye bye

0102

EXTRACT C

1.	Co.	hello Lifelners can I help you?
2.	Cl.	you couldn't put me in touch with a prostitute could you?
3.	Co.	a prostitute? I'm sorry I couldn't no ((3 secs.))
4.	Cl.	do you know where I could
5.	Co.	er no I'm sorry I don't think I do ((3 secs.))
6.	Cl.	alright thank you
7.	Co.	is there can I do anything else for you?
8.	Cl.	no that's (all) I wanted
9.	Co.	no
10.	Cl.	alright thank you
11.	Co.	alright thank you

Part II
Education

6. On the Necessity of Collusion in Conversation*

R. P. McDermott
Teachers College, Columbia University

Henry Tylbor
New York, New York

INTRODUCTION

> Language . . . lies on the borderline between oneself and the other. The word in language is half someone else's. (M. M. Bakhtin, 1934–35)

In 1928, V. N. Volosinov[1] complained that "all linguistic categories, per se, are applicable only on the inside territory of an utterance" and are of no value "for defining a whole linguistic entity" (1973, p. 110). This paper begins with a whole linguistic entity by going beyond the utterance to the social scene in which it is embedded for a unit of analysis. Unlike some recent linguistic analyses that acknowledge that speech acts do not in themselves provide for discourse cohesion but nonetheless are restricted to speech acts for a primary focus of investigation, we start with the properties of social activities as the essential guide to analysis.

We start with some assumptions that are, by now, well informed: participation in any social scene, especially a conversation, requires some minimal consensus on what is getting done in the scene; from the least significant (strangers passing) to the culturally most well formulated scenes (a wedding or a lecture), such a consensus represents an achievement, a cumulative product of the instructions people in the scene make available to each other; and, because no consensus ever unfolds simply by predetermined means, because social scenes are always precarious, always dependent on ongoing instructions, the achievement of a consensus requires collusion.

Collusion literally means a playing together (from the Latin *col-ludere*). Less literally, collusion refers to how members of any social order must constantly help each other to posit a particular state of affairs, even when such a state would

* Reprinted with permission from TEXT, 1983, 3,277–297. The present version replaces a final section on formality with some remarks on power in discourse. Other changes are minor.

Acknowledgements: This paper was prepared in anticipation of the late Erving Goffman liking it.

[1] Under the guidance and likely authorship of M. M. Bakhtin (Holquist, 1981).

be in no way at hand without everyone so proceeding. Participation in social scenes requires that members play into each other's hands, pushing and pulling each other toward a strong sense of what is probable or possible, for a sense of what can be hoped for and/or obscured. In such a world, the meaning of talk is rarely contained on the "inside territory of an utterance"; proposition and reference pale before the task of alignment, before the task of sequencing the conversation's participants into a widely spun social structure. The necessity of collusion in conversation has wide-ranging implications not only for how people use their talk in conversation, but for how linguistics might profitably locate units for an analysis of conversation.

In this paper, we build a case for the importance of collusion in the organization of talk ("The Case for Collusion") and offer a brief example of how collusion operates in a conversation ("An Example: From Precarious to Treacherous"). From a transcript taken from a videotaped seven-person reading lesson in grade school, we try to give a sense for the complex contexting work people do to arrange for utterance interpretations consistent with, and not disruptive of, the situation the people are holding together for each other. With an example in hand, we attempt to highlight the dimensions of a collusional stand on conversation by contrasting it to the now dominant propositional approach and the recently popular illocutionary approach to language behavior ("Three Ways of Appreciating Language"). Each is discussed in terms of its definition of such fundamental notions as units of analysis, their function, the role of context in their organization, and the theoretical prize won by their description. The relation between collusion and power is addressed in a final note.

THE CASE FOR COLLUSION

> Discourses on humility give occasion for pride to the boastful, and for humility to the humble. Those on skepticism give occasion for believers to affirm. Few speak humbly of humility, chastely of chastity, few of skepticism doubtingly. We are but falsehood, duplicity and contradiction, using even to ourselves concealment and guile. (Blaise Pascal, 1670)

We build on two common observations on language behavior to develop the claim that collusion is necessary for any conversation. The first observation has it that everyday language is irremediably indefinite, that every utterance indexes or builds on a wide range of knowledge about the world that would require a potentially endless expansion for precise application. The second observation, seemingly contrary to the first, has it that talk is so amazingly exact that participants can often talk their way to long-term concerted activities and well-shared ideas about what they are doing together (often far beyond any agreements immediately obvious in a transcript of their talk).

During the past decade both observations have been secured with much data. Under the banner of pragmatics, we have been shown how much a person must know about the world to understand even brief utterances, and, urged on by sociologists interested in conversational analysis, we have been shown an amazing variety of interactional mechanisms that conversationalists have available for directing and specifying utterance interpretations.

The collusion claim takes both observations seriously. It starts with an appreciation of how much unspecified, and likely unspecifiable, knowledge people must have in order to understand each other. At the same time, the collusion claim recognizes the powers of conversationalists to use local circumstances to shape their knowledge into mutually perceptible and reflexively consequential chunks. This marriage of indefiniteness and precision in utterance interpretation both requires and is made possible by conversationalists entering a state of collusion as to the nature of the world they are talking about, acting on, and helping to create. With a little help from each other, by defining what can (or must) be left vague or made precise, they can shape their talk to fit the contours of the world in which they are embedded, a world they can prolong to make possible further interpretations of their talk.[2]

At its cleanest, conversational collusion is well tuned to people's finest hopes about what the world can be—this often despite the facts, despite a world that sometimes offers them little reason for harboring such hopes. Examples include "we really love each other" or "We can all be smart." Although making believe that such statements are true does not insure our being loved or looking smart, it is an essential first step.

At its dirtiest, people's collusion amounts to a well-orchestrated lie that offers a world conversationalists do not have to produce but can pretend to live by, a world everyone knows to be, at the same time, unrealizable, but momentarily useful as stated. Examples of collusion as treachery can be cut from the same utterance cloth we used to illustrate collusion as hope. "We really love each other" can still be said when both know the statement as a cover for a relationship that offers only protection from the imagined world beyond the relationship; we have it from marriage counselors that under such conditions demonstrations of love can further lock the participants off from the world and further limit the possibility of their loving each other. Similarly, "We can all be smart" has as its most frequent occasion of utterance the classroom, the very place, as

---

[2] Garfinkel (1963) has advanced the same point with his work on "trust" as a condition of stable concerted activities. Various other terms glossing the same phenomenon with varying degrees of consistency and success are "context," "frame," "key," and "working consensus." The term "collusion" adds to these, as Garfinkel would appreciate, a sense of institutionalization and even treachery that we believe essential (institutionalization as the arrangement of persons and commodities that have us necessarily trusting reciprocally in the ways we do; treachery as a measure of how far we will drive ourselves and others to believe in a world not well connected to our experiences).

"Collusion" has the further advantage of plurality, as is essential to any analysis of social behavior such as conversation. One cannot collude alone; it takes at least three persons (as if two to collude and one to interpret).

we shall see, in which people organize significant moments during which smartness, and its opposite, must be alternately displayed, recognized, hidden, and held back, in which displays of smartness and stupidity must be choreographed into the relations people have with each other. Without resources for organizing conditions for making possible an experience of love or intelligence, their invocation points more to oppression than to hope.

By lies, we refer to a phenomenon far more prevalent than those in which speakers must first remind themselves what not to say on a future occasion, in which "one has to remember the truth as well as the lie in order to bring consistency to a recriminatory future" that could disprove the lie (Lang, 1980, p. 535). We think this kind of conscious lying is rare relative to the amount of treachery in the world at large. One way of understanding social structure, in fact, is that it offers differential protection from confrontations in which pure lies must be told.[3] Institutional authorities are afforded various shelters from unpredicted accountability. It is possible to live lies without having to tell them. Our institutions secure such lives for us at every turn. Starting with the generalized gender configurations available in a culture to specific institutions built around informational entanglements (Hanunoo or Mehinaku courtship, Kpelle secret societies, Mediterranean honor codes, or a therapeutic halfway house for drug offenders in America, and so on), we can find people choreographing each other's behavior according to scores that remain ad hoc and tacit and which, if made explicit, would render the behavior that seems to service them useless. We should never allow ourselves to forget the warning of Nietszche: "To be truthful means using the customary metaphors—in moral terms: the obligation to lie according to a fixed convention, to lie herd-like in a style obligatory for all . . ." (1873, p. 47).

The collusion stand on conversation not only unites apparently disparate facts about language behavior (indefiniteness and precision), but holds out the promise

---

[3] As Harvey Sacks (1975) has noted, there are numerous statements across varying occasions to which the "contrast set true-false" is not sequentially relevant. A description of the distribution of occasions for which the contrast set is relevant (and of the various statements that invite its application) might give us a revealing key to social structure. The important point is that talk seems well designed for making delicacy, avoidance, mitigation, and duplicity generally possible. Against this background, it appears that inviting a lie, lying, and catching a liar are socially structured games in which people together ignore the obfuscating powers of language to construct scapegoats and degradation ceremonies. The "outraged jeremiad is the mark of a moralistic rather than a moral society" (Shklar, 1979, p. 24). In this view, conversational "delicacy," for example, an attempt to insure that "the fact that an answerer is not giving [some requested information does] not constitute a recognizable refusal to give it" (Jefferson, 1978), represents a first attempt to escape the onslaughts of a true-false contrast set; lying is a next step for people in situations with fewer social resources for doing delicacy. An appreciation of this fact can help move us from a cynicism about individual morality to a political involvement for making different kinds of morality possible; at best, the outraged jeremiad "is not without affect, because this type of antihypocrite does at least have a sense of what is wrong, rather than an urge to spread the blame" (Shklar, 1979, p. 24).

of a linguistics that could be useful to an understanding of the social situations in which people do their talking. Although it is a century since George Simmel told us that secrecy is at the heart of any social order and William James told us that hope is a human possibility only by spitting in the face of the odds, our social sciences have proceeded pretty much as if the conditions organizing our lives were well ordered, shared, available for common understanding, and easy to talk about.[4] The social sciences have proceeded oblivious to the basic conditions of our lives together. In the language sciences, this has translated into a focus on the sentence as if truth value or illocutionary force could be found in the utterance.

Now it appears that to account for even the simplest conversations, we have to take seriously the moment-to-moment hopes and lies that connect our utterances into coherent parts of the social order. Language analysis can lead us back to social structure. To the extent that collusion is essential to conversation, then its exploration cannot leave too far behind an account of the institutional constraints that have us colluding in the ways that we do. It will leave us in the long run wondering about the constraints we are working against that, if we are making up so much of our lives together, we manage often such impoverished versions of what is possible.[5]

Our discussion of the necessity of collusion in conversation could proceed from first principles: All action, said John Dewey, "is an invasion of the future, of the unknown. Conflict and uncertainty are ultimate truths" (1922, p. 12). This is no less true for speaking and listening actors than it is of acrobats and subway

---

[4] The alternatives to the natural attitude have been important (Bernstein, 1976). Robert Murphy has offered us a helpful guide in what he calls the first principle of Irish (at least in the sense of not British) social anthropology: "My theories do fit with the well-known Irish trait by which there is little correspondence, and indeed much contradiction, between what a person thinks, what he says, and what he does. Perhaps I can best explain the tenets of Irish Social Anthropology by reversing Durkheim's formulation of the relation between restless, shifting sensate activity and the collective world of norms. My own resolution of the problem, then, is: All things real are ephemeral; all things enduring are false" (1975, p. 55).

Edward Casey has directed a similar insight to our understanding of a descriptive enterprise as linguistics must be: "The surface at stake in description is a moving surface. It changes in and through time; and even if such changes are not detectable in a given time interval, their description is itself a temporal event" (1981, p. 199).

[5] Grand theories of the world usually include an account of what has to be lied about. Timpanaro has offered a lovely account of a Marx-Freud contrast on the nature of the world that organizes collusion: "It is intriguing to imagine Freud's reaction if one of his patients—a neurotic, but a politically lucid one—in reply to the question which according to Freud was the best means of 'ensnaring' the patient: 'What would you consider was the most unlikely thing in the world in that situation? What do you think was the furthest thing in the world from your mind at the time?—had answered: 'I consider the most unlikely thing in the world would be to see a capitalist renounce his own privileges without any use of force on the part of the workers he exploits.' At this point, there would surely have been an exchange of roles: Freud would himself have succumbed to the behavior typical of a 'patient,' he would have lost his temper or changed the subject—in short, have revealed 'resistances' so strong that he would not even have been aware of their existence" (1976, p. 59).

riders (whatever the differential in risky outcome). Without a tentative agreement about what the future is (no matter, for the moment, how fanciful or harmful it might be), how else could conversationalists achieve precise understandings from ambiguous materials without ever really saying what is going on? Clearly, conversationalists have to be working together, tripping over the same defenses, stumbling into the same understandings, and working to the same ends (if only to reach the silence at the conversation's end). How they do this work should represent an answer as to how their collusion is both made necessary and subsequently organized.

AN EXAMPLE: FROM PRECARIOUS TO TREACHEROUS

> All lies are collusional; all truths are collusional. The nature of the truth is always bound by the shape of the context. . . . Truth and falsity are matters of agreement. . . . The conditions of sending the signal which arranges for deception may rest in a variety of places within the deception system. (Ray L. Birdwhistell, in McDermott, 1980)

For an example of collusion in conversation, we can offer some talk between a teacher and her first-grade students filmed and analyzed in some detail by McDermott (1976). It is a reading lesson, and much of the interaction is around the issue of getting turns to read. Unlike turns to talk in most conversational clusters, turns to read are not just managed in the pursuit of other conversational goals, but are often the focus of the group. It is in terms of turns to read that the group's talk is made directional, that it takes on meaning and carries social facts. The details of the taking turns to read system are constantly put up for noticing, analyzing, and interpreting, and their organization helps to curb the indefiniteness of talk, to make clear, for example, that "Me" is a call for a turn to read or that "Not me" is a request not to read while constituting simultaneously a display of an agreement to listen to another child reading. Collusion is visible in the ways the members have of instructing each other in the use of turns in organizing their interaction and is essential to their production of group order.

The case for the necessity of collusion in conversation is perhaps most arresting in the talk of one child, Rosa, who is often treated as if she had said something different than a literal interpretation of her words would indicate. That is to say, her words, imprecise on their own, are made precise by those about her in ways not well predicted by their propositional content. Literalness aside, how her words are used by the group seems much better described by the conversationalists' situation together as a particular kind of reading group within a particular kind of classroom, school, and wider educational community.

Rosa constantly calls for a turn to read by shouting "I could" or "I could read it." In addition, she complains when she is bypassed, "G . . Go around" or (long later and still without a turn) "I wanna go around." But Rosa almost never gets a turn to read; she is understood to be not very good at reading, and her status as a turn-taking reader seems to be problematic enough to be commented on at various times during the children's half-hour at the reading table with the teacher. Upon careful examination, it seems that Rosa is doing much work to arrange *not getting a turn:* everyone is on page 5, Rosa on page 7 (as everyone can tell with a first grade illustrated reader); as the teacher begins to call on another child, Rosa calls for a turn, just a fraction of a second behind; as the other children move up from their books to face their teacher and to call for a new turn, Rosa lowers her head into the book with her face turning away from the teacher. The ploys are numerous in kind and fast in occurrence.

Linguists have not had enough trouble with the kind of duplicitous talk just described. It has been unfortunately easy to put aside. Propositional analysis can chalk it up to the abominations of actual use in social scenes. However great the evidence to the contrary, no matter how much conversationalists seem to rely on meaning one thing by saying another, traditional linguistic analysis remains intact by claiming that the *literal* meaning of an utterance must remain the point of departure for describing how speakers understand each other.[6] The argument is that the meaning of Rosa's calls for a turn to read are quite clear; how else could have they been transformed into something systematically different from a literal reading. In addition, such a transformation in use would have been most likely signaled linguistically by some marked appeal to irony or subterfuge. However transformed by the situation, for most linguists, propositions remain meaningful in their own terms.

Illocutionary analysts would take Rosa a little more seriously. They would try to extrapolate the actual conditions of the social actors that their intentions could protrude without anyone having very literally put them into words. Again, the propositions would be understood on their own, albeit in a series. In either case, Rosa would be understood cognitively, as a strategist, who was manipulating the social scene and the people in it with her words. What would have organized her words or their systematic interpretation would have been left undiscovered. Neither Rosa nor linguistics would have been well served.

The collusional approach to Rosa's talk forces us to take her situation much more seriously. We are not interested simply in speakers, or even speaker-hearer pairs and the ways they react to each other. Rather we are interested in ongoing social scenes into which people walk and talk their lives together. As Arthur Bentley said well long ago:

> Terminology has been poor in the social sciences, drawn as it has been from the language of everyday life—from the vocabularies of the manipulation of one man

---

6. Owen Barfield (1947) has pointed out that the best of our talk, metaphor and poetry, thrives on saying one thing to mean another; the more one meaning lives as a modification of another, the richer the metaphor. Linguists have managed to avoid a careful look at how such talk is used in social life by giving great sway to the grammatical and referential workings of language. Nietzsche has bemoaned how deep this trend runs: "I am afraid we are not rid of God because we still have faith in grammar" (1889, p. 34).

by another. But not the point of view of one toward another is what we seek, rather the very processing itself of the ones-with-others. (1926, p. 457)

We are not interested in Rosa the strategist, but Rosa the participant. Rosa's words, Bakhtin reminds us, are only half hers. They must be brought to completion by the group. And all their words together, if well enough studied, belong to the conversation which is in turn a moment in a far more extensive conversation we might call American education (Varenne, 1983).

A collusional approach takes it that Rosa does not act on her own; that the very machinery used to transform, reframe, or to put into a new key Rosa's talk is group-produced; that every member of the group helps to instruct Rosa to say what she says in favor of what she did not say, which, in fact, if she did say would break the conditions for the group being together in an order that they can recognize, use, and perpetuate.

The collusional stand further takes it that the work members do to construct a consensus (that we are all learning how to read) while allowing, ignoring, and hiding important exceptions (namely, that some of us are here only to not get caught not knowing how to read) is a direct product of the institutional conditions under which the teacher and children are asked to come to school. Their production and interpretation of talk must be understood as a product of their collusion in response to a complex institutional setting that requires that they talk as if they could all learn while they arrange much of their day catching each other not learning (Hood, McDermott and Cole, 1980). In taking up utterances that seem to mean the opposite of what they would on their own appear to say, we have moved from collusion as a necessary solution to the precariousness of everyday life situations to collusion as a defensive tactic against the treachery of everyday life. There are reasons for "using even to ourselves concealment and guile." When further pressed, there are reasons for lying even to others, although we must remember, before hunting down liars, that "the conditions of sending the signal which arranges for deception may rest in a variety of places within the deception system."

It is not easy to describe an instance of collusion in conversation. One effort, particularly directed to linguists, is available in a recent paper by Dore and McDermott (1982). The dedicated reader can examine that data analysis in the light of the more radical arguments of the present account. The argument of that paper is that a particular "I could read it" by Rosa, by virtue of how it is said and its timing, is seemingly accepted as such by everyone in the group while they simultaneously act as if she had said that she could not read it and that a particular someone else had been given the turn to read. Rosa's claim for a turn appears at a time when the group is somewhat at bay for a clear definition as to what they are doing together. By interpreting Rosa's utterance as something different from what it seemingly proposed, an interpretation Rosa helped them to, the members of the group used Rosa's call for a turn to establish both a turn and a reader (other than Rosa) for the turn. The point is that everyone used the primary practice of the scene, namely, the constant evaluation of every reader's skill and the avoidance of such evaluation by different members at various times, to understand Rosa's call for a turn as a suggestion that she be bypassed. The very conditions that allowed for the methods Rosa used to instigate her subterfuge were not only well recognized by the group, they were maintained and supported by every member's involvement with evaluation.

The present paper offers a different fragment of talk from Rosa's reading group (Table 6.1). The scene opens with the teacher calling on Child 4 (numbered in order around the table). Child 1 and Child 2 have read page 4 to the group. Rosa is Child 3. As the teacher and the children raise their heads as Child 2 finishes page 4, the teacher turns her head towards Rosa, who has moved her head further down into the book and right, away from the teacher's advancing gaze. The teacher continues turning her head left, past Rosa, until she reaches Child 4. She calls on him, "Alright. Let's see you do it." He moans a complaint, "Unnh." Rosa begins to suggest that they take turns in order: "G . . Go around". She is supported almost immediately by Child 4 screaming, 'What about Rosa . . Sh . . She don't get a turn." Child 5 begins to chide Rosa, "You don't get a . . .", while Child 2 also calls for a more rigorous linear order, "Yeh. Let's go around." The teacher then, after a nonvocalized false start and a nervous glance away, addresses Child 4 very softly, "Jimmy. You seem very unhappy. Perhaps you should go back to your seat." Simultaneous with the teacher's attribution of Jimmy's feelings, Rosa begins to lay out the order of the going around that she has called for; in none of the two or three versions she

Table 6.1.   Transcript of Procedural Positioning, Getting a Turn 3

Teacher:	Alright. Let's see you do it.
Child 4:	Unnh
Rosa:	G . . . go around
Child 4:	What about Rosa (screaming) Sh . . she don't get a turn.
Child 5:	(to Rosa) You don't get a . . .
Child 2:	Yeh. Lets go around.
Teacher:	Jimmy (very softly). You seem very unhappy. Perhaps you should go back to your seat.
Rosa:	Back to Fred, then back to me. No. Back to Fred, back to Anna, and back to Fred and Maria and back to me.
Teacher:	Alright, Fred. Can you read page 4?

suggests is there any discernable, going-around order. After Rosa has her say, the teacher calls on Child 6, "Alright, Fred. Can you read page 4?"

How can we understand Rosa's talk? Is she calling for a turn, seeming to call for a turn, simply showing that she knows some rules about turn-taking in rounds, or, as we suspect, arranging to not read while nonetheless appearing to be part of the group? The point of this paper is that there is no one answer to this question. Rosa's "G . . . Go around" may contribute all the readings just listed. Some are more interesting than others in supplying insight to life in classrooms, and some are used more than others at various subsequent moments by group members. We should not expect Rosa to have a uniform stand serviced by her words. In the complex role that teaching-learning scenes play in the lives of young children, could we expect Rosa to be free of all the tensions of her community around the issues of relative skill, smartness, competitiveness, and the like?

As we flee from utterance complexity to a consideration of social context for some key to what Rosa might be talking about, we are offered some relief by the fact that Rosa's utterance does not stand alone. The question of meaning must be rephrased: What instructions are available in the scene for the participants to organize an interpretation of Rosa's utterance? Part of the instructions, of course, is Rosa's utterance; her talk reflexively arranges its own context and helps to organize the conditions for its own interpretation. And what does Rosa's utterance have to work with in arranging a hearing?

First of all, the group is organized posturally into a procedural focus or positioning well suited for activities such as getting a turn to read (for criteria establishing postural-kinetic events and their importance to the structure of interaction, see McDermott, Gospodinoff and Aron, 1978, and Scheflen, 1973). That they are at a getting-a-turn-to-read relevant moment is everywhere available in their body alignments and attentional structure. Second, that such moments are delicate can be seen in the work members do to preserve them; for example, they all attend carefully to the beginning and endings and hold each other accountable for any disruptions of the apparent order. Third, within any positioning, alternative formulations of what might be going on between the participants are often attempted and usually abandoned; for example, while most are still calling for a turn-to-read, someone might start reading. Fourth, while working hard keeping a focus organized and rejecting rival formulations, members of the group constantly make available for use the dimensions along which they can understand each other; for example, a child who does not follow the pattern of a procedural positioning may be considered a management problem, whereas a child who does not follow a pattern in a pedagogical positioning may be understood as a learning problem. Fifth, there appears to be a strong preference for how and when different dimensions can be applied; for example, the smart-dumb continuum is constantly applied in classrooms, and much interactional delicacy must be organized to apply the continuum only in cases when someone can be called smart. The application of the continuum to instances of ''dumb'' behavior does occur, but participants usually work hard to have it not noticed. Sixth, a getting-a-turn positioning does not usually attract the application of a smart-dumb contract set, and it is accordingly used as a moment safe from intelligence evaluations. By virtue of its comparative safety, it is used often as a place in which the participants prepare for some next intelligence display, including preparation for who might be subject to an upcoming evaluation. It is therefore a perfect umbrella under which to perform covert, unspoken evaluations that organize for more public contests in the next moment.

With all this going on (and the reader, for purposes of this paper, has only to agree that such events could be at work; it would take a volume to complete a description of the behavioral background), Rosa's utterance enters the world pregnant. As Bakhtin noted well: ''Language is not a neutral medium that passes freely and easily into the private property of the speaker's intentions; it is populated—overpopulated—with the intentions of others. Expropriating it, forcing it to submit to one's own intentions and accounts, is a difficult and complicated process (1934–35, p. 294).

The utterance is shaped to fit its occasion. The conditions that organize its production and interpretation are distributed throughout the system.

To the extent that ''G . . . Go around'' represents a hope, the possibility (no matter how improbably at the moment) of Rosa learning to read well enough to perform must be organized by all the participants. To the extent that it represents an institutionalized lie, a delicate way to avoid a confrontation with a smart-dumb contrast set, that too has to be organized across persons. Indeed, the lie has to be told against the background that everyone is still hoping, or at least making believe that they are hoping, that Rosa can learn to read.

Instead of asking whether Rosa is intending to get a turn—an unanswerable question anyway—if we asked about the social constraints to which Rosa's remark might be an appropriate and constitutive reaction, then we have to ask how the participants are playing into each other's hands (that is, more literally, colluding) to organize the world Rosa gets systematically instructed to avoid. If we could ask more questions about what issues our every institution has us avoiding, we would have not only a better account of social structure, but a better account of the language tools people use to build social structure.

THREE WAYS OF APPRECIATING LANGUAGE

> The salient aspect of the social fact is meaning; the central manifestation of meaning is pragmatic and meta-pragmatic speech; and the most obvious feature of pragmatic speech is reference. We are now beginning to see the error in trying to investigate the salient by projection from the obvious. (Michael Silverstein, 1981)

There are a number of dimensions along which to rank different approaches to language behavior. Silverstein (1979) goes to particular pains to point out what cannot be accomplished with traditional analyses that focus on reference and what might be accomplished if we were to concentrate more immediately on the social facts produced with talk. This paper proceeds in that spirit. By starting with the collusion required of conversationalists, the social facts of which the people are a part move to the center of analysis and their language can be understood for what it does within the social order. This approach gives us a different way of appreciating language behavior. It also requires a shift in some of the tools we have used to do language analysis.

In the following chart (Table 6.2), we offer a simple scheme for contrasting a collusional approach to appreciating what people do with their talk with the more traditional propositional and illocutionary approaches that dominate contemporary linguistics. At its best, the chart should offer a snapshot of what each of the approaches is trying to accomplish and its underlying conceptual assumptions.

The propositional approach focuses on the sentence for a unit of analysis, understands sentences in terms of their referential potential, and asks questions about their clarity and possible truth value. Propositional analyses produce statements of the type, Sentence X can mean *a, b,* or *c.* The variation in meanings available in the sentence is understood as contained within the sentence. Context is irrelevant and invoked only in the face of the abominations of actual use; it has no systematic bearing on utterance interpretation. Meaning is framed by the capital and the period without any reference to how, as Frake (1980) reminds us, plying frames can be dangerous or in any other way consequential for speakers.

An important, if partial, advance is made in the linguistic sciences when analysts start to look at the consequences of talk, at the effects speakers have one upon another. For a unit of analysis, speech act theorists stick closely to the sentence although they focus on what the sentence is doing in conjunction with other sentences. The utterance exchange is the purported unit of analysis, although the descriptions are deemed complete with the attribution of intentions. Talk is understood as being about the expression of intentions, and variations in utterance interpretation are chalked up to the complexities of organizing an identity in social situations; thus, hedging and mitigating can rule the discourse. The analytic product gives an appearance of being more complete than propositional analyses.

Dimensions of context are considered crucial to the description of the illocutionary force of speech acts. However, the use of context in the analysis is nonetheless an afterthought. There is still a reliance on a soup-in-the-bowl approach to context. According to this model, the soup has a life of its own; it is the substance which is placed in a bowl and accordingly shaped. In speech act analysis, propositional meaning is the soup (an alphabet soup, most likely, good for monologue, reference, and description) and the social statuses and roles of the speaker-hearer pairs are the contexts that organize the rewrite rules allowing the referential power of talk to be obscured enough to meet the demands of the social situation. Reference remains primary in the analysis, and the conditions of

Table 6.2. Three Ways of Appreciating Language

	Units of Analysis	Function of Talk	Role of Context	Analytical Accomplishment
Propositional Analysis	Speaker's propositions	Reference	An occasionally necessary afterthought to cover possible transformations under supposed conditions of actual use.	Utterance X means a or under special well-marked circumstances b or c
Illocutionary Analysis	Speaker-hearer propositions and intentions.	Expression and manipulation	A frequently necessary afterthought to explain how apparent social conditions regularly alter canonical propositional meanings to express speaker intentions.	Utterance X means a under conditions a, b under conditions b, c under conditions c, where the conditions are defined by phenomena beyond the talk, such as statuses and roles, that transform the talk.
Collusional Analysis	Scenes and social facts	Alignment and linkage, institutional maintenance and social change	An essential dimension of language analysis. As behavior reflexively organizes its own contexts, talk can be appreciated for how it organizes its own interpretation as a sequentially relevant element in a social scene.	Utterance X helps to preserve and organize the conditions for its own interpretation as a constitutive element of social scene. Institutional treachery and social transformation are constant possibilities around which interpretations are reflexively organized.

135

context are plied against what anyone could recognize as the canonical interpretation.

The problem with the soup-in-the-bowl approach is that it allows the assumption that the soup exists independent of the bowl, that the meaning of an utterance remains, if only for a moment, independent of conditions that organize its production and interpretation, that meaning exists "on the inside territory of an utterance." If, however, soup and bowl, behavior and its contexts, utterance and the hierarchy of scenes it serves, are all mutually constituted, then the utterance cannot stand alone; it cannot make meaning on its own any more than a fiber can make a rope, or a thread a fabric.[7] An utterance can only help to piece meanings together, and in so doing erases itself as the essential unit of analysis. Along with many other behavior sequences, an utterance becomes consequential in social facts, and it is to these facts we must turn for instructions on how to appreciate language as a social tool.

The collusion approach develops from a more reticular sense of context. It rejects the traditional notion of intention-to-mean as directly homing in on its object, but instead recognizes that the pathway of meaning of talk is by no means simple and assured. The behavioral stuff to which an utterance can make connections, and the connections the utterances make possible, are primary in the analysis. The irremediable absence of strict borders between persons and others, between acts and other acts, produces interactional puzzles that require constant alignment and collusion from participants (Plessner, 1965; Wieder, 1974). As we saw in some moments in Rosa's life, talk is primarily about alignments with others—alignments that run a moral order gamut from institutional manipulation to social transformation for the good of all, talk that runs the moral order gamut from hiding and lying to a will to believe and consciousness-raising. An appreciation of talk as collusional raises the most basic human issues for our consideration. It is demeaning to the richness of talk and its talkers to limit its description to anything less than a consideration of the most fundamental issues facing people in social life.

REMARKS ON COLLUSION AND POWER

The necessity of collusion in conversation raises two issues for the analysis of power in discourse. The first issue concerns how an analyst can find power in

7. Bateson is essential here: "It is important to see the particular utterance or action as part of the ecological subsystem called context and not as the product or effect of what remains of the context after the piece which we want to explain has been cut out from it" (1972, p. 338). Birdwhistell adds an equal wisdom in an account of what a context is: "I like to think of it as a rope. The fibers that make up the rope are discontinuous; when you twist them together, you don't make *them* continuous, you make the *thread* continuous . . . The thread has no fibers in it, but, if you break up the thread, you can find the fibers again. So that, even though it may look in a thread as though each of those particles are going all through it, that isn't the case. That's essentially the descriptive model" (in McDermott, 1980, pp. 4, 14).

talk. Linguists have not solved this problem, nor indeed have they tried very hard. The solution will not be easy. The interactional residue apparent in even the most obvious patterns of form use, for example, the use of address terms or honorifics (French "tu" and "vous" and Japanese "keigo" forms being classic), has produced little insight into the more complex constraints operative in a social structure. The more subtle interactional dynamics underlying differences in timing, for example, in the frequency of interruptions and strategic silences (as between men and women), although important for orienting us to power issues, have not been any more helpful in supplying us with an exact calculus for locating the dynamics of power in social relations.

By its emphasis on plurality, a notion of collusion suggests that we give up the question of *who* has particular powers and move instead to questions of how social institutions offer *access* to various kinds of power and how various conversational sequences supply instructions to their participants for acting consequentially for the institution of which they are a moment. We do not need to know who is powerful; rather, we need to identify the resources supposedly powerful people have available and the instructions within the power system that keep them, by simply following their nose, knowing how to wield their powers. By focusing on the collusion between the apparently powerful and the apparently impotent, conversational analysis may alert us to the institutional constraints on communicative activities.

By its emphasis on institutional treachery, a notion of collusion goes further to raise the question of what people have to arrange *not to talk* about in order to keep their conversation properly con-sequential with the institutional pressures that invade their lives from one moment to the next. Bateson once noted that the key question to be asked of any situation is what one would have to do to tell the truth while a participant (in Birdwhistell, 1977). This is a crucial remark, for a description of the constraints on people telling the truth, indeed of their even conceiving what a telling of the truth might be, represents a good description of the powers made available, fought over, or shied away from in a conversation (which is but a moment in the life of a more inclusive set of constraints called an institution). Institutional analysis might proceed by addressing conversational data with questions about what can be talked about while at the same time being kept quiet, handled delicately, lied about in a pinch, or confronted only under the most dire circumstances.

The second issue concerns what linguistics would look like if it were to take seriously that matters of institutional access and power are at the heart of most conversations. Gone would be a preoccupation with propositions that carry their own self-contained meaning, between sentence capital and period. The lonely speaker would give way to a community of voices, the proposition to the social fact. Gone also would be the speaker–hearer pair totally circumscribed within their own competencies, jockeying intentions back and forth in the name of felicity (although often behind her back). Speakers and hearers would instead merge a language collective, struggling to wrestle meanings to the ground and to sequence them into the harsh realities of institutional contraints.

This paper addresses both issues by way of an example of collusion in conversation taken from some classroom talk that is impossible to understand, at least as the participants understand it, without reference to the social structural constraints in terms of which some things not easy to say nonetheless seem to dominate the conversation. That it is an American school, first grade reading lesson conversation, as significantly different, for example, from an American family conversation, a Hanunoo or Balinese reading lesson conversation, or even an American school lunch conversation, makes a great difference in the understandings available to the participants in their interpretation and use of their own talk. In American schools, children must learn that the borders between competence and incompetence are not clearly defined, but subject to constant social rearrangement. Classroom discourse is dominated by questions of "Who can?" and, just as importantly, but far less often stated, "Who cannot?" This fact about classroom life is ubiquitous in transcripts from classrooms and the key to their interpretation (the same key the participants can be shown to be using in their orientation to both the said and the unsaid).

REFERENCES

Bakhtin, M. M. (1981). Discourse in the novel. In M. Holquist (Ed.), *The dialogic imagination*. Austin: University of Texas Press. (Original work published 1934–35.)

Barfield, O. (1962). Poetic diction and legal fiction. In M. Black (Ed.), *The importance of language*. Englewood Cliffs: Prentice-Hall. (Original work published 1947).

Bateson, G. (1972). *Steps to an ecology of mind*. New York: Ballantine.

Bentley, A. (1926). Remarks on method in the study of society. *American Journal of Sociology, 32,* 456–60.

Bernstein, R. (1976). *The reconstruction of social and political theory*. Philadelphia: University of Pennsylvania Press.

Birdwhistell, R. L. (1977). Some discussions of ethnography, theory and method. In J. Brockman (Ed.), *About Bateson*. New York: Dutton.

Casey, E. (1981). Phenomenological method and literary description. *Yale French Studies, 61,* 176–201.

Dewey, J. (1922). *Human nature and conduct*. New York: Random House.

Dore, J., & McDermott, R. P. (1982). Linguistic indeterminacy and social context in utterance interpretation. *Language, 58,* 374–398.

Frake, C. O. (1980). *Language and cultural description*. Stanford: Stanford University Press.

Garfinkel, H. (1963). A conception of, and experiments with, 'trust' as a condition of stable concerted activities. In O. J. Harvey (Ed.), *Motivation*. New York: Roland Press.

Holquist, M. (1981). The politics of representation. In S. J. Greenblatt (Ed.), *Allegory and Representation,* Baltimore: Johns Hopkins University Press.

Hood, L., McDermott, R. P., & Cole, M. (1980). Let's try to make it a good day. *Discourse Processes, 3,* 155–168.

James, W. (1967). *The writings of William James*. J. McDermott (Ed.). New York: Random House.

Jefferson, G. (1978). What's in a 'nyem'? *Sociology, 12,* 135–139.

Lang, B. (1980). Faces. *The Yale Review, 71(4),* 533–540.

McDermott, R. P. (1976). *Kids make sense: An ethnographic account of success and failure in one first grade classroom.* Doctoral dissertation, Anthropology, Stanford University (Ann Arbor: University Microfilms, 1977).

McDermott, R. P. (1980). Profile: Ray L. Birdwhistell. *The Kinesis Report, 2*(3), 1–4; 14–16.

McDermott, R. P., Gospodinoff, K., & Aron, J. (1978). Criteria for an ethnographically adequate description of concerted activities and their contexts. *Semiotica, 24,* 245–275.

Murphy, R. F. (1975). The quest for cultural reality: Adventurers in Irish social anthropology. *Michigan Discussions in Anthropology, 1,* 48–64.

Nietzsche, F. (1954). 1873. On truth and lies in an extra-moral sense. In F. Kaufmann (Ed.), *The portable Nietzsche.* New York: Viking Press. (Original work published 1873).

Nietzsche, F. (1968). *Twilight of the idols.* London: Penguin. (Original work published 1889).

Pascal, B. (1966). *Pensees.* London: Penguin. (Original work published 1670).

Plessner, H. (1965). *Die Stufen des Organischen und der Mensch.* Berlin: Walter de Gruyter.

Sacks, H. (1975). Everyone has to lie. In M. Sanches and B. Blount (Ed.), *Sociocultural dimensions of language use.* New York: Academic Press.

Scheflen, A. E. (1973). *Communicational structure.* Bloomington: Indiana University Press.

Shklar, J. (1979). Let's not be hypocritical. *Daedalus, 108,* 1–25.

Silverstein, M. (1979). Language structure and linguistic ideology. In R. Clyne, W. Hanks, & C. Hofbauer (Eds.), *The elements: A parasession on linguistic units and levels.* Chicago: Chicago Linguistic Society.

Silverstein, M. (1981). The limits of awareness. *Working Papers on Sociolinguistics,* no. 84. Austin: Southwest Educational Development Laboratory.

Simmel, G. (1964). *On individuality and social forms,* D. Levine (Ed.). Chicago: University of Chicago Press.

Timpanaro, S. (1976). *The Freudian slip.* New York: NLB.

Varenne, H. (1983). *American school language.* New York: Irvington Press.

Volosinov, V. N. (1973). *Marxism and the philosophy of language.* New York: Academic Press.

Wieder, D. L. (1974). *Language and social reality.* The Hague: Mouton.

7.

The Role of Language and the Language of Role in Institutional Decision Making*

Hugh Mehan
University of California, San Diego

INTRODUCTION

Decision making and problem solving are routinely thought to be cognitive activities. So, for example, Simon (1949), in his influential study of decision making processes in administrative agencies, depicts decision making in terms of "goal selection," "planning," and "design"—notions usually equated with cognitive processing. In a recent review of the field, Janis and Mann (1978, p. 11) outlined the seven procedural criteria involved in decision making: "canvassing," "surveying," "weighing," "searching," "assimilating," "reexamining," and "implementing." Each of these criteria are subsumed by Bartlett (1958) as "forms of thinking," which in turn, is a mental process that runs beyond immediate perception.

In this paper, a different approach to decision making is taken. I focus on the role that the *linguistic* process of persuasion plays in the *cognitive* activity of decision making in an institutional setting. In doing so, cognitive activities of decision making are made more visible, and the relationship between linguistic processes, cognitive activities, and social structures are made more explicit.

The context for this study is the decision making of committees of educators. Their task is to decide whether to place students into special education programs or retain them in their regular classrooms. Often, different committee members enter the committee meeting with different views of the student's case and its disposition. Yet, by meeting's end, one version of the student, that provided by representatives of the central school district, prevails. Furthermore, a striking feature of the educators' decision making activities is that they do not seem to be making decisions, or at least, they are not making them in the way that conventional theories of decision making have depicted them. They seem to *present* decisions rather than *debate* them.

This paper is addressed to the following questions: What discursive and

* This research was supported by a grant from the National Institute of Education, a part of the U.S. Office of Education. However, the contents of this paper do not necessarily reflect the policy of that agency, or the endorsement of the federal government.

This chapter is reproduced by permission from *Language in Society*.

Alma Hertweck and J. Lee Meihls assisted me in gathering the materials and conducting the analysis in this paper. James E. Heap, Dell Hymes, Gail MacColl and Alexandra Todd made many helpful comments on an earlier draft of this paper. I apologize for not always heeding their advice.

organizational arrangements provide for this manner of making decisions? How is it arranged such that committee members (including parents) are routinely induced to agree with school policy, and come to agreement in a relatively smooth and trouble-free way? An answer to those questions about the educators' decision-making activity is located in the role that language plays in committee meetings. The committee's presentational mode of decision making is grounded in the reflexive relations between the functions of language and the structure of role relationships among the committee members.

Students' Careers and The Special Educational Referral System

Under normal circumstances, students progress through school in a regular sequence. They enter school in the kindergarten and, at the end of each year, are promoted to the next higher grade. Not all students follow this routine career pattern through school, however. Under unusual circumstances, students are removed from their regular classroom during the school year, and are placed in a variety of "special education" programs.

The special education referral system.   These special career paths have been a longstanding feature of public schools in the United States. Recently, federal legislation has formalized the procedures involved in placing students in special education programs. Public Law 94–142, "The Education for All Handicapped Students" Act, mandates a free and appropriate public education for all handicapped children between the ages of 3 and 21, in the "least restrictive" educational environment possible. The determination of special education placements are not to be made solely by an administrator, but rather through consultation with many school officials and the children's parents.

In order to describe the decision-making process involved as students are referred from "regular" elementary school classrooms and are considered for placement in one of a number of "special" educational programs, we followed the progress of students' cases through the special education referral system mandated by PL 94–142. We gathered materials for this investigation in many ways, including reviewing official school records, interviewing educators, observing in classrooms and meetings, and analyzing the discourse between participants in key events.

A given case has the potential of progressing through a number of major decision-making points, including "referral," "appraisal," "assessment," "reappraisal," "evaluation," and "placement." The various "career paths" through the referral system are depicted in Figure 7.1.

Students' career paths.   A total of 141 first-time referrals were processed through the special education referral system during the 1978–79 school year in which we gathered material for this study. Table 7.1 summarizes the number of students, or rather, students' cases that traversed these paths.

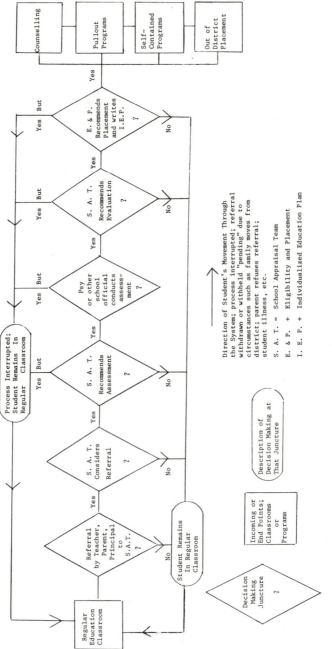

Figure 7.1. A Representation of the Special Education Referral Process

142

Towards a Description of the Processes of Educational Decision Making

This is some information about the products of the referral system, the educational "facts" of the referral process, if you will. (For more information, see Mehan, Meihls, & Hertweck, 1986.) We are interested in describing the institutional practices that constitute these educational facts. To this end, we have been conducting more micro, "constitutive," analyses of a number of key events at the referral, assessment, and placement phases of the referral system.

The grounds of teachers' referrals.   Since the referral process starts in the classroom, we have been attempting to uncover the grounds of teachers' referrals, and depict the relations between teachers' accounts and students' behavior. To do so, we have had teachers provide accounts of students behavior during videotaped lessons. We have been finding that teachers do not perceive students' behavior directly. Their judgments about referrals are mediated by culturally and experimentially provided categories that bear little relation to students' actual classroom behavior (Mehan, Hertweck, Combs and Flynn, 1982; Mehan et al., 1986).

Diagnosing students' performance.   When the referral process involves psychological assessment, we have been examining the procedures that assemble test results, and inform a diagnosis which is then used at later stages in the referral system. Videotape of actual educational testing situations and the test results and reports produced in them form the important data sources for this part of the overall study. Meihls (1981) has replicated the previously reported finding that test results are constructed jointly by teachers and students, and are not

Table 7.1.   Types of Placements

	Number	Percent
Regular Education		
Remains in classroom by decision	49	
Remains in classroom by default	29	
(interrupted in process)		
Total Regular Education	78	55.71
Special Education		
Counseling	6	
"Pullout" Programs[1]	41	
"Self-Contained" Programs[2]	15	
Out of District Placement	0	
Total Special Education	62	44.28
Total Referral Cases	140	100.00%

[1]Pullout special education programs: LDG, Speech Therapy, Reading, Adaptive Physical Education
[2]Self-contained programs are: EH, SLH, MH.

private productions. Diagnoses by school psychologists are informed by test results, to be sure, but in important ways, are influenced by teachers' informal opinions, and students' behavior in the informal aspects of testing situations.

Constraints on decision making. In another paper (Mehan, 1981), I continued the analysis to the Eligibility and Placement (E&P) Committee, which is the final stage in the decision-making process. In that paper, I examined the activities that occur before and surrounding the E&P meeting. I found that a number of economic, legal, and institutional factors constrain the referral process and the decision making about special education students. PL 94–142 indicates that 12 percent of the school-aged population will be served by special education programs. The compulsary thrust of this law provides an incentive to search for, identify, and place students into special education programs in order to meet mandated quotas. The legal incentive to search for special students is reinforced by financial incentives. School districts are provided funds from state and federal sources for each student in regular classrooms, and a greater amount of money for students in special education programs. This additional source of money also serves as an incentive to search for students to place in special education.

Just as there are incentives to locate and place students in special education in order to receive the maximum state and federal support, so, too, there are disincentives to find too many students. A funding ceiling is reached when a certain number of students are placed in certain special education programs; no additional money is provided if more students than the quota are assigned to particular classrooms. These financial and legal considerations constrain placement decisions, and influence the procedures for constructing individualized education plans.

Practical circumstances at the local level also limit placement options. The option to place students in special education programs outside the district at district expense was eliminated from consideration by administrative fiat because of the inordinate expense of such placements. Likewise, the district did not establish a separate program for mentally retarded students. Instead, students who met the clinical criteria for this designation were distributed to other programs such as "severe language handicapped."

The number of students already assigned to special education programs eliminated other options from consideration at different times in the school year. Programs that were "full," that is, had reached the funding ceiling, were eliminated from consideration, while programs that were "open," that is, had not reached the legally mandated quota, remained subject to consideration.

These legal, fiscal, and practical constraints influenced educational placements in the district during the year of this study. Educational placements were not made based solely on the basis of students' educational needs. Educational decisions were taken based on an interlacing of these factors and such factors as money and space available.

While this information about practical constraints and institutional responses to them is informative because it points out the influence of institutional structures on decision making, it did not tell the whole story. Most importantly, the emergent properties of decision making are left out when the analysis is restricted to the activities that surround and lead up to the final decision-making meeting. In order to understand the dynamics of institutional decision making while conveying a view of an organization as an intersubjective construction, constituted by the ongoing situated practices of its members, and not as an objectified reification (cf. Silverman, 1981), we found it instructive to study the actual language of the committee members during the final placement (E&P) meetings. That investigation is the topic of the balance of this paper.

Practical Decision Making in Committee Meetings

Decisions to place students into special education programs were made by the "Eligibility and Placement" (E&P) committee, a team at the district level composed of the referred student's parent(s), the school administrator in charge of special education, the school nurse, the district psychologist, the referring teacher, and a special education teacher. This committee had a number of placement options: it could recommend that the student be retained in the regular classroom, be placed in a number of special education programs, receive counseling, or be placed in a program outside the school district at district expense.

Methods of investigation. In order to study the process of reaching final placement decisions, we obtained permission from committee members (including parents) to observe, and in some cases, videotape, committee meetings. We transcribed the audio portion of the videotape. Our observations, the videotape, transcripts, and reports written during the meeting provide the main sources of information for the analysis presented in this paper.

Our observations of meetings we did not videotape were instructive for a number of reasons. First, it provided us information about the routine conduct and order of activities in the meetings we did videotape. Second, it gave us a way to measure the so-called "reactive effect" of videotaping. By observing committee members' actions when we did not tape, we had a way to gauge the committee members' actions when we did videotape. As productive as this strategy is, it does not, of course, dissolve the "observer's paradox," that is, knowing about behavior when it is not observed by observing it when it does occur (Labov, 1972).

The decisions made. Fifty-three (53) cases were considered by the E&P committee during the year of our study. (See Table 7.2.) Twelve of 53 cases (23 percent) were referred to self-contained classrooms; 39 of 53 (73 percent) were placed in "pull-out" programs; no students were referred for private schooling, and in all but one case, the decision reached involved the placement of the

**Table 7.2.   The Disposition of
53 Cases Considered by E. &
P. Committee in Coast
District, 1978–79**

Placement	Number
EH	7
LDG	36
SLH	3
MH	2
Speech	3
Private Schooling	0
No Placement	1
Interrupted	1
Total	53

student in some kind of the special education program and not in a regular classroom.

Sequence of activities.   The committee meetings that we observed in the district during the year of our study had the following "segments"[1] which took place in the following temporal sequence:

1. *Information Presentation Phase:* information about the student was presented by the committee members
2. *Decision Phase:* the committee reached a decision about the appropriate placement for the child
3. *Parents' Rights Phase:* parents' rights to educational services and the range of evaluative services were explained
4. *Goals and Objectives Phase:* the goals and objectives were written based on the discrepancy between the child's actual and expected level of performance.

The decision making.   There are a number of striking features about the interaction among the committee members concerning the placement of students. Placement decisions were made quickly. After the school psychologist, classroom teacher, nurse, and parents provided information about the student (Phase #1), the student's placement was determined. The following transcripts are representative of the interaction in the second, or "Decision" phase of the meeting (Psy. = Psychologist; S.E.T. = Special Education Teacher; Prin. = Principal):

---

[1] See McDermott et al., (1978), Mehan (1978, 1979), and Erickson and Shultz (1977, 1980) for more information about the segmentation of naturally occurring events into their sequentially organized constituents, and Pike (1967) and Scheflen (1972) for the foundation under such efforts.

EDM #33

92	Psy.	does the uh, committee agree that the, uh learning disability placement is one that might benefit him?
93	Princ.	I think we agree.
94	Psy.	We're not considering then a special day class at all for him?
95	S.E.T.	I wouldn't at this point//
96	Many	No.

EDM #47

28	Psy.	Okay, in light of all the data that we have, I think that the program we want to recommend is the learning disability pullout program.
29	Mother	Pullout = I don't understand that//
30	Psy.	For Tracy. You know, that's the program we sort of talked about that day, where he would be pullout out of the classroom for specific work on the areas that he needs, that, you know, are identified today.

EDM #57

| 35 | Psy. | Okay. Now, okay, now then, let's, why don't we take a vote. Um, for the Learning Disabilities Group pullout program. Um, is there anyone, anyone who does not agree? (3) Okay. I think that was unanimous. (soft laughter) All right. Then what we have to do now is sign. But, um, before we sign I'd like to have, uh, Susan um, talk about the rights to private schooling and talk about your rights as parents. |

These exchanges do not have the features routinely associated with "decision making." Certainly this mode of reasoning varies considerably from descriptions of "rational" decision making, in both its "comprehensive" (Parsons, 1932; Weber, 1947, pp. 115–118; 1949, pp. 52–53; Schelling, 1950) and "bounded" (Simon, 1949; Watkins, 1970) forms, where rational decision making has been described as the presentation of a range of alternatives, the consideration of the consequences of any choice singly, and in combination with others.

One of the significant ways in which these activities differed from current theories of decision making concerns the range of alternatives. The entire range of possible placements was not discussed during these placement meetings. At most, the possibility of placement in one or two closely related programs was discussed, for example, an Educationally Handicapped (EH) or a Learning Disability (LD) program. And these possibilities were not debated or discussed. They were *presented* to the committee by the school psychologist without question or challenge by other members of the committee, including the parents.

We seek to understand this manner of reaching educational decisions, but without disparaging it. Hence, we will not make invidious comparisons to the rational models of decision making; instead we will try to describe the mode of reasoning in placement meetings in its own terms. That is, the inquiry is "recollective.'' It aims to recollect what is known by the participants in this practical activity, albeit tacitly known by them (Mehan, 1979, pp. 173–176; Heap, 1980).

In order to reveal the machinery that provides for this mode of reaching decisions, it is necessary to go beyond the texts of the decisions themselves, into the events that led up to them. One transcript of a committee meeting in which a student, Shane, was placed in an LDG program will be used to illustrate this point. In the course of the analysis which follows, references to the interaction among the committee members will be made.[2]

LAY AND PROFESSIONAL REPORTS

There are a number of striking patterns in the language of the four reports made to the committee during the initial ''presentation'' phase of the meeting. One set of these patterns involves relations among speaker and format, source of information and mode of presentation, mode of presentation and speaker, and speaker and topic. Another set of patterns involve the manner in which contextual features are referenced by committee members. The compilation of these form-function and contextual relationships leads to a distinction between ''lay'' and ''professional'' reports. This distinction indexes an important part that language plays in authority relations within the institutionalized order of the school, which, in turn, reveals the grounds upon which decisions are made in this context.

The Role of Language and the Language of Role

The discussion of form-function relationships begins with a consideration of speaker-format relations.[3]

Speaker-format relations. The information that the committee obtained from the classroom teacher and the mother appeared in a different form than the information made available by the school psychologst and the nurse. The information that the nurse and the psychologist had about the student was *presented to* the committee in a single uninterrupted report.

The meeting was started by the school psychologist. She introduced the purpose of the meeting as follows:

1 Psy.:   Um. What we're going to do is, I'm going to have a brief, an overview of the testing because the rest of, of the, the committee has not, uh, has not an, uh, been aware of that yet. And uh, then each of us will share whatever, whatever we feel we need to share.

2 Prin.:   Right.

---

[2] The complete transcript of the meeting and the transcript conventions used in it are available from the author.

[3] See Hymes (1974) and Ervin-Tripp (1973) for the original seminal statements about the importance of form-function relationships for an understanding of language in society.

3 Psy.: And then we will make a decision on what we feel is a good, oh (3) placement (2) for an, Shane.

The school psychologist immediately provided the committee members with the information she had about the student:

3 Psy.: Shane is ah nine years old, and he's in fourth grade. Uh, he, uh, was referred because of low academic performance and he has difficulty applying himself to his daily class work. Um, Shane attended the Montessori School in kindergarten and first grade, and then he entered Carlsberg-bad in, um, September of 1976 and, uh, entered our district in, uh, '78. He seems to have very good peer relationships but, uh, the teachers, uh, continually say that he has difficulty with handwriting. 'kay. He enjoys music and sports. I gave him a complete battery and, um, I found that, uh, he had a verbal I.Q. of 115, performance of 111, and a full scale of 115, so he's a bright child. Uh, he had very high scores in, uh, information which is his long-term memory. Ah, vocabulary, was, ah, also, ah, considerably over average, good detail awareness and his, um, picture arrangement scores, he had a seventeen which is very=high

4 S.E.T.: Mmmm

5 Psy.: =very superior rating, so he, his visual sequencing seems to be good and also he has a good grasp of anticipation and awareness of social situations. Um, he (5) (she is scanning her notes) scored in reading at 4.1, spelling 3.5, and arithmetic 3.0, which gave him a standard score of 100 in, uh, reading, 95 in spelling, and 90 in arithmetic. When compared with his *overall* score, it does put him somewhat ah below his, you know, his capabilities. I gave him the Bender Gestalt (clears throat) and he had six errors. And his test age was 7–0 to 7–5 and his actual age is nine, so it, uh, he was considerably beneath his, uh, hisuh, age level. (2) His, I gave him the, uh VADS and his, um (5 or 6) (looking through notes) both the oral-aural and the visual-written modes of communication were high but the visual oral and the oral written are low::, so he, uh, cannot switch channels. His expressive vocabulary was in the superior range (6). Uh, visual perception falls above age level, so he's fine in that area (6). And fine motor skills appear to be slightly lower than, uh, average, (voice trails off slightly), I saw them. (3) He read words very quickly when he was doing the academics but I didn't see any reversals in his written work. Uh, I hgave him several projective tests and, um, the things that I picked up there is that, um he *does* possibly have some fears and anxieties, uh, (5). So I had felt ah, that perhaps he might, uh, uh, benefit, um, (3) from special help. He also was tested, um, in 1976 and at that time he was given the WISC- and his I.Q. was slightly lower, full scale of a 93 (3 or 4). His, um, summary of that evaluation, uh, was, uh, he was given the ITPA and he had high auditory reception, auditory association, auditory memory. (2) So his auditory skills are good. (3) He was given

another psychol—psychological evaluation in 1977. He was given the Leiter and he had an I.Q. of 96 (6). And, um (3 or 4) they concluded that he had a poor mediate recall (2) but they felt that was due to an emotional overlay and they felt that some emotional conflicts were, uh, interferring with his ability to concentrate.

At the end of this presentation, the psychologist asked the student's teacher to provide information (CLT = classroom teacher):

5 Psy.:   Kate, would you like to share with u:s?
6 CLT: What, the problems I see ( ) Um . . .
7 Psy.:   Yes.
8 CLT: Um. Probably basically the fine motor types of things are difficult for him. He's got a very creative mi:ind and expresses himself well (   ) orally and verbally and he's pretty alert to what's going on. (2) Maybe a little bit *too* much, watching EVERYthing that's (hh) going (hh) on, and finds it hard to stick to one task. And *mostly* I've been noticing that it's just his writing and things that he has a, a block with. And he can rea:ad and comprehend some things when I talk to him, *but* doing independent type work is hard for him.
9 Prin.:   mhmmm, putting it down on paper . . .
10 CLT: Yeah::, and sticking to a task//
11 Princ.:   mmhmmm
12 CLT: =and getting it done, without being// distracted by (hehhehheh) . . .
13 S.E.T.: How does he relate with what the other kids do?
14 CLT: Uh, very well (slight stress). He's got a lot of frie:ends, and, uh, especially, even out on the playground he's, um (3), wants to get in on the games, get on things and is well accepted. So::, I don't see too many problems there.

In this sequence, we have the classroom teacher beginning to present some of the characteristics of the student, and being interrupted by the principal, before the special education teacher took the floor. From that point on, the special education teacher asked the classroom teacher a series of questions about the child's peer relations, reading level, performance in spelling, and math. The school nurse also participated in the questioning of the teacher. She asked the teacher how "she handled the reading problem." After the school psychologist moved the discussion away from these academic concerns to a more personal one: how the student handles failure, the questioning shifted to the mother. The special education teacher asked the mother about his fine motor control at home:

46 S.E.T.: How do you find him at *home* in terms of using his fingers and fine motor kinds of things? Does he do//
47 Mother: =He will, as a small child, he didn't at all. He was never interested in it, he wasn't interested in sitting in my lap and having a book read to him, any things like that//

48	S.E.T.:	mhmmm
49	Mother:	=which I think is part of it you know. His, his older brother was just the opposite, and learned to write real early. *Now* Shane, at night, lots of times he comes home and he'll write or draw. He's really doing a lot
50	S.E.T.:	( )
51	Mother:	=he sits down and is writing love notes to his girl friend (hehheh). He went in our bedroom last night and turned on the TV and got out some colored pencils and started writing. So he, really likes to, and of course he brings it all into us to see//
52	S.E.T.:	=mhmmm
53	Mother:	and comment on, so I think, you know, he's not *NEGAtive* about//
54	S.E.T.:	=no
55	Mother:	=that anymore
56	S.E.T.:	=uh huh
57	Mother:	He was before, but I think his attitude's changed a lot.

These transcript inserts are representative of the manner in which information about the student was made available to the members of the committee by the psychologist, the teacher, and the mother. They show that the information that the nurse and the psychologist had about the student was presented to the committee in a single, uninterrupted report, while the mother's and teacher's information was elicted from them by other members of the committee. In fact, the classroom teacher's presentation and the mother's presentation took the form of an interrogation. Information from the mother and the teacher became available to the committee in the form of answers to questions posed by the committee members.

The format of the classroom teacher's report and the mother's report is different from the psychologist's and the nurse's in another respect. The psychologist provided a summary of the results of a given test or subtest in a standard format. She named the subtest, reported the student's score, and gave her interpretations of the results. For example:

3.9   I gave him a complete battery, and I found that, uh, he had a verbal I.Q. of 115, performance of 111, and a full scale of 115, so he's a bright child

3.11 He had very high scores in, uh, information, which is his long term memory.

3.14 His, um, picture arrangement scores, he had a seventeen, which is very high, very superior rating.

Thus, the educational test results provided the grounds of the psychologist's assertions about the student.[4]

Perhaps because the mother and the teacher were being interrogated, their

---

[4] Turn #5 contains many other tokens of this presentational format. Alternative forms are to be found in turn #3.

information was not presented to the committee in a standard format. For example, the teacher provided general statements "he's got a very creative mind and expresses himself well," as well as some more specific assertions: "He can read and comprehend some things when I talk to him, but doing independent type work is hard for him." The format of the mother's presentation is different from both of these. Her turns at talk were lengthy answers to immediately preceeding questions and were embedded in commentary on previous discussions.

Source-mode relations. The sources of information for the classroom teacher's report and the mother's report are also different from that of the psychologist and the nurse. Whereas the nurse and psychologist reported information about the student based on educational tests, the classroom teacher and mother based their reports on first-hand observations. While the classroom teacher's observations were confined to a relatively short temporal unit (a school year) and a circumscribed spatial and social arrangement (the classroom), the mother's observations concern the child's actions in a wide variety of situations, and span a lifetime. Thus, the information gathered by systematic albeit indirect observations (i.e., that gathered from specialized tests) was *presented* to the committee, while information that was gathered by direct albeit unguided or unstructured observation (which included information about classroom experiences and home life) was *elicited* from participants.

Mode-speaker relationships. The mode in which information was presented to the committee varied according to the status and official expertise of the participants in the meeting. In terms of the official table of organization in the district, the psychologist and the nurse are ranked higher than the classroom teacher (and the mother is not an official part of the educational system). The nurse and the psychologist work for the district office; the teacher works for one particular school. Technical expertise is coupled with this status ranking. The nurse and psychologist have advanced degrees, and represent technical specialties.

Furthermore, the school psychologist has an institutionally designated role responsibility. Part of the role of school psychologist involves accumulating all the information available about the child being considered by the committee. To do so, the psychologist had discussed the child with the teacher and his mother, and observed him in the classroom. As "case carrier," then, she had more knowledge about the child than any single individual attending the meeting. While the mother knows the child at home, and the teacher knows him in the classroom, only the psychologist has this information compiled in a single place.

Not only does the psychologist have "more" information, calibrated in terms of quantity or amount, the school psychologist has "official," that is, qualitatively different, information about the child. She has administered official and professional tests to the child. This official information is coupled with the information gathered from many other sources to compose the "case."

This combination of technical expertise and organizational rank is manifest in the stratification of talking arrangements present in the meeting. The most highly technical information (that from tests) was made available by the most highly trained people in attendance at the meeting, while the personal observations were made available by the participants with the least technical expertise. Speakers of officially higher rank and who spoke with their authority grounded in technical expertise, *presented* their information, while speakers of lower rank, who spoke with authority based on first hand observations, had information *elicited* from them.

Topic-speaker relationships.   There is another interesting form-function relationship in evidence in this phase of the meeting, a correlation between topic of discussion and speaker (see Table 7.3). Academic information (including educational test results, academic performance in class) is the domain of educators. It is discussed by teacher, nurse, and psychologist. Emotions and feelings (including attitudes toward school and a new educational program), are the province of mothers and teachers. In fact, with one exception, the mother is only asked about the emotional aspects of the case before the committee. The one exception was the topic of her son's small motor control activities at home. And this issue was raised after the committee had established the fact that this was the source of the student's difficulty. Thus, the mother's contribution was *post hoc,* and not decisive in reaching a decision.

Summary.   These constellations of relationships among the structure and function of language provide the first strands of evidence to distinguish between lay and professional reports. A further distinction between them is found in the way that context, in both its situational and biographical sense, operates in the presentations to the committee.

Contingent and noncontingent reports

The main issue before the committee was the student, his educational performance, and an appropriate learning environment. Perhaps as a consequence of the differences in the grounds of the reports made by the mother, the teacher, the psychologist, and the nurse, the issue before the committee is discussed differently by its members.

Categorical assessments of student performance.   The student is characterized by the psychologist as having "troubles" and "problems." For example, the school psychologist says:

"He has difficulty applying himself to his daily work."

"He cannot switch channels."

"He has some fears and anxieties."

Table 7.3.   Topic-Speaker Relationships in Information Presentation Portion of E & P Meeting

	Topics of Discussion	Transcript Line	Source of Information (Speaker)	Mode of Presentation
1.	Results of ed. testing	a)3.2–5.30 b) 91	School Psychol. Nurse	Reading report; informative speech act reading report; informative speech act
2.	Academic performance in class	8–34	Classroom Teacher	Elicitation; responsive speech acts
3.	Student's reaction to failure	40–45	Classroom Teacher	Elicitation; responsive speech acts
4.	Student's feelings in class	58–61 82–89	Classroom Teacher	Elicitation; responsive speech acts
5.	Student's reaction to Special Ed.	a)73–74 b)71–72	Classroom Teacher Mother	Elicitation; responsive Elicitation; responsive
6.	Fine motor problems at home	46–57	Mother	Elicitation; responsive
7.	Student's sensitivity at home	62	Mother	Informative speech act
8.	Student's attitudes toward school	63–68	Mother	Elicitation; responsive speech act
9.	Student's feelings	71–81	Mother	Elicitation; responsive speech act
10.	Reason for problem	a)8–12 b)37	Teacher Learning Disability Teacher	Elicitation; responsive speech act; informative speech acts

At some points in the meeting, the classroom teacher characterizes the problem in a similar way:

"the problems I see"

". . . the fine motor types of things are difficult for him"

"doing independent work is hard for him"

Thus, the issue before the committee is the child and his problem. The child's problems were characterized by both the classroom teacher and the psychologist as being private and internal to the student. They are treated as if they are his private and personal possession. This is a prime example of the use of dispositional properties in the search for the explanation of other people's behaviors

(D'Andrade, 1974; Shweder, 1977; Cantor and Mischel, 1979). This "person-ological" or individualized defect (Lopes, 1979) metaphor places the source of the problem "squarely on the back, or rather in the head of the child" (Coles, 1978, p. 333).[5] The purpose of the meeting, indeed the entire referral enterprise, is to solve the student's problem, and to do so by altering or modifying the internal states of the student.

Situational contingencies of student performance. While the student's problem is the focus of attention for the entire committee, the lay people in attendance at the meeting introduce information about the student which is different than that offered by the professionals. Notable in this regard are comments about the student's motivation: the teacher says "he enjoys math" (28) in response to the special education teacher's request for information about his math performance. She comments: "he enjoys handwriting and wants to learn it," "he seems to enjoy handwriting and wants to learn it," "he really tries at it hard and seems to wanna learn it better."

She also discusses some of the circumstances surrounding the student's "problems." She introduced a number of contingencies that influenced the student's performance:

1. His performance varies as a function of preparation: "If he studies his spelling and concentrates on it he can do pretty well."

2. His performance varies according to the kinds of materials and tasks: (1) "It's hard for him to copy down [math] problems . . . if he's given a sheet where he can fill in answers and work them out he does much better," (2) he does better on group tasks, "but doing independent type work is hard for him," (3) if the tasks at hand are a means to some other end desired by the student, then his performance improves: "if there's something else he wants to do and knows he needs to do and knows he needs to get through that before he can get on to something else, he'll work a little more dilligently at it."

3. The teacher's remediations are contingent upon the kind of work and the importance of the task. When the nurse asked her how she dealt with the "writing problems," the teacher indicated that her response varied. She either had him redo work if the task was important, or if it was a "rush job," then she would only have him clean it up a bit.

The classroom teacher provides more details about the circumstances surrounding the problems. When the classroom teacher was asked by the special education teacher about the student's reading level, the teacher responded: "about middle third grade," an answer presumably based on the results of a reading test or the reading series used with the student. She then embellished this response with some details about his performance: "He's a good reader, . . . but as far as comprehending it and being able to recall sequences of a story and

---

[5] See Lakoff and Johnson (1980) for an explication of the structure and power of "metaphors we live by."

things like that. . . ." She identified two components of the reading task, and provides some sense of the particulars of the reading process upon which her assessment is based.

When the special education teacher asked her about the student's work in spelling (21), she did not only comment on his level of performance; she also provided information about the aspects of the spelling process that cause him difficulty—namely final consonants and silent letters.

When the special education teacher asked the teacher about the student's handwriting, even though presented with a "choice question," she did not respond with either a yes or a no answer. She exceeded the minimal demands of this question by indicating frequency of use, by comparing this student to other students that she knows who "slip back into printing." And, once again, she mentioned his motivation—"he tries to learn" and performs academic tasks.

The classroom teacher also made observations about the manner in which the student performs his work, that is the process, and not just the outcome or product of his work:

"He's got his multiplication tables down pretty well, but not as quick as I'd like to see him have them."

Here, the speed of processing is discussed along with the student's knowledge of the academic task.

". . . doing independent type work is hard for him . . . sticking to a task . . . and getting it down without being distracted."

Here, his perserverance and concentration are discussed along with the kind of academic task he has been assigned.

The psychologist has introduced the topic of "peer relations" in her report: "He seems to have good peer relationships." The special education teacher returned to this topic in her questioning of the teacher.

The teacher provided some more detail about his relations with classmates in her answer. She provided more particulars later in the meeting, explaining that he's been elected a class officer and gets along well with girls.

In sum, the teacher, like the psychologist, characterized the issue at hand as "the student's problem." However, the teacher's characterization, unlike that of the psychologist, had a contingent quality; she emphasized the situational variability of the student's problem.

Historical and biographical contingencies of student performance. If it can be said that the classroom teacher is expanding the range of information available to the committee spatially by providing situational or local contextual information, then the mother's report adds a temporal dimension by providing historical and biographical contextual information. She continually contrasts her son as he was at an earlier age with how he is now. In each of these contrasts, she emphasizes improvements and changes for the better. Thus it seems she is working to redeem her child. While she seems to acknowledge the official committee position that there is a problem, she attempts to legitimate her child by emphasizing improvements and by providing an alternative explanation of the source of the problem. For her, the locus of difficulty is not within him, (''it's not physical,'' ''it's not functional''), but it is to be found in his past experience, and the situations he has been in.

Summary. Thus, the reports provided by the psychologist, classroom teacher, mother, and nurse can be placed on a continuum from the contingent to the noncontingent. The mother's report is at the contingent end of the continuum because she provides particulars about the biography and history of her son, and references situational circumstances. The classroom teacher's report sits next to the mother's because she tempers her report with statements about local circumstances, but does not provide historical particulars. The nurse's and the psychologist's report are at the noncontingent end of the continuum, because these statements are presented stripped of all contextual features of the situational and historical variety.

The psychologist made absolute and categorical statements about the student's abilities. She placed the locus of the student's problem within him. The result is a view of a child who has a general, that is, ''context free'' disability. In responding to the questions asked by other members of the conmittee, the classroom teacher tempered her report with contingent factors of a situational sort. She said that the student's performance was influenced by his state of motivation, kinds of classroom tasks, and types of materials. The result is a ''context bound'' view of a child, one who has specific problems in certain academic situations, but who operates more than adequately in other situations.

The Distinction Between Lay and Professional Reports

In sum, the mother's and the teacher's reports have the following features in common:

1. They were elicited.
2. They were made available by people who occupy either low status or temporary positions (both in terms of institutional stratification and distribution of technical knowledge).
3. Their claims to truth were based on common sense knowledge.
4. Their reports were based on direct albeit unguided or unstructured observations.
5. They offered contingent assessments of student performance.
6. They resulted in a context-bound view of student disability.

By contrast, the psychologist's and the nurse's reports had the following features in common:

1. They were presented, not elicited.
2. They were presented by people who occupy high status and permanent positions.
3. Their claims were based on technical knowledge and expertise.
4. They were based on indirect albeit guided or structured observations.
5. They offered categorical assessments of student performance.
6. They resulted in a context-free view of student disability.

I will call the first "lay reports" and the second "professional reports." The former have many features in common with what Irvine (1979) calls "informal events," and the latter have many features in common with what she calls "formal" events. The distinction between lay and professional reports is important for understanding how decisions are reached in these committee meetings. Both the professionals and the lay members make claims for the authority of their reports. The differences in the authority of the professionals and lay members recommendations are found in the differences in the structure of language used in assembling these two kinds of reports. The role that language plays in grounding the authority of accounts is explored further in the following section.

THE MYSTIFICATION OF LANGUAGE AND THE LANGUAGE OF MYSTIFICATION

There is a significant difference in the way in which professional reports (i.e., those offered by the psychologist and the nurse) on the one hand and the lay reports (i.e., those offered by the classroom teacher and the mother) on the other hand are *treated* by other members of the committee. The reports by the psychologist and the nurse are accepted without question or challenge, while those of the mother and the teacher are interrupted continuously by questions. No one asked the psychologist or the nurse to clarify the technical terms during their reports, while the classroom teacher and mother were often asked to provide further information or to clarify previous statements. I have already characterized the classroom teacher's report as an interrogation: the classroom teacher presented information, and either the special education teacher, the principal, the psychologist, or the nurse asked her for further information. Neither the mother nor any of the educators present asked the psychologist for more details, further information, or to clarify technical terms.

In fact, the mother made only one request for clarification during the course of the entire meeting—and that was at its conclusion, just as the formal business was being finished. Her question was about "PE":

422   SET   check over ((( ))) I don't think I addressed P.E.
423   Psy   I don't think we uh, *oh,* ok, we do not need that, okay, he does not need physical edu//

424 Mot ((I want to ask something about that while you mentioned P.E. You mean physical education/))
425 ?   mmhmmm
426 Mot Does the school have a soccer program/ or is that just totally separate from um, you know, part of the boys' club or::-
427 Prin =Right. It's a parent organized, um, association—
428 Mot Is there something at the school that would have information on it if it comes up in the season, because Shane really has expressed an interest in that

Mot = Mother

The Issue of Membership

One way to account for the differential treatment of the professionals and lay person's report, especially the differences in requests for clarification of technical terms and the grounds of conclusions is in terms of "membership." While the psychologist's and nurse's statements about educational test results and their interpretations may be obscure to noneducators (i.e., researchers), they are, in fact, comprehensible to the participants themselves. What seems to be a problem for outsiders is not a problem for members of this particular community.

However, that account does not explain the mother's request near the end of the meeting about the meaning of the expression "PE." If the technical terms used in this meeting were to be ranked in order from the most technical to the most ordinary, then "PE" would appear closer to the everyday usage end of the continuum than terms like "VADS," "Bender Gestalt," "aural oral channel of communication." Yet, the mother requested information about PE and not these other terms. The "membership" account also does not account for the points of clarification directed at the classroom teacher.

As a result of the weakness inherent in the membership account, I am inclined to consider another possibility: *the authority of the professional report resides in the very mode of its presentation.* The parents and other educators do not challenge the ambiguity of the psychologist's report because the grounds for doing so are removed by the presentational mode of the professional report.

In order to clarify this point, it will be necessary to discuss how people are said to come to understand each other in everyday conversation, and then compare this with what is happening in the committee meeting.

The Authority of the Office in the Discourse

In everyday discourse, meaning is said to be negotiated. Speakers and hearers both take responsibility for the construction of understanding. According to observers from a wide variety of perspectives, a first maxim of conversation is that speakers will speak clearly; they intend to make sense and they intend to be understood (Grice, 1975; Merleau-Ponty, 1964; Sacks, Schegloff, Jefferson, 1974). Hearers contribute to meaning in discourse by making inferences from the conversational string of utterances. They display their understanding actively, through "back channel work" (Duncan, 1972), which includes eye contact, head nods, and vocalics such as uh huhs, and even lexical items like "I see," "I understand." When the hearer does not understand "a request for clarification," the manifest purpose of which is to obtain more information, is in order. The request for clarification is generated by the hearers when they do not think that the speaker is speaking clearly.

The grounds for this kind of negotiation of meaning are removed from the committee both by the institutionalized trappings of the meeting, and the language used in the meeting. As indicated above, the psychologist had been designated "case carrier." As case carrier, the psychologist assembled the "file" on the student. The file represents the official, school-sanctioned version of the student being considered by the committee. The psychologist *presented* her report. In doing so, she is presenting the school's case concerning the student. The case is the culmination of institutionalized work. She is speaking for the institution in her presentation. The school psychologist's presentation of the case to the committee is augmented by officially sanctioned props. These include the case file itself (a bulky manila folder on display in front of the psychologist), test results, carefully prepared notes, and her designation as leader of the meeting. When she presents the case, she reads from notes. By contrast, the mother and the teacher have no such props. They speak from memory, not from notes. They call upon remembered knowledge of first-hand observations, not compilations of remembered information.

When the school psychologist speaks, it is from an institutionally designated position of authority. This authority is made manifest in the very language that the psychologist uses. The psychologist, through her report, is making a recommendation about the next step in a child's career. This recommendation is based on her professional expertise. The privileged status of the psychologist's expertise is displayed in the *technical* language of her report. The clinical language of the psychologist supports the discourse of everyday life with a technical vocabulary.

There is a certain mystique in the use of technical vocabulary, as evidenced by the special status that the technical language of doctors, lawyers, and businessmen is given in our society (Shuy, 1973; Philips, 1977; Shuy and Larkin, 1978). Technical language can be mystifying (Marcuse, 1964; Laing, 1967; Habermas, 1970). The use of technical language indicates a superior status and a special knowledge based on long training and specialized qualifications.

When technical language is used, and embedded in the institutional trappings of the formal proceedings of a meeting, the grounds for negotiating meaning are removed from under the conversation. Because the speaker and hearers do not share membership in a common language community, the hearer does not have the expertise to issue a challenge. To interrupt, to question, to request a clarification of the psychologist, then, is a challenge to the authority of the official position of the district and its representative concerning this child. The hearer is placed in the position of assuming the speaker is speaking knowledgeably, and the hearer does not have the competence to understand.

When technical language is used, even though the possibility for active negotiation of meaning seems to be removed, the guide of understanding remains. Yet the understanding is a passively achieved one, not the active one associated with everyday discourse. Instead of signaling a lack of understanding via such tacit devices as back channel work and manifest ones like requests for clarification, the committee members (including the mother) remain silent, thereby tacitly contributing to the guise that understanding has been achieved.

CONCLUSIONS

We now return to the question that was raised at the outset of this paper: How is it arranged such that committees of educators meet and make decisions without seeming to do so? The differences in the manner in which the professional and lay people in the committee reported information highlights the way in which the language that people use structures role relationships. And, the structure of role relationships found embedded in the language used by the committee members, in turn, provides the grounds of the authority of the claims and recommendations made. Despite the fact that they were composed of a highly technical vocabulary, the professional reports were accepted without challenge or question, while the lay reports were continually interrupted with requests for clarification and further information.

This differential treatment can be understood in terms of the authority that reports gain by their very mode of presentation. The ambiguity of professional reports is not challenged because the obscurity of professional language removes the grounds for the negotiation of meaning from the conversation. The authority of the professional report comes from its very incomprehensibility and its obscurity. The psychologist and the nurse gain their authority from the mastery and use of a technical language that others do not understand and do not question. The professional report gains its status and authority by virtue of the fact that it is obscure, difficult to understand, and is embedded in the institutional trappings of the formal proceedings of the committee meeting. And, it is this authority that contributes to the assembly of the "discourse of persuasion" (Silverman, 1981) observed in the committee meetings, such that decisions are "presented," not "discussed;" "credentialed," "not negotiated" (cf. Irvine, 1979).

Here we have yet another instance of the "politics of experience" (Laing, 1967; Pollner, 1975; Mehan & Wood, 1975, pp. 215–218). The various members of the committee experience this student differently. More specifically, the classroom teacher and the mother provide accounts about the student's performance that compete with the professional's version of the student's academic difficulties. Yet, by meeting's end, one version of the student, that provided by the psychologist and the nurse, prevailed.

In concert with others, people work to establish some unequivocal foundation beneath the "endless equivocalities" of everyday life (Pollner, 1975, p. 411). Often, consensual resolutions are achieved when one or another person relinquishes his or her experience of the world as the preferred version. In this case, the resolution was not negotiated. Instead, the members of the committee resolved the disjuncture between lay and professional versions by credentialing the professional version as the official version of this student.

These, then, are some of the ways in which the committee's mode of decision making are grounded in the reflexive relations among language and role, and in which a cognitive activity—decision making—is embedded in an institutional setting and made manifest in language.

REFERENCES

Bartlett, F. D. (1958). *Thinking*. New York: Basic Books.

Cantor, N., & Mischel, W. (1979). Prototypes in person perception. *Advances in Experimental Social Psychology, 12*, 3–52.

Coles, G. (1978). The learning disabilities test battery: Some empirical and social issues. *Harvard Educational Review, 48*(3), 313–340.

D'Andrade, R. (1974). Memory and the assessment of behavior. In (H. M. Blalock, Jr. (Ed.), *Measurement in the social sciences*. Chicago: Aldine.

Duncan, S. (1972). Some signals and rules for taking speaking turns in conversation. *Journal of Personality and Social Psychology, 23*, 283–292.

Erickson, F., & Shultz, J. (1977). When is a context? *ICHD Newslatter, 1*(2), 5–10.

Erickson, F., & Shultz, J. J. (1982). *The counselor as gatekeeper*. New York: Academic Press.

Ervin-Tripp, S. (1973). *Language acquisition and communicative choice*. Palo Alto: Stanford University Press.

Garfinkel, H. (1967). *Studies in ethnomethodology*. New York: Prentice-Hall.

Grice, H. P. (1975). Logic and conversation. In P. Cole & J. Morgan (Eds.), *Syntax and semantics* (Vol. 3), *Speech Acts*. New York: Academic Press.

Habermas, J. (1970). Toward a theory of communicative competence. In H. P. Dreitzel (Ed.), *Recent sociology #2: Patterns of communicative behavior*. New York: MacMillan.

Heap, J. (1980). Description in ethnomethodology. *Human Studies, 3*(1), 87–106.

Hymes, D. (1974). *Foundations of sociolinguistics*. Philadelphia: University of Pennsylvania Press.

Irvine, J. (1979). Formality and informality in communicative events. *American Anthropologist, 81*(4), 773–790.

Janis, I., & Mann, L. (1978). *Decision Making*. New York: The Free Press.

Labov, W. (1972). *Sociolinguistic patterns*. Philadelphia: University of Pennsylvania Press.

Laing, R. D. (1967). *The Politics of experience*. New York: Pantheon.

Lakoff, G., & Johnson, M. (1980). *Metaphors we live by*. Chicago: University of Chicago Press.

Lopes, L. (1979). "I'm sorry to have to put it that way." But it is the only way he can: Two Tiered Ethnography of a Couple in Therapy. Unpublished doctoral dissertation. Stanford University, Palo Alto, CA.

Marcuse, H. (1964). *One dimensional man*. Boston: Beacon Press.

McDermott, R. P., Gospodinoff, K., & Aron, J. (1978). Criteria for an ethnographically adequate description of concerted activities and their contexts. *Semiotica, 24*(3/4), 245–275.

Mehan, H. (1978). Structuring school structure. *Harvard Educational Review, 45*(1), 311–338.

Mehan, H. (1979). *Learning lessons.* Cambridge, MA: Harvard University Press.

Mehan, H. (1981). Practical decision making in naturally occurring institutional settings. In B. Rogoff & J. Lave (Eds.), *Everyday cognition: Its development and social context.* Cambridge, MA: Harvard University Press.

Mehan, H., Hertweck, A., Combs, S. E. & Flynn, P. J. (1982). Teachers' interpretations of students' behavior. In L. C. Wilkinson (Ed.), *Communicating in the classroom.* New York: Academic Press.

Mehan, H., Meihls, L., & Hertweck, A. (1986). *Handicapping the handicapped.* Stanford, CA: Stanford University Press.

Mehan, H., & Wood, H. (1975). *The reality of ethnomethodology.* New York: Wiley Interscience.

Meihls, J. L. (1981). Handicapping students. (1981, March). Paper presented at Second Annual Ethnography in Education Forum. University of Pennsylvania, Philadelphia, PA.

Merleau-Ponty, M. (1964). *Signs.* Evanston, IL: Northwestern University Press.

Parsons, T. (1932). *The structure of social action.* Glencoe, IL.: The Free Press.

Philips, S. (1977). The role of spatial positioning and alignment in defining interactional units: The American courtroom as a case in point. Paper presented at the American Anthropological Association Meetings, Houston, TX.

Pike, K. L. (1967). *Language in relation to a unified theory of the structure of human behavior.* The Hague: Mouton.

Pollner, M. (1975). 'The very coinage of your brain': The anatomy of reality disjunctures. *Philosophy of Social Science, 5,* 411–430.

Sacks, H., Schegloff, E., & Jefferson, G. (1974). A simplist systematics for the organization of turn-taking in conversation. *Language, 50,* 696–735.

Scheflen, A. E. (1972). *Communicational Structure.* Bloomington: Indiana University Press.

Schelling, T. *Strategies of Conflict.* New York: Oxford University Press, 1950.

Shuy, R. (1973). Problems of communication in the cross-cultural medical interview. Paper presented at the American Sociological Association Meetings, New York.

Shuy, R., & Larkin, D. L. (1978). Linguistic considerations in the simplification/clarification of insurance policy language. *Discourse Processes* 1, 305–321.

Shweder, P. A. (1977). Likeness and likelihood in everyday thought: Magical thinking in judgments about personality. *Current Anthropology, 18,* 637–648.

Simon, N. (1949). *Administrative behavior.* New York: The Free Press.

Silverman, D. (1981). The child as a social object: Down's syndrome children in a pediatric cardiology clinic. *Sociology of Health and Illness, 3,* 254–274.

Watkins, J. (1970). Imperfect rationality. In R. Borger & F. Cioffi (Eds.), *Explanation in the behavioral sciences.* Cambridge: Cambridge University Press.

Weber, M. (1947). *Theory of social and economic organization.* Glencoe, IL: Free Press.

8. The Language of Attribution: Constructing Rationales for Educational Placement*

Alma Hertweck

Oceanside, California

In the course of a child's school career, a social identity is created. This identity is partially represented in school records, report cards, testing scores, and other official records concerning the child. However, this social identity is also comprised of much more subtle, and often more influential data than that contained in school files. Oral interpretations of school performance—both successful and unsuccessful—based on social perceptions concerning the child offered by testers, principals, teachers, and others follow the student through a schooling career and contribute to his/her social identity.

Often these more subjective components of the educational process are not considered in the research report, as they seem so far removed from the institutional demands of the educational system. This research explores the relationship of institutional demands to subjective interpretations of student success and failure. It shows how institutional demands and subjective interpretations merge at the interactional level through attributional accounts presented by educators. Ultimately, these features combine to contribute to student placement in particular programs in the school.

SOCIAL PERCEPTION AND EDUCATORS' JUDGMENTS

The topic of social perception has stimulated considerable interest in sociology and social psychology, contributing in part to the development of entire schools of thought, including those portions of "symbolic interactionism" (Blumer, 1969; Becker, 1973; Manis & Meltzer, 1969) concerned with the development of self, labeling theory, and those portions of social phenomenology and ethnomethodology concerned with the social construction of reality (e.g., Berger & Luckman, 1967; Garfinkel, 1967; Cicourel, 1964, 1973; Mehan & Wood, 1975) and accounting practices (Garfinkel, 1967; Weber, 1947).

A more recent development in the area of social perception research has centered around attribution theory. Attribution theory provides a framework for considering educators' judgments of students, since it is concerned with the

---

* This research was partially supported by a grant from the National Institute of Education. However, the contents do not necessarily reflect the views or policy of that agency. I wish to thank Sue Fisher, Hugh Mehan, and Alexandra Todd for their helpful comments on drafts of this chapter.

processes through which we assign causes and attributes to ourselves' and others' behavior. Weiner and his associates (1971; Weiner, 1972a, 1972b, 1974) extended attribution theory into the educational domain. They examined the influences of attributions on teacher and student behavior, specifically student motivation and achievement.

An assumption underlying trait theory in psychology and prevalent personality theories is that attributions index actual underlying conditions. Attribution theorists challenge this assumption. They maintain that the dispositional consistency lies not so much in the person or the environment. Rather, it lies in the labels used to describe these persons or their environments. This perspective takes consistency out of the personality of the individual, and places it in the social perception of the attributor and in the semantics of the language used to describe people.

This paper examines the language used to describe students in an elementary school setting. The focus is on the attributional description provided by educators during decision-making meetings concerning students who were potential candidates for certain special education programs. Through an analysis of the discourse in these decision-making meetings, dimensions are uncovered which comprise the rationale for placement that has been created for these students in order to make them eligible for special placement. This analysis will suggest some of the ways institutional demands are enacted in interaction through the attributions made by educators.

THE CONTEXT OF THE STUDY

With the advent of Public Law 94–142, "The Education for All Handicapped Students Act", school districts across the country have made a concerted effort to formalize their procedures in the identification of children for special education programs. The purpose of P.L.94–142 was to facilitate the integration of handicapped individuals into the mainstream of American life. This law mandates a free and appropriate public education for all handicapped children between the ages of three and 21, and sets up a system of federal financial support to states in implementing the law. Special funds are provided to each school system for each child who is enrolled in a special education program, until the number of students reaches 12 percent of the school population, after which no further funds are made available.

Programs in school districts are instituted in order to find children requiring special education. Prior to any special education placement decision the law mandates a full individual evaluation of the referred child. Certain standards must be maintained to insure the nondiscriminatory evaluation of suspected disabilities. Information from a variety of sources including psychological and educational tests, teachers' and nurses' opinions, and information about the child's cultural or social background must be carefully documented when considering a special education placement.

The referral process normally begins in the classroom when a student is perceived by the teacher as having a "special problem." In the district considered in this study, if the teacher decides to refer a student, a standard form is completed, which provides a rough profile of the student's performance in the classroom, and states the reasons for the referral, such as, below grade level in reading, lack of fine motor coordination.

The referral process continues if a school-based committee (called a "School Appraisal Team", SAT) finds the referral warranted. At this time, detailed educational and psychological assessment of the child is authorized. If the results of assessment are such that the SAT feels the student is eligible for special education, the case is referred to a district-wide eligibility and placement committee. Throughout this process of assessment, school personnel are making judgments and attributions concerning the student being considered for a special education program.

Methodology

This research was conducted in conjunction with a larger study of the educational decision making of one southern California school district that traced the entire process by which children are referred and placed in special education programs. (For more information, see Mehan, 1981, 1983; Hertweck & Mehan, 1981, Hertweck, 1981, Mehan, Hertweck, Combs, & Flynn, 1981; Mehan, Miehls, Hertweck, & Crowdes, 1981.)

The study participants are 15 teachers and 31 students, and 19 placement committee members. Placement committee members include two psychologists, three teachers, three mothers, one father, two nurses, two special education teachers, three principals, and two assistant principals. This article focuses on three of the students.

After a referral was made, the classroom teacher was contacted and observations scheduled if he/she agreed to participate in the study. Once teacher permission was obtained, the classroom was observed in order to obtain a sense of classroom routine and typical patterns of classroom life. Once general observations were completed, representative classroom events which included the referred student as part of a regular work group were videotaped.

The teacher was then interviewed. During the course of these interviews, the teachers were given an opportunity to provide their accounts of the referred child and other children in the videotaped groups. These interviews were tape-recorded, transcribed, and submitted to an attributional analysis. (For more information on this aspect of the study, see Hertweck, 1982a, 1982b, 1983; Hertweck & Mehan, 1981.)

The data utilized for the analysis presented in this paper is derived from videotapes of meetings held for the purpose of evaluating the placement of children in special education programs. The audio portion of each videotape was transcribed, and the transcript was indexed. The transcript then served as a basis for the analysis of attributions made by committee members. The transcripts were searched for statements that educators made about students' school performance. These statements were isolated, extracted from the transcripts, and transferred to a coding form which I devised for attribution analysis. These accounts then became the materials upon which the attributional analysis was conducted. The accounts were then analyzed against the background data gained through interviews conducted with teachers and other placement committee members, school records, and observation by the researcher.

Attribution Categories

It would be helpful to briefly describe how I determined the coding categories used in the attributional analysis. Ability, effort, task, and luck have been proposed as the most frequent attributions made about children in achievement situations (Weiner, 1974). A group of researchers has sought to discover other perceived determinants of success and failure (Frieze, 1976; Cooper & Burger, 1980; Medway, 1979; Bar Tal & Darom, 1979; Bar Tal, Ravgad & Zilberman, 1978). Several researchers have recognized that perceived determinants are not limited to the four "original" factors (Weiner, 1974; Weiner, Russell & Lerman, 1978).

A preliminary analysis of the data gathered from educators' descriptions revealed that attributions were indeed quite varied and much more numerous than the four elements first identified. After considering various categories, 20 categories were chosen. The choice of these categories was guided by information emerging from the data.

While prior studies of teachers' perceptions of children's achievements provided a success or failure condition (actual or hypothetical) to subjects, in this study attributions which were offered in the context of discussion concerning the child's perceived success or failure in school were extracted from the naturally occurring narratives in decision-making meetings. This paper examines these attributional narratives describing students who were potential candidates for special education programs.

THREE CASES

In this paper, case studies for three of the referred children are analyzed. The cases were followed from the point of referral by the teacher through the educational placement meeting. For this discussion, I will focus on a particularly important event concerning each of these children—the placement committee meeting—in which four major participants are involved (psychologist, teacher, special education teacher, and parent[s]). Brief histories of the cases will be presented and comparisons made that reveal some patterns in the attributional process surrounding referred children.

Brief Synopses of Cases

Terry. Terry's case was first brought to the attention of the school assessment team on October 26, 1978, at which time it was recommended that he receive the full psychological battery of tests, that a developmental report be presented by the nurse, and that his previous school records be reviewed. Terry was officially referred on November 3, 1978, for the following reasons:

1. low academic performance
2. does not apply himself to daily class work
3. history of behavioral problems and truancy in previous district.

The teacher also recommended that he receive one-to-one teacher-student help.

Educational tests were administered by the psychologist on December 6, 1978, and January 2, 1979. On January 4, 1979, the case was again brought up at the school assessment team meeting. At that time it was decided that the psychologist should finish testing. The committee also recommended that the case go before the Eligibility and Placement Committee for possible placement in an Educationally Handicapped or Learning Disability Group program. On January 4, 1979, further tests were administered. On February 16, 1979, the placement committee assigned Terry to a Learning Disability Group.

Terry entered his class in the latter part of September, 1978, after the school year for that track had been in session for two months. He had moved in from another district which was on a traditional September–June schedule. Thus he was two months behind the other students in terms of class work. Four days after entering the class, he was truant for one and one-half weeks while his parents were away on vacation and he was in the care of an older brother. After Terry returned to school, he was in the class approximately three weeks when his case was first presented to the school assessment team. He entered the Learning Disability Group program February 20, 1979, and went to that program for one hour per day for three months until the end of that academic year.

The Eligibility and Placement Committee reviewed his case in June, 1979. The committee recommended that he attend a regular classroom full time at the beginning of the next school year. During the course of her work with Terry, the learning disability group teacher tested the child. These tests indicated that his achievement was at a level that would enable him to return to the regular classroom on a full time basis.

Milo. Milo, a first grader in a bilingual class, was referred by his teacher on October 8, 1978, for the following reasons:

1. perceptual motor difficulties
2. behavior problems

Milo's case was first brought to the attention of the school assessment team on November 16, 1978. At that meeting, suggestions for the modification of aggressive behavior were made to the teacher. On November 30, Milo was again discussed, and it was decided that the teacher should do some testing and report the results back to the committee. On December 7, 1978, it was recommended that Milo receive a battery of psychological tests and be considered for possible Learning Disability Group placement. On March 16, 1979, placement in the Learning Disability Group was recommended. Milo was ultimately retained in first grade because the teacher felt he had not made enough progress to go on to second grade.

Sean. The third case is Sean, a second grader. Sean was referred by his teacher for the following reasons:

1. constantly frustrated with second grade work
2. easily disrupted
3. low self concept
4. lacks fine motor coordination

Sean was first brought to the attention of the school assessment team on October 19, 1978, at which time it was recommended that the nurse make a home visit to check afternoon supervision. It was recommended to the teacher that the child be tutored and also that she confer with the parents. On December 4, 1979, it was decided that the psychologist should administer some tests to the child, and on March 15, 1979, further testing for special education placement was recommended. The child was tested further and on April 27, 1979, the Eligibility and Placement Committee recommended placement in a Learning Disability Group.

As these case synopses show in considering their referral and progress through the system, all three children considered in this paper were referred within approximately three months after entering their respective teachers' classes. They each received a battery of psychological tests and were ultimately placed in a learning disability program. All three of the cases took at least four months to be resolved before placement. In two of the cases it was approximately six months, so it was well into the school year before they received assistance.

During this time, teachers are expressing frustration at not being able to get the children whom they have referred placed in special education programs. It should be noted here that there is a demand to fill special education classes to capacity, but not overcapacity. This creates an ebb and flow in the rate of placement of children in education programs. When there are vacancies in the special education programs, cases in the system are facilitated. When classes are near capacity, there is an ebb in the rate of placement. At the beginning of the year, teachers were briefed on the referral process and given suggestions on criteria for referring children. There were quite a number of referrals at that time as teachers were sensitized to look for learning disabilities. As the year progressed and programs became filled, referrals were discouraged, and those in process were delayed due to heavy case load of the psychologist.

Thus there is constraint or facilitation depending on whether there are openings in certain programs or whether certain programs are filled to capacity. (For more information, see Mehan, et al., 1981; Mehan (Chapter 7, this volume); Hertweck, 1982a, 1982b.) This demand to keep the enrollment figures more or less constant in these classes is an institutional demand of the educational system which is enacted eventually in the attributions made during the placement meetings.

Relationship of Meeting Context to Dimensions of Attributions

The placement meeting can be viewed as an attributional event. Educators assemble for the purpose of making attributions about the referred child, for example, why is Terry having problems in school, why does Sean have difficulty with second grade work? It is of particular importance to consider how these attributions, made at the interactional level, are influenced by the contextual features of the educational environment in which the meeting is situated.

I focus on three dimensions of the attributional process to reveal some of the constraints imposed by the macrosociological structure: first, the frequency of attributions, that is, who makes the most attributions in the placement meetings and what is the impact of these attributions; second, the valence of the attributions, for example, more positive or more negative; third, the locus of attributions, that is, where they locate the source of the students' difficulty.

I will show how certain contextual factors enter into the type of attributional language that is used in the meetings. The frequency of attributions by committee members and the degree to which attributions are either positive or negative and either internal or external may depend on the circumstances surrounding the event. Due to certain contextual features, school personnel may wish to make attributions concerning the child which portray a certain picture of the situation.

The attributions provided by the teacher in the course of referral have special prominence because they provide a frame of reference for the other committee members to assess the child. However, although his/her attributions are vital to the social identity which will be constructed for the child in the process of referral, the attributional portrait is completed by (1) the psychologist as he/she tests the child, formulates results, and makes recommendations concerning placement; (2) the special education teacher, as he/she observes the child and adds his/her interpretation to the portrait from his/her point of view; (3) the parents, as they present information about the child in out-of-school contexts; and to a lesser degree, (4) other school personnel—the nurse, the principal, and (5) attributions in absentia, that is, educational and psychological reports from previous districts.

This plethora of data coalesces in the meeting where the disposition of the case is decided. The committee members come together and present their information about the referral student. The form and content of these presentations provide a rationale for the placement of the child. The attributional language extracted from their presentations emerges from a particular context reflective of educators' perceptions of the child and district policy. These features inform the interaction and the decision-making process.

Frequency of attributions.   Table 8.1 shows the comparison of percentages of attributions for each committee member for each child. For school personnel the respective teachers made the highest percentages of attributions in the meetings concerning Terry and Sean. The teacher had the same percentage as the psychologist concerning Milo.

Of the four committee members, the special education teachers have had the least contact with the children. Their contact has usually been limited to a classroom observation. In light of lack of contact, their contributions to the attributional profile are quite significant. In Milo's and Sean's cases, they contributed 28.8 and 20.4 percent of the attributions.

Although in Terry's case, the contribution was only 6.7 percent, given the context of the situation, which I will describe, this is quite remarkable. The special education teacher had never had any contact with Terry and was asked to attend the meeting in the place of another special education teacher who had been unable to attend at the last minute. Yet, 6.7 percent of the attributions made concerning Terry were contributed by the special education teacher. Her* attributions were made on the basis of answers to questions she put to other committee members and information presented in the meeting.

The psychologists made 27.3 percent of the attributions about Terry, 35.0 percent about Milo, and 14.3 percent about Sean. Although not usually the most frequent attributor in the meetings, the psychologists' attributions have a powerful force behind them. Everyone at the meeting knows that the child has received a battery of tests under the direction of the psychologists. The assumption is made that the attributions made by the psychologists are based upon an accurate, quantified assessment of the child's abilities and propensities. Her recommendation is of utmost importance. In each of these three cases, after testing, the psychologist recommended that the child be placed in a special education program and indeed they were.

The frequency of parents' percentages of attributions varied. The parent with the highest level of education (a graduate degree), Sean's mother, had the highest percentage of attributions (42.9 percent). In the meeting, she asked questions and volunteered her assessments of where Sean's problems might lie. The parents with the least contribution were Milo's parents with the lowest level of education.

---

* In this section of the paper, I will use specific gender designations, because the special education teachers and classroom teachers are women in each of the three cases, and the students considered are boys.

Table 8.1. Percentages of Individual Committee Members Contributions to Meetings

Psychologist			Teacher			Spec Ed Teacher			Mother		
Terry	Milo	Sean	Terry	Milo	Sean	Terry	Milo	Sean	Terry	Milo	Sean
27.3	35.0	14.3	46.9	35.0	22.4	6.7	28.8	20.4	19.1	1.3	42.9

Usually frequency of speaking would indicate that a person was in a powerful position in a situation. It would seem also that the teacher would be in a powerful position in the meeting, having spent the most academic time with the child. Indeed, the percentages of teacher attributions are equal to or exceed those of the psychologist and special education teacher.

However, when attributions were coded according to whether they were ''elicited'' or ''spontaneous,'' I found that a great deal of the attributions were made in response to interrogations by others. In two of the cases, over 50 percent of attributions by the teacher were made under an interrogation condition. In the other case, the amount was 27.3 percent. Mehan (Chapter 7, this volume) has focused on the ''role of language'' and the ''language of role'' in these placement meetings. He contrasts the type of report given by the teachers and mothers in these meetings to the type of report given by the psychologist and special education teacher. He identifies the teacher's as a lay report and the psychologist's as a professional report, due to differences in format, mode of speaking, source of information, and topics discussed. He also notes that the teacher occupies a low status position in the institution, while the psychologist occupies a high position in the institution. Their respective authority is grounded in the differences in the structure of their two kinds of reports.

The analysis of frequency of attributions bears this observation out. Even though the teacher is a more frequent attributor, her attributions do not carry as much weight as the psychologist or special education teacher. Thus, the frequency of attribution is modified by the context in which the attribution was produced to reveal the effect of differential vesting of professional authority within the institutional structure.

Mehan has emphasized the part that language plays in authority relations within the institutionalized order of the school. The attributions emerging from the enactment of the teacher role do not carry the same force as the attributions emerging from the enactment of the psychologist role. Blau (1964) has noted in his analysis of authority and power relations that the person who can provide the most benefits to other group members becomes the leader. Eventually shared values emerge which give the leader the right to expect compliance. At this point one starts to see differentiation of status. Participants see that one person is going to do more work and have a larger role in the group. Others start to draw back and everyone comes to terms with the stratification. They learn to live with it, and at that point there is cohesion. As Mehan has noted, the psychologist has been appointed "case carrier." There is an unstated agreement that she has done the most work in assembling the data. In addition, the data she presents carries institutional prestige. It is in the form of what Mehan has termed a "professional report," which has more status, while that of the teacher is in the form of a "lay report," which has less status.

Valence of attributions and context.   The attributional analysis of the placement meetings revealed that the percentages of positive and negative attributions were comparable. One might assume that if a child is being referred for academic rehabilitation, an overwhelming percentage of attributions about the child's performance would be negative in tone.

Using Terry's case to illustrate, Figure 8.1 shows the valence of attributions for each of the four committee members. The portion of the graph above the "O" line indicates the positive attributions. The portion of the graph below the "O" line indicates the negative attributions (see Figure 8.1).

Column 1 of this figure shows that the psychologist discussed the student's ability in positive terms 32.1 percent of the time and discussed his ability in negative terms 39.6 percent of the time. The teacher discussed the student's ability in positive terms 9.9 percent of the time and in negative terms 16.5 percent of the time. The special education teacher made 53.8 percent of her attributions to negative ability and 23.1 percent to positive ability. The mother made 13.5 percent of her attributions to positive ability and 8.1 percent to negative ability. These positive-negative percentages are reflective of the effort to "find cause" for placing Terry in a special education program.

The teacher indicated during the interview that she referred Terry in the hope that he would be placed in a learning disability group (LDG). As she stated, "He would either have gone to LDG or he wouldn't (have been placed in any program) at all" (11–740.2).[1] There was a question in the teacher's mind if he would be placed, as the following excerpt indicates:

Interviewer: . . . did you feel like a decision was made *there* or do you feel like a decision was made before the meeting?

Teacher: No, I feel like well (pause) well I know in this case that it was made *there* because there was a question or, before the meeting whether he would be placed or not.

Interviewer: Before the meeting began.

Teacher: Yeah.

Interviewer: How was that? What did you do?

Teacher: Well, in earlier contact with them, I kept bugging her (psychologist) about,

---

[1] Line numbers (e.g., 11–740.2) refer to the full transcript of the interviews from which this summary has been made.

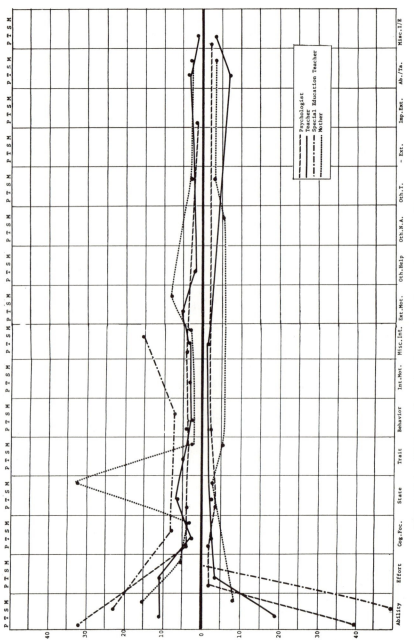

Figure 8.1. Valence of attributions by categories for committee members

um, giving him testing and what's going on. It was like, "Oh, well, I don't know if he's going to qualify or not. I don't think he's low enough. Well, his test scores aren't going to come out like you want them to, you know." The poor kid, he, you know, he would benefit by this extra help. An uh, so, you know, Janet (the psychologist) said, "Well, we'll have to wait till we get to the meeting, and we'll talk about it, and we'll *see*." Cause they have rejected students (11.715.1–720.15).

The teacher is a strong advocate for Terry's placement. However, in order to be placed, he must qualify for special education. The district's policy clearly states the conditions which must exist for any student to qualify for educational handicapped classrooms and the "learning disability group."

1. EH—Educationally Handicapped Self Contained Classrooms. A child may be considered EH when he/she fails in one or more of the following categories:
    (a) Whenever there is a severe discrepancy—at least two years—between the child's capacity and his/her school achievement. This discrepancy can be for either one or more academic subjects.
    (b) Whenever there is evidence of a severe skill deficit, for instance, in motor perceptual development.
    (c) Whenever there is a behavior disturbance of such degree that the child is unable to profit from the regular classroom experience.

    A child is placed in the EH classroom per recommendation of a committee *after* the psychologist and SAT member(s) have completed a case study report.
2. LDG—Learning Disability Grouping (regular classroom placement with pullout assistance). A child is considered LD if he/she meets the requirements of (a) and/or (b) of the EH category. Actual placement is recommended by a committee upon completion of the psychologist's and/or other SAT member(s) case report(s). The EH or LD placement recommendation is based on the consideration of how severe the learning deficit is, the discrepancy between capacity and achievement, and/or the overall child's behavior.[2]

In the portion of the teacher's interview cited earlier, she indicated that the psychologist did not find the discrepancy of the magnitude required in paragraph (1a) of the above-cited guidelines for placement. Therefore, the teacher expected that the placement decision would be made in the committee meeting. The criteria set forth by the district interacts with the information presented by committee members to develop a rationale for placement.

---

[2] Information extracted from Coast District Policies (1978–79).

According to local school policy, Terry or any elementary school student could be placed in the LDG program:

1. if he had "a severe discrepancy (at least two years) between his capacity and his school achievement."
2. If there were a "severe skill deficit, i.e., motor perceptual development."

The two tests most commonly used in this district to assess children are the Wechsler Intelligence Scale for Children (WISC) and the Wide Range Achievement Test (WRAT). In reporting Terry's WISC test results to the committee, the psychologist stated, "He had a verbal I.Q. of 115, performance of 111, and a full scale of 115, so he's a bright child" (3:10–11).[3] She reported that the results on the subtests on the WISC are utilized when considering placement possibilities; therefore, if there had been a two-year discrepancy, this fact could have influenced Terry's placement.

The psychologist reported the following about Terry's WRAT results (5.1–5.5).

	Standard Score	Grade Rating
Arithmetic	90	3.0
Spelling	95	3.5
Reading	100	4.1

She stated, "When compared with his overall score, it does put him somewhat, uh, below his, you know, his capabilities" (5.6–5.7). However, at most, Terry is one year below grade level in arithmetic and five months below grade level in spelling. He is not two years behind grade level. These two educational test results did not establish Terry's eligibility for LDG or EH placement.

The psychologist then reported the results of the Bender Visual Motor Gestalt Test. "His test age was 7–0 to 7–5 and his actual age is nine, so it, uh, he was considerably beneath his, uh, age level" (5.6–7). This statement provided a criteria for placement in the area of "skill deficit" which implies a physiological problem. She supported this "deficit view" by presenting augmenting data: he "cannot switch channels" (5.13), and "his fine motor skills appear to be slightly lower than, uh average . . . I saw them" (5.15–5.16).

This "search for cause" is reminiscent of Heider's (1958) rationale for the "naive analysis of action" in everyday life. But, we must keep in mind that this search for cause is occurring in an institutional context. That is, it is reflective of instrumental action to "show cause" for the decision to place the child in a "special education" learning situation. In order for Terry to be placed, he must be labeled, and in order to label, the committee must "show cause" for labeling.

---

[3] Quoted from transcript of committee meeting; available upon request from the author.

The information is thus presented in a manner that reflects the effort to construct a rationale for placement that will fit into the policies of the district and meet the legal requirement to find students for special education programs.

The "mirror image" of success and failure attributions shown in Figure 8.1 shows the frequency and structure of within-child comparisons. Terry's optimal performance is used as a base line for comparison. The committee members work to show that the child is performing below this optimal level. Terry's performance at 4.0 grade level in reading and 3.0 in spelling is presented as a discrepancy between potential and performance. The need for placement is demonstrated by comparing the child to himself in some optimal state. The decision-making committee discourse reveals narratives concerning the child in failure conditions, then disconfirming evidence is presented that portrays the child in success conditions. A case is thus built for a discrepancy between optimal performance and poorest performance. If the discrepancy cannot be inferred from subtest scores on the WISC or if criteria for eligibility cannot be established by standard scores on the WRAT, it appears the psychologist resorts to another test to substantiate the conceptualization of the child as a candidate for a special education program. At no time is disconfirming evidence offered as a rationale for not placing the child in a special education program.

It would be an exaggeration to say that the committee made a giant leap from the Bender-Gestalt data to the diagnostic label of "learning disabled," but these test results do seem to have provided the bridge across the gap. However, the test data presented in the meeting is augmented in terms of a personality description of the child, an attributional portrait which presents the child as having a potential which is not being realized. The committee members have presented a case for placing this child through the negative portrait that has been created. Nevertheless, there is a child who has an I.Q. of 115 (which is one S.D. above the mean), who scores at grade level or, at most, is one year below grade level on academic achievement tests. Thus, in order to draw comparisons, a positive attributional portrait must be created as well. All of this information, confirming and disconfirming, is rallied to provide a rationale for diagnostic categorization. The child must be shown to be learning disabled in relation to himself.

My analysis of the other two cases reveals the same pattern as Terry's case: positive and negative attributions are fairly well balanced or even slightly more positive than negative for most committee members considered. In Milo's case, every committee member had 14 percent or more positive attributions than negative attributions. Table 8.2 shows where emphasis was placed according to the various committee members, on an internal or external locus of control, on a positive or negative valence (see Table 8.2).

As with Terry's case, the "mirror image" of success and failure attributions reflect the within-child comparisons. A child's optimal performance is used as a base line for comparison. Effort is made in the committee meeting to show that the child is performing below this optimal level. However, in reviewing the three

Table 8.2. Locus of Control and Valence of Attributions in Placement Meeting

Locus	Percentage Positive				Percentage Negative			
	Psych	Tchr	SET	Mthr	Psych	Tchr	SET	Mthr
Milo								
Internal	46.4	35.7	34.8	100.0	39.3	32.1	30.4	.0
External	10.7	10.7	21.7	.0	.0	7.1	13.0	.0
Interactional	.0	10.7	.0	.0	3.6	3.6	.0	.0
Total	57.1	57.1	56.5	100.0	42.9	42.9	43.5	.0
Sean								
Internal	42.9	54.5	20.0	23.8	42.9	27.3	20.0	42.9
External	.0	.0	20.0	.0	.0	.0	.0	19.0
Interactional	.0	9.1	40.0	9.5	14.3	9.1	.0	4.8
Total	42.9	63.6	80.0	33.3	57.1	36.4	20.0	66.7
Terry								
Internal	47.2	49.5	46.2	59.5	49.1	31.9	53.8	16.2
External	1.9	5.5	.0	10.8	.0	.0	.0	8.1
Interactional	.0	4.4	.0	2.7	1.8	8.8	.0	2.7
Total	49.1	59.3	46.2	73.0	50.9	40.7	53.8	27.0

placement committee transcripts, in no case was a child two years below grade level as measured by the Wide Range Achievement test,[4] or with a mental age two years below their chronological age as measured by the WISC. The most that the children were below grade level was one year. I have discussed the use of the Bender Visual Motor Gestalt test in the assessment of Terry. This test was also used in presenting the case for Milo to be placed. The psychologist in Milo's case stated:

> He got, um a developmental range of five years, two months on the Bender Gestalt test and a developmental age of five years, seven months on the Berry Developmental Test of Visual Motor Integration, which indicated a developmental range of about one and a half to two years below the expectations for his chronological age. . . . His reading achievement score is significantly below what we would expect for his, um, for his chronological age and his I.Q. (she indicated earlier he was of average intelligence based on the WISC "with high and low areas") . . . so basically what we have is a little boy who has average to above average abilities who has a de-um, a deficit in visual motor integration skills, um, and in reading, specifically (1.24–3.26).

The within-child comparison in Sean's case is reflected in the following statement by the psychologist: "The rationale, the discrepancy, is his ability level and achievement level, and his ability level is really quite high" (83.1–3).

---

[4] Interviews with school personnel has revealed that two S.D. below the mean on the WRAT can be considered reaon for placement.

However, the psychologist also stated that he was "on a grade scale of 1.7 on the WRAT" (90.1), which at the very most could only be construed as one year below grade level, not the stipulated two years.

For each of these three cases, enough positive attributions are presented to provide a baseline, but enough negative attributions are presented to show a deficiency exists.

Locus of control of attributions and context.   Referring again to Table 8.3, the most frequent internal attributions made by committee members were for Terry, followed by those for Milo and finally, those for Sean. The most attributions were made for Sean. What particularly stands out, however, is the relatively high number of external positive attributions for Milo made by school personnel, for example, influences outside of the child which result in success. I have found that the number of external positive attributions are usually quite low unless a special circumstance prevails. In this case, the psychologist and the teacher each made 10.7 percent attributions of this type, while the special education teacher made 21.7 percent positive external attributions which is high compared to the other cases.

This may be explained by considering the context—the history of this child and the history of this teacher in this class. Milo had been in this teacher's classroom for most of the year, with only two months remaining in the academic year. Milo's parents had been displeased with his placement in a bilingual class, particularly since a school employee had voiced the opinion that he should not be in a bilingual class. Bilingual classes in this district are viewed as having more of an open structure with more movement and "noise" than other classrooms. Bilingual classes must maintain a certain ratio of English-speaking to other language-speaking children in order to obtain funding. This balance is difficult to maintain, because the parents are often not anxious to have their English-speaking children placed in a bilingual program. Milo's classroom was no exception to this dilemma. It would be reasonable to assume that school personnel wished to keep this English-speaking child in the classroom to maintain the language balance.

As is the case with all placement meetings, as indicated by the psychologist in interviews, meetings with various members of the committee are held beforehand, particularly with the parents, to discuss any problematic areas which might otherwise arise in the meeting. At the meeting with these parents, it was pointed out that since there was so little of the school year remaining, it would be advisable to leave Milo in his assigned classroom and place him in an LDG pullout program rather than disrupt him by placing him in an entirely new class.

There is evidence in the transcript that an attempt is made to assuage these apprehensions concerning the child being in this particular classroom when particular attributions are made. Attributions imply that certain conditions exist within or for a child and that particular classroom characteristics would have a positive effect on any undesirable characteristics of that child. This can be noted in an attributional narrative being presented by the special education teacher where he appears to be presenting a case for the suitability of this particular classroom for Milo, even given his "problems."

Mmmmm. Yeah, I've observed Milo Friday. I think it was last Friday, or Friday before. No, last Friday, uh, at Marva's classroom. Uh, I observed him for *about* a total of an hour and a half, I think. And he uh, he seemed to be working very well in the classroom situation was ah, very well structured, and it was as quiet as I've seen a classroom, especially since Milo's *auditory* attention seems to be (1) so limited, ah it was, any slight noise in the classroom and he, it pulled him away. You know, like when Marva was giving instruction in the corner of the classroom just the normal sounds of work and paper shuffling and people getting things out of the desk seemed to draw his attention away for a moment and those were the times that he tended to miss out on what was going on. As I noticed part of, at the end of the instruction as he was kind of pulled away by just the classroom noise which *wasn't* exceptionally loud, it was he just happened to fix into it. He missed out on the last instruction. It wasn't real, real *strong* for him and he went back and he did the first two parts of the assignment and didn't know what to do the last, the last piece. But I noticed also he was getting attention at *intervals*. Marva and her aide Alice were coming to Milo on an interval basis so that he was always *getting* some feedback as to what he should be doing, and where he was supposed to be. And you know the math—the math was very appropriate for you know, his level. He was working at pretty much at what the other kids were doing, uh, and seemed to be able to stay with it. He was distracted usually with this classroom activity that would pull his attention away but with the attention of the teacher and the aide he seemed to really enjoy that, to know that they were interested and wanted to see what he was doing and it only took maybe once every 15, not even that, once every 10 minutes, 15 minutes, they'd come and see how he was doing and what was going on. And he responded really strongly (10.1–32).

In essence, the special education teacher is saying Milo has problems in following the classroom agenda and he needs the help of adults in the classroom to do this, and, indeed, he is receiving the treatment that he requires. Yet in the interview with the classroom teacher, she indicated that there was not enough time to attend to all of the children in the classroom and that ideally a class should consist of 15 children with an aide. In Milo's case, a "system" problem, that of too few adults and too many children in a classroom, is obscured in the attributional narrative that is presented in the meeting.

When the psychologist viewed the videotape segment cited above, she indicated that the special education teacher was "validating" the teacher. She also indicated that it was important for committee members to be careful what they say.

Interviewer: . . . One of the things I was trying to do is watch Ms. Cattell's (the teacher) face while Mr. Jensen was talking about Ms. Cattell's class and see how she felt about that. . .

Psychologist: Well, Mr. Jensen was validating her.

Interviewer: . . . cause he wanted to say it was an organized classroom and at the same time indicate that Milo, Milo's not doing very well otherwise you wouldn't be meeting on that. So it was a very delicate balance as an instructor?

Psychologist: You know that's always part of the PR work that you do beforehand. And when I even present the information, you know to the committee, you know I always tell the parents there'll be a whole group of people there and they'll be talking . . . about their children . . . you really do have to monitor what you say and before this meeting (during a meeting with the parents) they were going to pull the child out of the classroom (84:11–12).

To present negative attributions in a context of favorable extenuating circumstances places more emphasis on the locality of the problem within the child. If the child does not perform under the best possible situation, he/she definitely is in the possession of a problem that is not solvable by merely changing the environment. Thus attributions must be presented in a context where "fault" may not be attributed to school personnel. The committee is there to "treat" the child, not the teacher nor other school personnel.

Here we have two institutional demands which are enacted in the attributions made during the placement meetings. First, the demand to keep quotas of Anglo students in bilingual classrooms is met by assuring the parent that the child is in a favorable environment and attributing the difficulty to the child. Second, the demand to fill a special education class is met by creating a discrepancy between optimal performance and poorest performance for the child.

CONCLUSIONS: THE TYRANNY OF THE DISCREPANCY SYNDROME

Although federal law (Public Law 94–142) has given a legal mandate to identify children for special education programs, it does not set forth specific guidelines for the constitution of "learning disability." This determination is left to the discretion of the individual school district. The "learning disability" is socially constructed at the organizational and interactional level of the school.

A learning disability ideology which legitimates the existence of special education programs for school children has evolved around a succession of disability categories. Children must be certified as eligible according to the current categories in order for them to be subsumed under the categories. The certification process results in the mystification of practices of allocation which obscures the social, perceptual, interactional, and institutional factors in the identification of children for special programs. Further, beliefs concerning the suitability and effectiveness of disability programs for particular children obscure the functional significance of placing children in special programs.

Common psychological practice is to associate clusters of behaviors with certain diagnostic labels, with implications for the type of treatment the child will receive and for the type of behavioral and academic performance which can be expected by the child. In most diagnoses the implication is made that the child is his disease. Dispositional attributions are made which contribute to a personal stigmatization. Learning disabled ''states'' are inferred from what the child says or from what school personnel, parents, and so on report about what the child says or does.

When observing most of these 31 children in the classroom in interaction with their teachers and with their classmates, one is most often struck with the difficulty in ascertaining what makes the referred child different from the nonreferred child in the classroom. One assumes that the referred child must have some type of deficit, an anomaly, or if that is too strong a word, some type of departure from the rest of the children in the class. However, general behavior and lesson performance is often indistinguishable between referred and nonreferred children.

Earlier I listed the qualifications whereby a child could be considered for a special education classroom. One of these was ''Whenever there is a severe discrepancy, at least two years, between the child's capacity and his/her school achievement.'' This discrepancy can be for either one or more academic subjects. Thus it is not necessarily the case that the child must be shown to be below grade level in relation to other children at his/her grade. He/she may be shown to be learning disabled in relation to his/her self.

Most of the children considered in this study appear to be marginally, if at all, in need of special assistance. In the majority of cases, we are not discussing severe disabilities. These are children who often score well above the mean on the Wechsler Intelligence Scale for Children (WISC) in several areas on which they are tested. However, they may also score low in one or more areas in relation to their other scores (as children perceived as ''normal'' often do).

Conceivably a fourth grade child could be placed in a learning disability program if he/she demonstrated a seventh grade proficiency in math and a fifth grade proficiency in reading. It is also conceivable that the highest achieving child in a class might be placed in a learning disability group because there was a discrepancy in his/her abilities in certain subject areas.

Most children view special education programs negatively, so in a sense the child could be penalized for being precocious in certain areas. While it is not likely that a child would be referred if she/he were indeed at grade level or above in all subjects and the teacher perceived no behavior problems or psychological problems, such data can make the difference if a child is say, less than a year below grade level in a particular subject area. On the other hand, a child who is struggling in every area of the curriculum, but is not the required two years below grade level and fits quietly into the classroom agenda structure might not be referred at all.

Success and failure deviations are quantified in order to justify placement through showing a discrepancy in potential and performance or grade level discrepancies in subjects. Testers do succeed in finding discrepancies in test scores as discussed concerning Terry's case.

Although normative comparisons can be made, all that is actually required is within-child comparisons. The need for placement is often demonstrated by comparing the child to himself. As my discussion of placement meetings discourse revealed, narratives concerning the child in failure conditions, then disconfirming evidence were presented that portrays the child in success conditions. A case is thus built for a discrepancy between optimal performance and poorest performance. If the discrepancy cannot be inferred from subtest scores on the WISC or if criteria for eligibility cannot be established by standard scores on the WRAT, it appears the tester resorts to another test to substantiate the conceptualization of the child as a candidate for a special education program. At no time is disconfirming evidence offered as a rationale *for not placing* the child in a special education program, only as a rationale for discrepancy. Thus, in order to draw comparisons, a positive attributional portrait must be created as well. All of this information, confirming and disconfirming, is rallied to provide a rationale for diagnostic categorization. The child must be shown to be learning disabled in relation to himself.

Test data presented in placement meetings is augmented in terms of a personality description of the child, an attributional portrait which presents the child as having a potential which is not being realized. The committee members present a case for placing a child through the negative portrait created in contrast to a foil, a positive portrait. This converts attributional statements to instrumental factors (the need not only to find cause, but to "show cause") as I have shown in the analysis of the placement meetings.

What appears to be occurring in most cases is that an informal decision to place the child in a special education program may be made before the formal placement committee meeting. Even in Terry's case discussed earlier where the teacher was indefinite whether he would be placed or not, there appears to be a very early consensus in the meeting that he will be placed. Analyzing the decision-making process in that meeting, Mehan (Chapter 7, this volume) notes how quickly placement decisions are made and the limited options which are presented in the meeting (even though there are other options actually available).

Even though an informal decision to place a child in a special education program may be made before the formal placement committee meeting, the rationale for placement must be formalized in the context of the placement meeting (Cf. Mehan, 1981). Before a placement meeting is scheduled it is fairly well understood that a placement will be made and what that placement will be. What remains is for a dialogue to take place in the meeting that will be supportive of (1) placing the child and (2) doing so within the stated policy of the district.

In looking at the process whereby children are identified as having learning disabilities it is vital to discover how those involved in this process—the teachers, the psychologists, the special education teachers, and other placement committee members are constrained by legal and institutional demands. It appears that placements may be discouraged or facilitated depending on whether there are openings in certain programs or whether certain programs are filled to capacity. Committee members are also faced with the fact that state law and district policy require that a rationale be provided for placing a student in a special education program. Within the framework of the practical circumstances discussed in this paper, committee members must proceed to construct the rationale for placement. They provide reasons for their decision to place that will coincide with law and stated policy. Thus institutional demands are inacted at the interactional level through the language of attribution utilized by school personnel in placement meetings. This dynamic interaction between the social perception of participants, their role in the event, and the enactment of institutional demands in the participants' attributions has far-reaching consequences for students' careers in school.

REFERENCES

Bar Tal, D. (1979). Interactions of teachers and pupils. In I. Frieze, D. Bar Tal, & J. S. Carroll (Eds.), *Attributional theory: Applications to social problems*. San Francisco: Jossey-Bass.

Bar Tal, D., & Darom, E. (1979). Pupils' attributions of success and failure. *Child Development, 50*, 264–267.

Bar Tal, D., & Frieze, I. (1977). Achievement motivation for males and females as a determinant of attributions for success and failure. *Sex Roles, 3*, 301–313.

Bar Tal, D., Ravgad, N., & Zilberman, D. (1978). Development of causal perception of success and failure. Unpublished manuscript, Tel Aviv University. Israel.

Becker, H. S. (1973). Labeling theory reconsidered. In H. S. Becker, *Outsiders*. New York: The Free Press.

Berger, P. L., & Luckman, T. (1967). *The social construction of reality*. Garden City, NY: Doubleday.

Blau, P. M. (1964). *Exchange and power in social life*. New York: Wiley.

Blumer, H. (1969). *Symbolic interactionism, perspectives and method*. Englewood Cliffs, NJ: Prentice-Hall.

Cicourel, A. V. (1964). *Method and measurement in sociology*. New York: The Free Press.

Cicourel, A. V. (1973). *Cognitive sociology: Language and meaning in social interaction*. London: Penguin.

Cooper, H. M., & Burger, J. M. (1980). How teachers explain students' academic performance: A categorization of free response academic attributions. *American Educational Research Journal, 17*(1), 95–109.

Frieze, I. H. (1976). Causal attributions and information seeking to explain success and failure. *Journal of Research in Personality, 10*, 293–305.

Freize, I. H., & Weiner, B. (1971). Cue utilization and attributional judgments for success and failure. *Journal of Personality, 39*, 591–606.

Garfinkel, H. (1967). *Studies in Ethnomethodology*. New York: Prentice-Hall.

Heider, F. (1958). *The psychology of interpersonal relations*. New York: Wiley.

Hertweck, Alma. (1981). Attributional analysis in context. In *Educational decision making in students' careers, end of year (1979–80) report, Part II: Prospectus for year three, 1980*. Unpublished manuscript, University of California, San Diego.

Hertweck, Alma. (1982a). Constructing the ''truth'' and consequences: Educators' attributions of perceived failure in school. Ph.D. Dissertation, Department of Sociology, University of California, San Diego.

Hertweck, Alma. (1982b, April). Mandate for the discovery and social construction of disabilities: The tyranny of the discrepancy syndrome. Paper presented at Pacific Sociological Association Meeting, San Diego, California.

Hertweck, Alma. (1983). Teachers' theories of success and failure. Paper presented at annual meeting of the American Educational Research Association, Montreal, Canada.

Hertweck, A., & Mehan, H. (1981, April). The three ''R's'': Referral, rehabilitation, and ramification. Paper presented at American Educational Research Association Meeting, Los Angeles, California.

Manis, J. G., & Meltzer, N. (1969). *Symbolic interaction.* Boston: Allyn and Bacon.

Medway, F. J. (1979). Causal attributions for school-related problems: teacher perceptions and teacher feedback. *Journal of Educational Psychology, 71* (6), 809–818.

Medway, F. J., & Lowe, C. A. (1976). The effect of stimulus person valence on divergent self-other attributions for success and failure. *Journal of Research in Personality, 10,* 266–278.

Mehan, H. (1973). Assessing children's language using abilities. In J. M. Armer & A. D. Grimshaw (Eds.), *Methodological issues in comparative sociological research.* New York: John Wiley and Sons.

Mehan, H. Accomplishing classroom lessons. (1974). In A. V. Cicourel, K. H. Jennings, S. H. M. Jennings, K. C. W. Leiter, R. MacKay, H. Mehan, & D. R. Roth (Eds.), *Language use and school performance.* New York: Academic Press.

Mehan, H. (1979). *Learning lessons.* Cambridge, MA.: Harvard University Press.

Mehan, H. (1981). Practical decision making in naturally occurring institutional settings. In Barbara Rogoff & Jean Lave (Eds.), *Everyday cognition: Its development and social context.* Cambridge, MA.: Harvard University Press.

Mehan, H. (1983). The role of language and the language of role in institutional decision making. *Language and Society.*

Mehan, H., Hertweck, A., Combs, S. E., & Flynn, P. J. (1981). Teachers' interpretations of students' behavior. In L. C. Wilkinson (Ed.), *Communicating in the Classroom.* New York: Academic Press.

Mehan, H., Hertweck, A., & Meihls, L. (1981). Educational decision making in students' careers, Part II: Prospectus for year three. Unpublished manuscript. University of California, San Diego.

Mehan, H., Meihls, L., Hertweck, A. L., & Crowdes, P. (1981). Identifying handicapped students. In S. B. Bacharach (Ed.), *Organizational behavior in schools and school districts.* New York: Praeger Press.

Mehan, H., & Wood, H. (1975). An image of man for ethnomethodology. *Philosophy of the Social Sciences, 5,* 365–376.

Weber, M. (1947). *The theory of social and economic organization* (trans. by A. M. Henderson & T. Parsons). New York: Free Press.

Weiner, B. (1972a). Attribution theory, achievement motivation, and the educational process. *Review of Educational Research, 42,* 203–215.

Weiner, B. (1972b). *Theories of motivation.* Chicago: Markham Publishing Company.

Weiner, B. (1974). *Achievement motivation and attribution theory.* Morristown, NJ: General Learning Press.

Weiner, B. (1977). Attribution and affect: Comments on Sohn's critique. *Journal of Educational Psychology, 69,* 506–511.

Weiner, B. (1979). A theory of motivation for some classroom experiences. *Journal of Educational Psychology, 72* (1), 373–81.

Weiner, B., Frieze, I., Kukla, A., Reed, L., Rest, S., & Rosenbaum, R. M. (1971). Perceiving the causes of success and failure. In E. E. Jones, D. E. Kan, H. H. Kelley, R. E. Nisbett, S. Valins, & B. Weiner (Eds.), *Attribution: Perceiving the causes of behavior*. Morristown, NJ: General Learning Press.

Weiner, B., Russell, D., & Lerman, D. (1978). Affective consequences of causal ascriptions. In J. H. Harvey, W. Ickes, & R. F. Kidd (Eds.), *New directions in attribution research* (Vol. 2). Hillsdale, NJ: Lawrence Erlbaum Associates.

9.

Writing, Sexism, and Schooling: A Discourse-Analytic Investigation of Some Recent Documents on Sexism and Education in Queensland*

A. W. McHoul

James Cook University, Australia

POLICY STUDIES AND OPPOSITION

This paper examines some recent attempts by the Queensland Department of Education to introduce what appears on the surface as "non-sexist" (or, on another reading, even countersexist) policy provisions for state schools. To that extent, the paper might be taken as a contribution to "policy studies." But, from the outset, it should be clear that what has traditionally passed under that title will not be found in these pages. Instead a shift in the terrain of policy analysis is developed.

Firstly, the site of analysis is policy documentation. But this does not mean a narrowly formalistic look at the "linguistics" of policy statements. It acknowledges from the start that policy texts (both policy-making texts and their partially transformed rewritings in "policy studies") constitute nodal points in webs or networks of signifying practice generally; networks of discourse which constitute a field of power and knowledge. That is, it acknowledges that a social fabric is constituted and saturated by discursive formations; that "policy," "policy making," "policy writers," "policy studies," and so on are effects of determinate techniques of signification, and that these techniques provide the "rules," the conditions of possibility for policy. So, we are beginning with the assumption that "policy" is not the *expression* of some pre-existing collective will-to-act, and nor is it the presaging of actions and practices yet to emerge. This much may be the self-understanding of policy makers and policy theorists. But, we want to argue, that self-understanding (including especially its notion of linear temporality: problem → policy-solution → new practice) is only *part of* the conditions of possibility that policy techniques constitute; for to indulge in that self-understanding is to see policy texts as relatively neutral linguistic matter which merely "stands on behalf of," "corresponds to" some more underlying and significant "trouble" or "object" which is taken to be inherently prediscursive.

---

* This paper is part of a joint research project undertaken with Dr Sandra Taylor. Sociohistorical background on the development of educational policy on sexism in Australia can be found in her paper 'Ideology, Policy and the Education of Girls' (1982).

Texts do not emerge as the effects of pregiven ideal or ontological objects in this way. Rather they discursively create those objects. So policy does not stand in any "relation" to a domain of practice from which it is ontologically severed; rather it constitutes a domain of practice in itself: a field of signifying practice. We believe that traditional "policy studies" has been fundamentally misguided by reproducing the above mentioned "correspondence" position on policy making and that it can and ought to be radically separated from such techniques. Those techniques, we argue, should instead become a critical topic for policy analysis.

Hence we propose to focus on texts and textuality—on the conditions of possibility of the signifying practice of policy texts. For us, these become sites whose conditions of possibility must be investigated and whose practical effectivity (destinations) must be opened to strategic intervention. To critique policy texts, then, is to make a critical intervention at the level of signifying practice—that is, at the level of policy discourse itself.

Policy texts cannot be examined within their own frames, for they necessarily interarticulate with other material social practices—in the classroom, in the boardroom, in departmental offices, and in other textual and nontextual sites—and they interarticulate with these precisely in and as their readings and writings. So the question "how do we read/write policy?" is no longer an anaemic matter of "point of view," of some "mere ideology" divorced from material practice. It is critical, to use Althusser's (1970) terms, in the sense of a critical situation.

Policy texts work to police other specific material practices, to allow and to deny certain cohorts access to particular practices and social spaces. Who is allowed to do what and where are effects of readings and writings. A critical intervention, therefore, must seek other-than-dominant (oppositional) modes of reading/writing policy; other modes of determining the forms of access that are "permitted" or "denied" to particular social cohorts—in the present case, women.

Policy texts thereby become strategically analyzable for their potential as elements in either dominant or oppositional cultures. Their existence as either incorporated or as critical-emergent discourses (Williams, 1976) depends on forms of signifying practice: and that depends not on any inherent "meaning" they contain in and of themselves but on how we read/write them. Thereby policy texts are rendered (for they always already are, if in repressed form) constituents of political calculation and agency. The form of calculation, however, depends crucially on whether we read/write them according to the techniques of policy making's own self-understanding or by means of techniques oppositional to them.

To do "discourse analysis" on policy texts, then, is no neutral or merely formal matter. Discourse analysis entails

> analysing the material effects of particular uses of language in particular social conjunctures . . . [A] theory of specific signifying practices—above all, of the

discursive practices of the juridical, political and religious apparatuses of the state. (Eagleton, 1982, p. 103)

So, policy constitutes a highly elaborate and complex state machinery whose common techniques infiltrate and saturate both bureaucratic and popular-informal (''everyday'') settings, triggering some further practices while repressing some others and so forth. But this is by no means automatic. The policy text does not ''act'' by virtue of some internal structure given to or inhering in it. Policy texts do not have single, monolithic, endogenous ''meanings'' which, ''whatever happens,'' relay to certain automatic practical consequences. Rather it is the constancy of policy techniques which can be more or less relied upon by state agencies for the production of stable (''normal'') readings and their effects. ''It is policy, thus it will be read *this* way—as policy has always been read.'' The point of an intervention is to disrupt this assumption in process—an assumption or wager that nearly always comes off, for ''other readings'' are marginal and simply not regularly available outside other trainings, and other trainings are not available because the institutions of training (families, schools, universities, factories, army barracks, hospitals, etc.) are keenly policed and self-policed. And ''policy,'' by a neat turn of etymological fate, partly determines that policing of training itself (Donzelot, 1979). The web is, in principle, self-repairing in this respect. But at the same time it is fraught with contradictions and fissures— many of which are poorly sutured. The point of a critical intervention in policy studies is to discover those cracks and to prise them open. That work is precisely the work of finding other possibilities of reading/writing. Discourse being inseparably linked with power, interventions into power-effects are constituted by the search for discursive transformations at such critically weak sites. We argue below that certain policy documents of the Queensland Education Department constitute just such sites.

So it is already ''critical'' that we should resist ''correspondence'' versions of policy in the form of those readings which treat policy texts teleologically, as shadows of practices passed or yet to come and instead play upon the available but routinely repressed *performative* (Austin, 1965) aspects of policy discourse. As we shall see, policy texts almost always consist in transformations of other discourses, for example, in this case, the discourses of feminism, liberal humanism, and prior policy making. Their work is precisely to transform those discourses such that some are effectively neutralized while others are reproduced unhindered or even amplified. So critical work might begin by examining those transformations as practices and so perform still further (but oppositional) discursive transformations on the policy texts themselves. It becomes important, then, to see how policy texts which promise emancipation in various forms actually exist as practical strategies for the normalization and cooptation of a population (in this case, women). To see that, it is crucial to see that text and action are not separate elements bound together only by a temporal teleology of ''change.''

Text-action is one; and the point of policy critique is not to set up alternatives in the face of dominant policy but to *do* oppositional text-action.

THE POLICY STATEMENT

There is no "starting point" or origin for the Queensland Policy Statement on "sex equality" (1981). But it can be noted that the document appeared some six years later than the (now acknowledged as seminal) document *Girls Schools and Society* drawn up as part of International Women's Year (Australian Schools Commission, 1975). It is almost impossible, then, not to read that statement (reproduced below) as the effect of growing pressure in Australia since the early 1970s to acknowledge and promote "women's rights." Certainly indirect pressure can be discerned in the sheer existence of parallel texts internationally and in most other Australian states' policy decisions, as well as those of, for instance, the Catholic Education Authority, teachers' unions, and private schools' groups. But how does the statement articulate exactly with feminist *discourse?* What transformations of feminist discourses does it make?

Departmental Policy Statement

Queensland society is characterised by a diversity of values and wideranging social, economic and technological changes. These factors are contributing to an increasing range of roles for men and women in both the family and the wider community.

It is a societal responsibility, shared by the family and other social institutions, including schools, to provide equal opportunities for all girls and boys so that they can develop skills and abilities, and effective participation in such a society. Failure to accept this responsibility and provide equality of opportunity, limits the potential attainments of students and, therefore, of Queensland society in the future.

At times, an individual's potential attainments are inadvertently constrained by educational practices. The various roles and labels ascribed to students because of their particular sex, background or ability are illustrative of such constraining practices. These practices channel students in certain directions and contribute to discrimination contrary to the ideal of equality of opportunity.

Of increasing concern in this regard is discrimination on the basis of sex. An expression of such discrimination is sex-role stereotyping whereby students are expected to pursue interests, careers and lifestyles which are based on sex differences rather than on individual potential and talent. Such expectations constrain the life-views and experience of students and are incongruent with the provision of equality in education.

Educational policies alone cannot be effective in eliminating sex-role stereotypes and their related inequalities. Nevertheless, changes can be effected in schools in such ways that the individuality and equality of all students are accommodated. Schools need to examine the assumptions and values underlying sex-related expectations and the limitations these place on students.

In particular, efforts need to focus upon the analysis and correction of stereotyping in curriculum development and implementation, the selection of resource materials, subject choice and career counselling, discrimination in school and class organisation, and in teacher practices.

Schools should assist all students to develop a sense of self-worth and a range of skills and abilities in order to meet their individual needs and interests. Most importantly, schools should open up rather than foreclose the range of life choices available to individuals in a changing society. The pursuit of these goals will help to promote the attainment of equality of opportunity in education. (Queensland Department of Education, 1981)

The first thing to note is not anything "internal" to the text itself. Rather, we should turn to the competing and contradictory conditions of possibility at work in its production. For it is not simply the discourse(s) of feminism that are invoked and transformed here, but also the discourses of previous state policy. When we look at that previous policy, it becomes possible to see the statement as the effect not of any single discourse ("bourgeois liberal humanism"?) but of a contradiction between oppositional (feminist) discourses as culturally dominant ones (antifeminism). And that antifeminism is evident in the terms of reference for schooling policy in Queensland since 1980—the Ahern Report.

4.14 The Committee has received recommendations that a special programme should be introduced to 'combat sexism' in the schools. We do not approve of discrimination on the grounds of sex. However, we believe that equality should be based on opportunity rather than outcomes. We also believe that the wish of a majority of women to accept family and caring roles should not be discouraged or in any way denigrated. We reject the concept of 'role reversal' featured in certain book and poster material and recommend that this material not be used. (Queensland Legislative Assembly, 1979, p. 10)

This delivers to the machineries of policy making their apparently baseline conditions of possibility. The guidelines of Ahern cannot be openly transgressed; for they can be (and, as we shall see, have been) cited as a *force majeur,* as a ruling which overrules any nonsexist practice or policy.

Note how the quotation marks work in this Ahern text. The terms "combat sexism" are duly relegated to the space of someone-other-than-the-Committee's speech. This Committee makes it plain that it could not subscribe to such terms. It could not put itself forward as moving against sexism and could especially not entertain the strategy labeled "combatting"—for that carries with it a certain militantism. However, *rights* are to be considered within the Committee's scope. But not specifically *women's* rights. Instead: "We do not approve of discrimination on the grounds of sex." Now "sex" is a categorization device which traditionally carries two members: male and female. And this has not been lost in the departmental policy statement; for that statement does not directly address the problems of women in schooling and society. Instead it makes reference to "an increasing range of roles for *men and* women", to "roles and labels ascribed to students because of their *particular sex.*" In fact, at *no point* does the statement make direct reference to women (unless they are, as ever, accompanied by "men

and. . .''). It is as though the document were a discursive analogue of those
exclusive male clubs and masonic temples where an accompanying male is a
necessary passport.

So the device, "sex," is clearly available and regularly used to do transfor-
matory work on the discourse(s) of feminism. It rewrites the discourse on
"women and education" as one of "education and sexual equality"—at no
point noting or implying the obvious point that it simply is not men who suffer
from patriarchal forms of domination in education and elsewhere but that on the
contrary they flourish at the expense of women. "Sex" (unlike, say, "race")
being a two-category device makes the emancipatory gloss very easy to accomplish.[1] So, in the statement's advocation of *rights,* which is a rewrite of Ahern
and which appears emancipatory, there is a consequent relegation and absenting
of the more pertinent (to feminism) concept of *liberation.*

Are "sexual equality" and "women's liberation" identical? Quite simply
they are not—for one is a concept in the discourse of liberal humanism and the
other a concept in the discourse(s) of feminism. For Ahern, while that text allows
the bourgeois discourse on individual equality to become one on sexual (m/f)
equality, it will not extend the transformation far enough for it to become a
discourse on the *in*equality of women specifically, let alone their possible liberation from that inequality. That is why "sexual inequality" is not coterminous
with "women's liberation" and why, in fact, "sexual equality" is a form of
practico-discursive obstacle to women's liberation. So it is not that the policy
statement offers less than was demanded (e.g., 12 points from a 20 point list),
but it in fact alters the *demand* in the first place before "granting" it. So no
effective "granting" is performed at all. It appropriates the discourse(s) of
feminism, transforming the demand for a reconstruction of sociosexual relations
as a whole into the demand for individual rights. And this is an effect of the
conditions of possibility of policy making locatable in, inter alia, Ahern.

Ahern also generates a discourse on "equality of opportunity" rather than of
"outcomes," in a single sentence which stands almost unconnected with the rest
of the text. (The prefatory "However," however, makes it clear that a caveat
against discrimination is upcoming.) The sentence stands there, free-floating as a
cryptic signal to those policy makers who have the training to read it, constraining by its large margin of indexicality the possibilities of any antisexism policy.
For any "policy" reading of that sentence, there are circumscribed possible
rewritings having a number of specific political effectivities. Firstly, it constrains
policy in a way which prevents it from invoking programs of positive discrimination. And that fits, like a hand in a glove, the protection of "individual equality"—for *both* sexes; and in so doing obstructs discourses on any general recon-

---

[1] The notions "device," "categorization" and "membership categorization device" were initially worked on by the late Harvey Sacks, and his two papers on the subject can be consulted for
further details—see Sacks (1972, 1974).

struction of sociosexual relations in educational sites controlled by the state which are presently shot through with forms of patriarchal domination. This trace, this small, marginal, and fragmented remark reverberates through policy discourse to countercheck the passage of any feminist discourse. Secondly, it reinaugurates for policy an already dominant picture of the world; for it shows (even though it may not say) that we live in a world where a certain population (women), no matter how much its "opportunities" are equalized, will simply not achieve outcomes equal with another (men). And the interrogative "Why?" is left unasked and unanswered, leaving only one possibility—namely that women will achieve poorer outcomes, given equal access to the same trainings, because they *inherently* must fair worse than men. That, for Ahern, is in the Nature of things. That is what the Ahern text shows behind its saying (Silverman & Torode, 1980).

We can see how these dual constraints operate in the policy statement itself. Firstly, we can read that "Education policies alone cannot be effective." Policy writing demands that it be read as only a partial "influence" on practice. It does not ask to be read as signifying practice in itself, and in fact attempts to cut off that reading. Secondly, we can read that there are to be "equal opportunities for all girls and boys," reiterated numerous times as, for example, "equality of opportunity" and "the ideal of equality of opportunity." The stress here leaves unspoken the second possibility that the Ahern document spells out clearly: "equality of outcomes." The policy statement shows (though *it* does not say) that no guarantees are to be made about outcomes. Equal opportunity is to be "provided" for the realization of "individual needs" for both sexes. This ironing out, "at the start," so reminiscent of Parsons and other conservative apologists, repeats and amplifies not a feminist Weltanschauung but the Ahern picture of the world in which inherent differences, supposedly prior to, and constraining upon, social trainings, just "are" and so must inevitably pervade educational practice and so cannot be legislated for. At the bottom level, the raw material (which is now to be processed "equally") just *is* differentiated prior to the processing. No responsibility can be taken by the management for that. The promise is "to do our best" with an inherently hierarchized and stubborn Nature. The discourse, that is, *creates* a space outside itself which is—on a "policy" reading—prior to and untouched by policy discourse. But we should remember, in our readings, that the space of the "given," of the "datum" is not discourse-neutral. Policy discourse creates that Nature as one of its specific effects, but at the same time, produces the reading-effect that that unequal Nature is *not* its own product. Technically, this is fetishism: the alienation of discursive work from its product. And one possible effectivity of that fetishism is that the cohort "women in education" remains shackled—in educational practice—to an unfortunately recalcitrant Nature: one specifically created, here in this discourse (as well, no doubt, in staffrooms, across the breakfast table, in the bedroom, and other sites of sexist discourse in "common sense" and "everyday life")) exactly for the purpose of policing and retaining women's diminished consumption of educational goods. It is a technique for ensuring that, for some, for women, the goods are no good.

So we can now see how the surface reading of "emancipation" is in fact one of repression; and how that repression works primarily through the overt policy of sociosexual homogenization, an homogenization which self-effaces when confronted by "Natural" hierarchies. What, above all, cannot be entertained, what must remain unspoken, is that women *are* different but in the sense that they are differently produced in sites of material social practice and in signifying practices like this very one. It is not what the policy statement says that generates this reading, but rather an attention to what it does.

Lastly, Ahern tackles "role reversal," only to discover that this perfectly common sense piece of sociologizing backfires in its practical effectivity. The document here is, at least, "up front." Its sexism is overt and gives counter-discourses something definite to come back at (perhaps, at the limit, even by a reappropriation of the very liberal humanist discourse which pervades the policy statement itself). At the same time, these last two sentences expand the Natural picture built up so far. For now Ahern is to respect the "wishes" of women to accept "family and caring roles"—as they traditionally and Naturally do (at least on his picture). This new baseline of (female) Human Nature is the "wish," the desire. What is pertinently absent here is any scene in which wishes and desires are themselves the products of desire-producing mechanisms and trainings, the very "desiring machines" (Deleuze & Guattari, 1972) which policy produces and maintains. It does not take enormous (or perhaps even any) sociological insight to see that choices are never unconstrained choices. As Taylor (1980) points out, the mechanisms and techniques of family discourses, their repetition and acceptance in the cohort often alluded to as "peers," along with educational mechanisms such as the timetable and cultural machineries such as the "culture of femininity" all act (in concert with a galaxy of other mechanisms) upon and constrain the specific mechanisms glossed by the term "choice." Families, for instance, when "choosing" subjects or schools are

> constantly reminded of their fate by a direct or indirect intuitive grasp of the statistics of the failures or partial successes of children of the same kind, and also less directly, by the evaluation of the . . . school teacher who, in his role as counsellor, consciously or unconsciously takes into account the social origin of his pupils and thus, unwittingly and involuntarily [?], counterbalances the over-theoretical nature of a forecast based purely on performance. (Bourdieu, 1976, p. 111)

Hence the repetition of dominant discourses on sex and schooling which have come to be known collectively, in an overgeneralized way, as "reproduction." The effect of Ahern's text is to show that that reproduction is a quite Natural process. Girls, it seems, just *want* to be carers and maintenance engineers in domestic labour processes. What Ahern cannot see is that it is the repetition of this very variety of discourse in sites such as reports to the Queensland Legislative Assembly which *is* that reproduction—or a fraction of it.

The "backfire" alluded to above consists of transformations of the Ahern discourse on "role reversal" made between the Interim and Final Reports. As a simple indicator, 4.14 above was read to over 50 first education students who were asked to repair the indexicality of the term "role reversal" in that context. Almost unanimously, the rewrites contained elements such as "women doing traditionally male work," "men working in the home," "women getting the important jobs men usually get," and their limited variants. This fragment of initially feminist discourse which has now come into general usage is simply *not* mistakeable for anything else. "Reversing roles" is as plain and open a matter for competent speakers as "betting on the TAB," "making coffee," and so on (if not as widely practiced). Its routineness as a piece of everyday discourse in contemporary Australia is not subject to any great semantic debate. Yet, facing this "backfire," Ahern's final report rather lamely tries to wriggle away by invoking just such semantic techniques:

> 6.6. In paragraph 4.14 of the Second Interim Report, the Select Committee stated that 'we reject the concept of "role reversal" featured in certain book and poster material and recommend that this material not be used.' This has apparently created some confusion in the minds of some teachers for whom the term 'role reversal' has a technical connotation which is rather wider than we had appreciated. Our intention was, and is, to discourage the use of material which portrays women who elect to remain at home and devote their time exclusively to household duties, as being of lesser value in the community than those who enter the work force. We have seen material, particularly cartoons, in use in some schools, which portrays the housewife as frumpish and stupid, and is constrasted with the working woman who is portrayed as elegant and intelligent. It is this sort of material which we recommend should not be used in Queensland schools. (Queensland Legislative Assembly, 1980, p. 20)

We pass over the Report's peculiar categorization device in which domestic labour is distinguished from the workforce and housework is not counted as working and note simply that the "normal" reading of "role reversal" is duly castigated and its readers turned into judgmental dopes (Garfinkel, 1967, p. 66). The technique is familiar enough: where there is error it is not the reporting that is responsible for it but those reported on. Teachers were, apparently, "confused" in their "minds" by the Committee's use of the term. They, it is indicated, did not use the "everyday" sense of the term (which of course they blatantly *did*), but chose instead a "technical connotation." And, presumably unlike every other "technical connotation" in the language, *this* particular one was *wider* ranging than the usual usage. Ahern plainly knows that it is his report's hastily revised use which is forced into being technical and "narrow" while the teachers in question had obviously used its more common reading. The semantic game which Ahern plays involves shifting the terrain of "role reversal'' so that it covers differential images of ''womanhood'': the smart executive ''lady'' (who works) vs. the houshold drudge (who, peculiarly, does not). *That* oppositionality is, quite plainly, by no means one which ''role reversal'' carries with it. For that term is (perhaps to Ahern's chagrin) articulated in a discourse which envisages a reconstruction of sociosexual relations as a whole—the very thing which Ahern so carefully, in other places, keeps distant from the policy agenda. Something has slipped in by the back door, or by general incompetence with everyday language—and now there is no getting out of it. It is plain that Ahern is not going to tip the wink to policy making for a discourse on change in general sociosexual relations and, more importantly, it is not just an *absence* of that ''permission'' from the Interim and Final Reports which is in question now (that being the routine policy strategy) but rather that ''permission'' has been specifically excluded, materially, in black and white.

Consequently the policy statement's discourse is constrained to repeat Ahern's world centered on the subject, a world in which the individual personality, mind, psyche, or consciousness is the baseline. Likewise, the task of ''equal'' education becomes the *educatio* (leading out) of ''essential'' elements of Naturally disparate individual personalities. Hence the statement talks of the ''accommodation'' of ''the individuality and equality of all students'' and of ''individual potential and talent'', all of which are taken as seemingly inevitable starting points. Yet it is bizarre in the least that individuality *and equality* should be taken as Natural in this respect because, for them both to be givens would obviate the need for a policy on equality. Further, that baseline of the individualized subject holds across and irrespective of sex-classes (Cass, 1978) in this document. The sociosexual division of labour and *its* inherent inequalities are consequently rendered unmentionable: they must be passed over in silence. Instead, the attack is marshalled against further personalist elements: the ''assumptions and values underlying sex-related expectations and the limitations these place on students,'' these being presumably under the control and will of autonomous subjects of educational practices. The product of such a policy aims to be an amelioration of equally personalist traces, namely the development of (1) ''a sense of self-worth,'' presumably in a world where the self is presently far from ''worthy'' given predominant (but, here, unspoken) *social* conditions and of (2) ''a range of skills and abilities in order to meet . . . individual needs and interests.'' Along with this is an attack not on the current absence of liberatory strategies for women in education but on ''sex-role stereotyping''—that is, not just a weaker version of ''the same thing'' but instead a discursively different object, one created by policy discourse's transformation and effective annulment of feminist discourse. So the state is to be ''no change'' over the liberal humanist discourse of *Girls Schools and Society* which feminists such as Jepson (1976) saw for what it was. Jepson's conclusion

> is that the power of radical educational and radical feminist ideas has been co-opted and defused. The original feminist critique which aimed at a ''new'' set of social

relationships between men and women, and thus a radical transformation of society, has been diminished to a critique of inequality emphasising sex-role socialisation as its agent. (Foster, 1981, pp. 302–303)

This transformation of a discourse on liberation as a sociopolitical practice into a discourse on individual rights and needs as a psychopersonalist practice entails what Williams (1976) calls the incorporation of oppositional cultures. It is a specific mode of operation of hegemonic discourses that they do not produce discourses overtly *counter* to marginal and oppositional forms. Rather they seek to incorporate them by a process of discursive transformation rendering them residual and neutralizing their emergence prior to any possible mass adoption. It is a tactic of appropriation at the level of signifying practice, and one which could be examined not just in relation to policy on sexism but also those on sex-education, multiculturalism, and so forth where, we may suspect, potentially oppositional knowledges are incorporated and policed. Williams goes on to say that this policing of "cultural forms" at a highly penetrative and keen level is a feature of late twentieth century capitalism, a recent turn in that mode of production which could not be discerned in its classic form:

It may be true of some earlier phases of bourgeois society . . . that there were some areas of experience which it was willing to dispense with, which it was prepared to assign to the sphere of private or artistic life, and as being no particular business of society or the state . . . But I am sure it is true of the society that has come into existence since the last war, that progressively, because of developments in the social character of labour, in the social character of communications, and in the social character of decision, it extends much further than ever before in capitalist society into certain hitherto resigned areas of experience and practice and meaning. Thus the effective decision, as to whether a practice is alternative or oppositional, is often now made within a very much narrower scope. (Williams, 1976, p. 206)

So, for oppositional policy studies, it is clear that liberalist documents like the policy statement should be seen for what they are—appropriations and incorporations of radical discourse which neutralize those discourses' effectivities—and not, for example, celebrated as the thin end of the emancipatory wedge.

POLICY STUDIES AND INCORPORATION

Some versions of policy studies might not operate in this way. And they are consequently in danger of the kind of incorporation which Williams outlines (either this or they are already incorporated). For example, such studies often use discursive forms identical with those of the policy *statements* they could, in other circumstances, critique—forms such as "X is happening, Y must be done in order to bring about Z" (the diagnostic-therapeutic mode). This involves a statement of *the* problem with no concern for the reality that that "mere" *de*scription produces, followed by a *pre*scription based on the prior, unquestioned ontology.

> Policy-making, aimed at solving problems, is in this light inherently subject to administrative and logistical difficulties in its implementation. There must be a considerable refinement of procedures and managerial techniques to ensure the more efficient coordination and operation of policy. (Smith, 1982, p. 4)

In this fragment, we find a useful representation or typification of policy discourse mimicking state bureaucratic discourse.[2] It constitutes a repetition of policy discourse *upon* policy problems. As with other policy discourse, the supposed generation of action *from* discourse (as opposed to a consideration of discourse *as* action) is so embedded in an ultimately prescriptivist mode that the equally necessary descriptive premises are overlooked. They are taken to constitute an unproblematic domain: "how it happens to be." Policy language forgets its own responsibility for the creation of ontological effects by repeating the positivist technique of "merely describing the facts" in some unexplicated way. Yet, as we have seen, it is precisely how policy concocts "what is" (let alone "what should be") that is problematic and critical. It is through such ontologico-discursive strategies that policy is able to "sell" us its version of the "real." And that is, characteristically, how hegemony works, for hegemony does not produce debates and counter-debates about what "ought to be" but, on the contrary, gags effective debate by saturating a society's initial starting points, its "agreement" about "what is." It

> supposes the existence of something truly total, which is not merely secondary or superstructural, like a weak sense of ideology, but which is lived at such a depth, which saturates the society to such an extent, and which, as Gramsci put it, even constitutes the limit of common sense for most people under its sway, that it corresponds to the reality of social experience very much more clearly than any notions derived from [for example] the formula of base and superstructure. (Williams, 1976, pp. 204–205)

The question becomes: how to resist policy discourse's narration of the real? Clearly no critical strategy would reproduce that subjectivist and metaphysical discourse upon rights and equality but would show precisely that that narration of one possible "real" is no more than that—a narration. "No more than that": but this does not mean it is a petty matter for it is precisely this apparently simple discursive strategy that underpins the signifying practice of policy discourse.

What is most pertinently absent from the policy statement is the social, despite its glances in the direction of structural functionalism (roles, values, the wider community, and so on). The social needs to be reinserted and reasserted. The statement's discourse is one of individualism, of the psychological subject,

---

[2] I am assured by Dr. Smith (personal communication) that this statement is in fact parodic and in no way represents his personal position on the matter.

"the whole man" who displays Natural individual difference as a mere fact of Nature which "just is" and, because it "just is," is the Natural starting point for policy. That level is irreducible for policy discourse. Yet it must be reduced (or reworked) to show the socio-discursive origins of the personal. But along with this discourse on the personal goes a parallel one on the nation or (in this case) the state. The policy statement makes frequent allusions to the effectivity of its proposals at the site of the nation/state: "Failure to accept this responsibility . . . limits the potential attainments of students and, therefore, of Queensland society in the future." Like advertising, the statement either penetrates the level of personal values ("even your best friend won't tell you") or the level of the nation ("Advance Australia," "Declare it for Australia"). The picture is clearly of a mythical nonsociety; of a society from which the social is absent. It is a nation composed of micropersonalities with all the "intervening" (though discursively quite alterior) stages omitted: no class, no sex-class, no division of labour and so on. As if the national/social fabric were entirely unfragmented—a piece of whole cloth woven from well-aligned and tightly knit fibers of multiple individual personalities. It is precisely the sociopolitical that is omitted in order to get maximum sociopolitical effect. Any form of sociopolitical discursivity is sequestered from radical social discourse (here: feminism) in its appropriation by bourgeois liberal humanist policy statements. This is the double-appropriation of policy: by transforming radical discourse it both incorporates it and alters its articulation of the "real." Thereby the cracks of social conflict can be papered over (or sutured). If the "surface" of society seems smooth on any "normal" reading of policy documents, that is only because a sufficient amount of discursive pressure is keeping the lid on.

TEXTUAL EFFECTS

If there remain any doubts about the neutralizing of radical discourse in the policy statement, we can turn to two specific textual effects which it actually produced. These are in the form of letters from the director general and acting director general of the Queensland Department of Education to principals of state schools. The first (chronologically the later) is anaemicized simply by the absence from it of radical forms of implementation. The second makes it quite plain that the policy statement is not to be taken as "permitting" counter-sexist practices and materials in schools. The first reads quite simply:

> The enclosed poster and print materials are being forwarded to all Schools to raise awareness of the Departmental Policy Statement on Equality of Opportunity in Education for Girls and Boys and of the project currently being implemented through the Curriculum Branch in this regard.
>
> Principals are requested to display the poster, to place the bibliography in the school library and to draw the attention of staff to these materials. (Letter of 25 August 1982)

The second is lengthier and treats the question of SENSE (Studies to Encourage Non-Sexist Education), a set of materials available to schools from the federal Curriculum Development Centre. These materials are "considered inappropriate for use in Queensland State Schools" and the reasons advanced for that inappropriateness form the first instance of the policy statement being put to reactionary use. Three reasons are advanced:

- When reviewed against the Departmental policy statement on 'Equality of Opportunity in Education for Boys and Girls' (Education Office Gazette, 30 January 1981), the materials are inappropriate, given their focus on the elimination of sexism as opposed to the promotion of equality.
- Given the statements made by the Parliamentary Select Committee on Education in Queensland and its Second Interim Report (pp. 8–10 in paragraphs 4.3, 4.4, 4.7, 4.10 and 4.12) which relate to teaching techniques including role playing and dilemma stories, the private lives of students and their families, and the consideration of controversial issues in schools, much of the student resource and work material in SENSE would be inappropriate for use in Queensland State Schools.
- Section II of the materials, which encourages examination of the school by students in relation to sexism practices, presents the potential for conflict between students, staff members and principals and could contribute to an undermining of school organisation and authority. (Letter of 6 May 1981)

Note the use of Ahern as *force majeur* to overrule the policy statement and the reiteration of Ahern's explicitly sexist policy—"the materials are inappropriate, given their focus on the elimination of sexism as opposed to the promotion of equality" (!). Here the possibility that any trace of radical discursive effectivity might remain in the government policy statement is flatly countered. If the message was not clear upon a first reading, now, in practical effectivity, it is blatant. And "blatant" is a term which the acting director general himself uses, but in referring to the radical nature of SENSE. He makes it quite obvious that, even if sexism is a product of conservative forces in the society, those conservative forces, according to liberal humanist doctrines of equality, are to be allowed their freedom, are to be acknowledged and deferred to:

> The objective of eliminating discrimination and stereotyping between the sexes is not to be achieved by the use of material which is patently overt in its intentions, and much of the material in SENSE is blatant in this regard. Indeed, the technique is likely to be counter-productive, particularly with respect to individuals or families with what might be described as conservative views, who could find a significant proportion of the material of questionable taste, if not directly offensive. (Letter of 6 May 1981).

Now it is quite plain that possible feminist policies have been neutered and incorporated by the policy's effectivity in some actual material domain. And that displacement is effected precisely through the techniques of liberalist discourse.

So we may assume that the return to '60s liberal education policies advocated by some writers will not only be ineffective in bringing about radical change but might in fact generate continuingly repressive policies. We should be reminded here of Marx's analysis of attempts at historical repetition: that they occur initially as tragedy and secondly as farce.

Finally, the strategy of radical policy critique to formulate counterpolicies may be equally ineffective, for the techniques of incorporation that we have witnessed here are in massive evidence. Instead of formulating counterprescriptions on the basis of consensus descriptions, it is the very formulation of "what the problem is" that needs intervention, at the level of discursive operations. To produce counterpolicy is analogous to the Maoists' attempts in Paris in the '70's to set up people's courts to try the police for their crimes. As Foucault (1980) points out, at the level of technique, that merely ensures a repetition of repressive formations. The new liberals call for a return to basic "justice," but as Foucault shows, in a passage where "policy" is eminently substitutable for "courts":

> When we talk about courts, we're talking about a place where the struggle between contending forces is willy-nilly suspended: where in every case the decision arrived at is not the outcome of this struggle but of the intervention of an authority which necessarily stands above and is foreign to the contending forces, an authority which is in a position of neutrality between them and consequently can and must in every case decide which party to the dispute has justice on its side. The court implies, therefore, that there are categories which are common to the parties present . . . and that the parties to the dispute agree to submit to them. Now, it is all this that the bourgeoisie wants to have believed in relation to justice, to its justice. All these ideas are weapons which the bourgeoisie has put to use in exercise of power . . . This justice must therefore be the target of the ideological struggle of the proletariat, and of the non-proletarianised people: thus the forms of justice must be treated with the very greatest suspicion by the new revolutionary state apparatus. (Foucault, 1980, p. 27)

An alternative is therefore to inaugurate oppositional techniques and a first step in that direction is to find oppositional reading strategies for policy texts. It is hoped that this paper has sketched the form of such an analytic strategy.

REFERENCES

Althusser, L., & Balibar, E. (1970). *Reading Capital*. London: New Left Books.

Austin, J. L. (1965). *How to do things with words*. New York: Oxford University Press.

Australian Schools Commission. (1975). *Girls schools and society*. Canberra: Australian Government Publishing Service.

Bourdieu, P. (1976). The school as a conservative force: Scholastic and cultural inequalities. In R. Dale, G. Esland, & M. MacDonald (Eds.), *Schooling and capitalism: A sociological reader* (pp. 110–117). London: Open University Press/Routledge & Kegan Paul.

Cass, B. (1978). Women's place in the class structure. In E. Wheelwright & K. Buckley (Eds.), *Essays in the political economy of Australian capitalism, III*. Sydney: ANZ Books.

Deleuze, G., & Guattari, F. (1972). *L'Anti-Oedipe, capitalisme et schizophrenie*. Paris: Editions de Minuit.

Donzelot, J. (1979). *The policing of families*. London: Hutchinson.

Eagleton, T. (1982). The end of criticism. *Southern Review,* 14 (2), 99–106.

Foster, L. E. (1981). *Australian education: A sociological reader*. Sydney: Prentice-Hall.

Foucault, M. (1980). On popular justice: A discussion with Maoists. In M. Foucault, *Power/knowledge: Selected interviews and other writings 1972–1977*. Brighton: Harvester, pp. 1–36.

Garfinkel, H. (1967). *Studies in ethnomethodology*. Englewood Cliffs, NJ: Prentice-Hall.

Jepson, P. (1976). *Women's education and feminism*. Arena, 44–45, 8–13.

Queensland Department of Education. (1981). Departmental policy statement. *Education Office Gazette,* January 1981, p. 15.

Queensland Legislative Assembly. (1979/80). *Second interim and final reports of the select committee on education*. Brisbane: Queensland Government Printer.

Sacks, H. (1972). An initial investigation of the usability of conversational data for doing sociology. In D. Sudnow (Ed.), *Studies in social interaction* (pp. 31–74). New York: Free Press.

Sacks, H. (1974). On the analysability of stories by children. In R. Turner (Ed.), Ethnomethodology: Selected readings (pp. 216–232). Harmondsworth: Penguin.

Silverman, D., & Torode, B. (1980). *The material word,* London: Routledge & Kegan Paul.

Smith, R. (1982). Policy studies in education: Problems and prospects, Unpublished paper. Department of Education, University of Queensland.

Taylor, S. (1980). Secondary school organisation and aspects of sex-role socialisation. Unpublished doctoral thesis. Department of Education, James Cook University.

Taylor, S. (1982). Ideology, policy and the education of girls. Unpublished paper, Brisbane CAE at Kelvin Grove.

Williams, R. (1976). Base and superstructure in marxist cultural theory. In R. Dale, G. Esland, & M. MacDonald (Eds.), *Schooling and capitalism: A sociological reader* (pp. 202–210). London: Open University Press/Routledge & Kegan Paul.

Part III
Law

10. The Verbatim Record: The Myth and the Reality*

Anne Graffam Walker
Georgetown University

One of the most common, and perhaps least examined, set of assumptions held in both lay and legal communities about the institution of American law concerns the association of verbatimness with the recording of trial proceedings. From the primary assumption—that a trial record will be made which will be verbatim—flow the others, which are that verbatim means word-for-word, and word-for-word implies exactness, completeness, and correctness. This concept, the assumptions continue, is insured by the making of a simultaneous recording of the event, most often through the offices of a court reporter, who is seen as the symbol of an objective and mechanistic process, and who, it is supposed, is impartially recording all speech of all speakers.[1]

The first of these assumptions—that the law requires a verbatim trial record—is certainly a fair one, stemming as it does from a statutory provision of the United States Code (28 U.S.C. §753(b)(1976)) for federal district courts, which calls for the making of a record "verbatim by shorthand or by mechanical means."[2] But the remainder of these assumptions, those which associate the notion of verbatimness and the presence of a court reporter with completeness, exactness, and pure objectivity—*insofar as they depend on a literal construal of verbatim as word-for-word*—are not so well founded. And when the word-for-word umbrella is extended to cover the belief that all speech of all speakers in a courtroom is equally represented in the record, the assumption fails altogether.

It is with the misconceptions that lead to these faulty assumptions that this chapter will deal, its purpose being to provide the reader with a more realistic understanding of the verbatim concept, and its capacity to illuminate our expectations about language as influenced by institutional power. Accordingly, in the

---

* This work is an expansion of a background paper which I did in the summer of 1983 for the Federal Judicial Center in connection with its *Comparative Evaluation of Stenographic and Audiotape Methods for United States District Court Reporting* (Greenwood, 1983). The citations to statutes and cases are the work of Deena Rabinowicz Dugan, to whom I extend my grateful appreciation, as I do also to Gordon Bermant of the Federal Judicial Center. His incisive criticism was immensely helpful.

[1] Some court proceedings are reported via electronic recordings instead of stenographic devices. Tape recordings, to be useful, however, require the services of a human monitor, and eventually must be translated into a written document. The principles which apply to either process are the same.

[2] This fact is, of course, not generally known by the layperson, whose expectations about trial records can better be traced to dramatic representation of legal processes in books and films.

paragraphs to follow, I will be touching on three issues which are importantly involved in applying a verbatim concept to the recording of natural speech in a court context: (1) the necessity to preserve what is essentially an oral event in a written form; (2) the legal world's concept of what constitutes information; and (3) the court reporter's model of English against which the incoming speech and information are measured. Since all three of these issues operate simultaneously in the recording process, I will be covering them in a nondiscrete way, as I propose them as explanations for a claim I will be making: that as presently understood, such a thing as a strictly constituted "verbatim" record is a myth. Not only does it not exist, but it would be unacceptable to the very community who requires it if it did. As might be expected, the court reporter will figure prominently in this discussion, since it is through that agent's understanding both of language and task that verbatim achieves its actual definition.

The data on which I base my claim are taken primarily from two sources: a comprehensive 1981 study I performed of transcription conventions and practices employed by approximately 115 professional court reporters in three eastern jurisdictions, and a follow-up inquiry in 1983 which included two nationally accredited reporting schools. I have made use as well of professional publications in the fields of law and court reporting, and have drawn extensively on insights generated by my own seven years of experience in the court reporting field. It was, in fact, as a novice court reporter that I first encountered the problems associated with verbatimness, problems that begin with the basic question of what a "record" is.

Technically speaking, the record of a trial consists only of the notes or audiotape made on the site, (28 U.S.C. §753(b)(1976); Bieber 1976) and does not include the transcript which results, but the common acceptance of transcripts as part of the record[3] has blurred the boundaries of the verbatim requirement set forth in the United States Code, leading to a generally unexamined association of verbatimness with both the original notes of the proceeding, and with their final typed form. That fact becomes important both legally (as when challenges are made to the accuracy of a transcript)[4] and theoretically, since a

---

[3] In an article entitled "Let Verbatim Be Your Guide," Seymour Bieber writes: ". . . what do we mean when we say 'the record'? To me as an attorney, and more particularly as one well acquainted (I believe) with the functions and duties of the verbatim court reporter, 'the record,' for the purposes of this discussion, has a double meaning. First there is the stenographic record, manual or machine, of what transpires in the courtroom—*made while the trial of the case is actually in progress.* Second, there is the typewritten transcript of these stenographic notes, made by or for the reporter *after he has left the courtroom.*" (Bieber 1976:27).

Waltz and Kaplan (1982:2), both professors of law, take a more inclusive, and perhaps more commonly held view of the record: "The record . . . has three basic parts: (1.) the litigation's paperwork [Complaints, Answers, Motions, and so forth], (2), the verbatim transcript of hearings, conferences, and trial testimony, and (3.) the tangible exhibits that the parties offered into evidence." Note the phrase "*verbatim* transcript".

[4] In United States v. DiCanio, for example, the court examined a transcript allegedly defective

further requirement of the same statute that calls for a verbatim record to be made is that the "transcript . . . certified by the reporter shall be deemed prima facie a correct statement of the testimony taken and proceedings had" (28 U.S.C. §753(b)(1976)).[5] Of the several implications inherent in this linking of the concepts of verbatimness and correctness, two will be of concern here now: (1) that "correct statements" of proceedings are based upon verbatim records; and (2) that there is such a thing as a verbatim record.

In the legal community, these two implications take on the status of the obvious, which perhaps explains the curious fact that in spite of the considerable importance which statutes and cases ascribe to faithful adherence to a verbatim standard,[6] there is no single definition in either the legal or court reporting profession that serves as the sole, officially sanctioned account of what "verbatim" entails. The result of this absence of explicit definition is that while everyone in the legal community agrees in theory that there is such a thing as a verbatim record (and by implication, verbatim transcript) there is in practice widespread disagreement[7] as to interpretation and application of a verbatim standard. A few courts have undertaken to supply a definition, but their efforts have been notably unhelpful. One court, for instance, wrote:

1. A verbatim record means the taking of the record word for word; all the dictionaries so define it. (In re DLF, 176 N.W. 2d 486,488 (S.D.1970)).

Another attempt was even less editfying:

2. Verbatim in this rule means *verbatim*. (Caffrey v. Chem-Ionics Corp., 499 P.2d 809,811 (Wash.1966)).

From these and other definitions of verbatim that I have elicted from members of both the lay and legal worlds, it is clear that it is the dictionary standard upon which they rely: "word-for-word." Such a literal construal, however, sets a goal

---

because of omissions. It concluded, however: "Most of the omissions are plainly mere colloquy, the sort of bickering between counsel that is often omitted entirely, by experienced court reporters." 245 F.2d 713,715 (2d Cir.1957).

[5] Although the courts are aware of the possibility of error, and rule 10(e) of the Federal Rules of Appellate Procedure contains the method by which corrections are to be made, the court reporter's transcript is "clothed with a presumption of correctness." United States v. Smith, 433 F.2d 149,151 (5th Cir. 1970).

[6] Compliance with 28 U.S.C. §753(b) is mandatory; e.g., United States v. Piascik, 559 F.2d 545 (9th Cir. 1977), and failure to do so can compel reversal. See, for example, Stephens v. United States, 289 F.2d 308 (5th Cir. 1961) (conviction reversed for failure to record voir dire and arguments to the jury). Neither of the latter is considered "evidence" in a trial.

[7] The widespread differences in interpretation at the judicial level primarily concern decisions as to what should be included in the record. Questions have arisen, for example, regarding the taking down by a court reporter of tape recordings played for the jury: United States v. Craig, 573 F.2d 455 (7th Cir. 1977); the portions of criminal proceedings to be recorded: Herron v. United States, 512 F.2d 439 (4th Cir. 1975); and whether the charge to the jury should be recorded as spoken by the judge or copied from the standard charge: United States v. Perkins, 498 F.2d 1054 (D.C. Cir. 1974).

which is not only unattainable, as I will demonstrate shortly, but actually undesirable[8] in view of the fact that court records are intended to provide a "clear account of the trial or hearing" (Bieber 1976, p. 27). This purpose requires both more and less than mere words, for whatever is spoken must be placed in time and space, and be assigned to a specific situation and speaker if any sense is to be made of it. For that reason, any serious attempt to apply the strict dictionary standard of word-for-word (and nothing else) to the recording of speech as it occurs naturally in court settings would ultimately result in a document that would be both virtually impenetrable to the reader and useless for the purposes for which it was intended.

To begin with, in being restricted to registering only what was spoken, a record in either electronic or written form would necessarily consist solely of a string of words[9] arranged primarily in linear fashion, bereft of punctuation, speaker identification, and nonverbal contextual cues. Features such as these are undeniably necessary for comprehension of the event depicted, yet they nevertheless are rarely if ever represented explicitly in naturally occurring speech. It would violate, for instance, the rules for normal conversational exchanges if speakers were to include verbally the commas, periods, or other orthographics which, on a written page, offer clues to meaning.[10] These clues could not, therefore, be relied upon to appear in either a strictly verbatim record, or in the transcript which resulted from it. And even should speakers identify themselves, as occasionally happens in legal proceedings, their speech when represented on paper would remain unintelligible without application in the notes and transcripts of the features mentioned above.

A sample exchange, taken from the files of my own transcripts, illustrates the problem. The colloquy represented took place among unusually conscientious counsel who were about to begin taking a deposition in a civil case. It is presented first in an undifferentiated form, then as it actually appeared in the official transcript filed with the court.[11]

---

[8] The fact of its undesirability may explain the little-recognized statutory language in 28 U.S.C.§753(b) (1976), noted above, which does not call for a "verbatim transcript."

[9] Without native speaker intuitions to help differentiate the words, the string would of course consist only of syllabic sounds.

[10] The recognition in the reporting field of the importance of punctuation is expressed in a textbook of the NSRA devoted entirely to that subject. Excerpts are as follows: "The overriding purpose of punctuation is to clarify the speaker's meaning, chiefly by separating certain words or groups of words. The comma, the semicolon, and the period merely separate, in varying degrees. Added overtones of meaning are provided by the question mark, the colon, the quotation mark, the dash, and the parenthesis." (NSRA 1971:3)

And: "*Where the speaker's manner clashes with his obviously intended meaning, we punctuate according to the meaning.*" (loc cit.)

[11] In this, as in all examples which appear in this chapter, identifying characteristics have been altered.

3. a) I guess the first item of business is to identify counsel my name is James Ballard and I represent the kaybe management company and kaybe management group Harry Emery you are the plaintiffs in the case my name is Harry Emery I rep I am counsel for all four defendants in the case

    b) MR. BALLARD: I guess the first item of business is to identify counsel. My name is James Ballard and I represent the K.B. Management Company and the K.B. Management Group.

    MR. EMERY: Harry Emery—

    MR. MARTIN: You are the plaintiffs in the case?

    MR. EMERY: My name is Harry Emery. I rep—-I am counsel for all four defendants in the case.

In both of the above passages, of course, the reader has been aided by an application of those writing conventions as to capitalization which would be immediately apparent to a listener who was a stranger to the participants.

The assumption has been made too, in the first example, that the hearer would be able to distinguish, for the most part, what constituted a word. But identification of words is not as simple an operation as it may seem, a fact which sets up a stumbling block for any who would claim that literal interpretation of "verbatim" is possible. This is because recognition of what constitutes a word in a language depends in large part on what the hearer is prepared to hear as a word, and its representation on paper depends in turn on the conventions the hearer has learned for reproducing what he or she believes to be that word. Spoken languages are notorious for their rapid-speech elisions, and so speakers and hearers must rely on one another to know the underlying forms, and how they are connected and separated. Given the right situation and mutual expectations, for instance, "Jeetyet?" is recognized by speaker and hearer alike to represent the question: "Did you eat yet?" But change either the situation or the expectations about what this or another string of sounds may or may not mean, and at least momentary misunderstanding can result. This explains the conflicts that arise when two speakers of different "accents" come together. "House," to a northern speaker, may be one short syllable (howse) but two long drawn-out syllables (haa/yuhs) for someone from the South. "Correct" separation of the syllabic sounds into a meaningful word will rely on the hearer's knowledge and/or belief in what the speaker "meant to say," and only when that is agreed upon will a message have been passed.

But if mutual expectations about what is meant are not shared, the result may be that a witness's "gross receipts," for instance, may be heard, and was, (Whitford 1898) to be "grocery seats"; a doctor's dictated phrase "male in extremis" may appear, and did, (McArdle 1981) in typed form as "male, an extremist." In cases like these, written transcripts of spoken forms could hardly be called "verbatim" if the standard of "word-for-word" also includes, as it is intended to, the added requirement of "correctness" (28 U.S.C. §753(b)(1976)), which implies exact correspondence between the words as they appear on the record and as they would ''appear'' in the speaker's mind. Nor, on a couple of grounds, could an appeal to the literal construal of verbatim permit spoken units like ''dju'' or ''whinecha''— forms common to conversation of even the best-educated speakers of English—to be translated by the hearer/reporter into their appropriate written representations. First, if verbatim requires correspondence of record to speaker meaning as well as sound, then there is a problem in that each of these phrases can represent two meanings: Do you?/Did you, and Why don't you?/Why didn't you? While context of speech will ordinarily supply differentiation between the two, an instantaneous choice, as must take place in court situations, may or may not represent the correct intention, and a literal standard of verbatimness will not be met.

If, on the other hand, the problem is finessed by simply making a phonetic record, the result is equally troublesome, for while these natural forms pass unnoticed for the most part in spoken English, no one expects to find them in written documents. Indeed, English teachers do their best to teach us to avoid them. Should they appear in a court transcript as coming from either counsel or witness, they would be generally considered inappropriate and incorrect, and should they be further combined with the verbatim features mentioned earlier, they would create a document that no one, in court or out, would ever accept. As Robin Lakoff (1981, p. 13) notes, writing more broadly on the subject of literacy:

4.   A unretouched transcript of authentic ordinary conversation is almost impen-
     etrable to us because we are so accustomed 1) to the conventions of ''ide-
     alized'' conversation as represented in writing and 2) to the oral, non-spon-
     taneous dialogue of the movies or television. We do not find false starts,
     interruptions, overlaps, and hesitations used in these forms which we do find
     in truly spontaneous discourse.

Lakoff's observations highlight another reason for the unacceptability of a word-for-word standard in court records: Americans, in this case the consumers of legal records, do not value an accurate written representation of their speech.

Implicit throughout the foregoing argument for the incompatibility of a dictionary definition of verbatim and useful court records of whatever type is the fact that a change in modalities is involved: what begins as essentially an oral event must be transformed into a written record. The importance of this problem cannot be overstated, since it involves both practical and theoretical considerations. On the theoretical side, apart from the fact that a written document stands in contrast to speech in being permanent, and thus available for storage, study, and selective review, the most salient difference between the oral and written modalities is that of context, briefly alluded to earlier. In face-to-face speech, the environment is rich in verbal and nonverbal cues which, by combining with or contrasting to the content of speech, help the participants attribute meaning to what is said.[12] The verbal cues include, among other features, false starts, stammers, hesitation sounds, speed, pitch, and intonation. The nonverbal cues include markers like eye gaze, gesture, posture, and so on. All these features of context are important in indicating to the hearer what the speaker takes seriously as information, but as might be expected, virtually all of them are lost in a shift to transcript form.

One practical problem involved in the shift of modalities is the mechanical one related to moving from a multichanneled event to a single channel of representation. In oral happenings, information is sent via a simultaneous selection of more than one of the cues discussed above. Given a too-generous loading of available channels, the result may be utter confusion, but generally the human brain, guided by past experience and present expectations of the participants and situation, is able to process the relevant cues all at once. Writing, however, whether by pen or machine, is linear in nature, and can handle only one channel at a time, so must pick and choose among the cues available for representation. This means that much of the context necessarily will be lost, and there will be discrepancies as a result between the occurrence and the fullness of its representation. In a court situation, a question or an answer, for example, delivered rapidly in a high pitch and loud voice, punctuated by gasps, or tears, or laughter, can be shown in the record as consisting only of the words spoken, thus presenting only a partial representation of what actually went on at the time. The problem is further compounded in the case of cospeech (simultaneous voices, Walker 1982a) in which even the words spoken may not appear in the record,[13] or may not appear in their actual order of occurrence. Consider the example below. I have typed it here, first using an ad hoc convention for indicating cospeech, to suggest what actually happened during the exchanges of question and answer. (The brackets show where cospeech begins; angled lines indicate no measurable pause between one voice and another.) The testimony is that of a plaintiff in a personal injury case (Bieber, 1976, p. 29).

5a.　Q.　When you approached the corner, did you look at the ⌈ traffic light? What
　　　　　color was the light—
　　　A.　　　　　　　　　　　　　　　　　　　　　　　　　　⌊Yes, I did.
　　　Q.　—when you ⌈ started to drive into the—
　　　A.　　　　　　⌊Green for me.

---

[12] Meaning as influenced by situation is the subject of study in many fields, including psychology, philosophy of language, sociology, and most particularly, sociolinguistics. For one discussion, see Gumperz, 1977.

[13] While electronic records can capture this simultaneous feature of natural speech (stenotype and shorthand cannot, being linear like typing) there is no guarantee that the transcriber will be able to distinguish either words or speakers. Even when differentiation is possible, there is as yet no accepted format for depicting it accurately. Some reporters do use a parenthetical in front of the cospeech, (such as [Interrupting] or [Interposing]) but have no conventions for showing clearly if one voice wins out, or if both persist simultaneously (Walker, 1981).

Q. —intersection? Did you see the defendant's car?
A. Yes, it was——⌐
Q.   ∠Wait a minute, please. Where was it when you first noticed
                it?⌐
A.   ∠He was about 50 feet to my left.
Q. Please, Mrs. R., let me finish before you answer. Where was defen-
     dant's car when you first saw it after your car had entered the inter-
     section?
A. I saw him⌐coming toward me fast;——
MR. N.:   └Your Honor, I object to—
A. —about ten feet from the corner.
     THE COURT: Objection sustained. Madam, just answer your lawyer's
     question; nothing else.

Next, the example is typed to represent the cospeech in a sequential fashion
(which is how I, and most reporters I interviewed customarily do it (Walker,
1981)). The elisions represent speech omitted from the original transcript.

5b. Q. When you approached the corner, did you look at the —
      A. Yes, I did.
      Q. —traffic light? What color was the light when you—
      A. Green for me.
      Q. —started to drive into the intersection? Did you see the defendant's car?
      A. Yes, it was—
      Q. Wait a minute, please. Where was it when you—
      A. He was about 50 feet to my left.
      Q. —first noticed it? Please . . . intersection?
      A. I saw him coming towards me—
           MR. N.: Your Honor, I object to—
      A. —fast; about ten feet from the corner.
           THE COURT: Objection sustained. Madam . . .

The conventions employed in this method of transcription succeed in replicating
the event insofar as indicating clearly to the reader that there was an obvious
breakdown in normal Q-A sequencing rules. The use of dashes at the beginning
of the lines shows continuation of an utterance. But while the affected questions
(in this case) are shown as continuous, this method is ambiguous as to the
continuity of the voice stream. That is, this method cannot make clear either how
many voices were speaking at once, or for how long. Of course, such a defect in
the transcript is unlikely to matter for any legal purpose. It is, however, a
deviation from the full, exact replication of the event which adherence to a strict
verbatim standard demands.

An obvious requirement for the production of either 5a or 5b above is,
naturally, that the reporter/recorder be able to hear and make sense of all these
incoming signals. If, however, all does not go well in the reporting process, and

not all the speech is heard or distinguishable, the resultant transcript might look like this:

5c. Q. When you approached the corner did you look at the traffic light? What color was the light when you started to drive into the intersection? Did you see the defendant's car?

  A. Yes. It was—

  Q. Wait a minute please. Where was it when you first noticed it? Please, Mrs. R., let me finish before you answer. Where was defendant's car . . . intersection?

  A. I saw him coming towards me fast; about ten feet from the corner.
   THE COURT: Objection sustained. Madam, just answer your lawyer's question; nothing else.

In this example, which treats counsel's questions as paramount, three of the witness's answers are missing, as is the objection made by the opposing attorney, making the judge's "Objection sustained" somewhat odd. Of course, it is extremely rare for a reporter not to be able to handle situations like the above, so neither transcripts nor records are likely to be as incomplete and obtuse as the example just offered. What is apt to happen, however, is that, in the interests of clarity of reading, the cospeech of participants, assuming it is all recorded in the original notes, is represented in the following fashion, which some reporters and lawyers consider more "correct" (Bieber, loc.cit.). This method too results in a less than accurate replication of the event, notably as to the coherence of the exchanges. The breakdown (as shown in this model) begins at the arrow. Note the oddity of the period.

5d. Q. When you approached the corner did you look at the traffic light?

  A. Yes, I did.

  Q. What color was the light . . . intersection?

  A. Green for me.

  Q. Did you see the defendant's car?

→ A. Yes, it was.

  Q. Wait a minute, please.

  A. He was about 50 feet to my left.

  Q. Where was it when you first noticed it? Please, Mrs. R., let me finish before you answer. Where was defendant's car . . . intersection?

  A. I saw him coming towards me fast; about ten feet from the corner.
   MR. N.: Your Honor, I object to—
   THE COURT: Objection sustained. Madam, just answer your lawyer's question; nothing else.

Except possibly for the idealized example as shown in 5a, each of the exchanges depicted above fails to present the whole picture of the event. One would assume, if in fact a literal standard for verbatimness were in actual operation, that partial representations like these would be totally unacceptable. But obviously that is not the case, since records of the sort shown in 5b. and 5d. above, which contain both more and less than actual words spoken in their actual sequence, are not only accepted, but expected. (Opinion among counsel is divided: some prefer b., and some d.) So why does the legal profession believe it wants and is getting a literal, word-for-word record? The answer lies, I suspect, in the equation of the word-for-word concept with information. Underlying this literate orientation of the legal system is a preference for the referential, as opposed to the expressive function of speech. It is content, not context, upon which the legal world relies for its primary source of information. This places the burden on what is said: not how it was said or what was meant to have been said, but only on the words themselves, and primarily, in fact, on words as represented in their printed form. This attitude is typical of cultures which value literacy over orality (Havelock, 1963), and in the context of legal processes, is buttressed by the fact that the only information which counts is information of *record*. Since this view of information as decontextualized content is nuclear in the institution of American law, being shared by all members of the profession, including court reporters, it plays an important part in shaping the character of all forms of the record, and has a significant effect on the belief as to what constitutes "verbatim."

The first of two forms which the record takes[14] is that indicated earlier as comprising the notes made concurrently with the event. By far the majority of the speech which a reporter hears during a legal proceeding is represented in these notes, but some is not. Those things not reflected—those which are added, subtracted or condensed—make a record either more, or less verbatim, and thus offer a greater or lesser opportunity for a reporter to exercise his or her concept of what counts as information. Since reporters do not agree among themselves as to what constitutes verbatimness, (on that subject, Bieber writes (27): "Only one thing is certain. Each court reporter arrives at his or her particular conclusion and thereafter remains immovable."), it is not surprising that this exercise arouses varying degrees of controversy.

On the level of uncontroversial at any stage of the record is the representation of features related to document design. These include, among other things, ritual events that use formulaic language (e.g., swearing in of witnesses) and speaker/event change, these features being either condensed ("Witness sworn") or added to the notes ("Cross examination by Mr. Daimler"). Still uncontroversial, but more dependent on the wishes of the lawyers and/or judge and less on the discretion of the reporter as to what enters the record, is the representation of

---

[14] For reporters who dictate their notes for a third party to transcribe, there is of course an intermediate step in the record which involves "speaking" the transcript, and giving appropriate directions to the typist as to speaker, spelling, document design, and so forth. For reporters who employ notereaders to type the transcript, an information sheet is sent along, which in addition to the above, gives translations of any special shorthand symbols employed on an ad hoc basis, and so on. In the case of original records which are tape recordings, the transcriber steps into the process at this point.

nonevidentiary events, such as discussions held off the record, conferences at the bench, and so on.[15]

Each of these deviations from strict representation in the record of the actual event is dictated by what the legal world considers to be important for its purposes. But when that guideline is further influenced by the reporter's own consciously and unconsciously held model of Standard English and those who speak it, changes to the record result that are the most open to individual application and thus to the most controversy. Among these are the changes so often characterized in the reporting field as "editing," and, in offering the greatest potential for discrepancy between what is said and what is read, they render the concept of verbatim most problematic, and merit further discussion here.

In many cases, editing of incoming speech is unconscious, as reporters, like all speakers of English, match what they hear to their own internalized model of their language, of how it ought to work, and how it ought to be spoken by speakers depending on their perceived educational and socioeconomic levels. One result of this process of matching models turned up in one of my own transcripts which I was analyzing for an earlier study (Walker 1982b).[16] The transcript was of a misdemeanor hearing involving a dispute between a hotel and a customer, and the model-related change I made is contained in the following excerpt. A prosecution witness is answering, and his speech reads as I reported it, with the correct spoken form placed in brackets.

> 6.   . . . The next thing I knew, the next thing my recollection was that, uh, she came back. They paid the bill. I heard the manager [management] say, or someone said, Well, she's finally paid—

It is true, of course, that I could simply have misheard the witness, confusing "manager" with "management." But a more probable explanation is that since I made it a practice, like many reporters, to write behind the speaker (lagging a few words behind so that sense could more easily be made of the utterances), when I heard the witness say "or someone said," I transformed the faceless, person-less noun of agency into a single human agent, capable of being present and saying something. This interpretation would better fit my model of how English grammar works.

In the foregoing example, it was my own personal model of English which was influential, and my knowledge of the speaker's social niche played no part

---

[15] Whether or not a discussion is considered by the participants to be on or off the record may itself be controversial, but its parenthetical representation in the transcript (e.g. [Discussion off the record]) is not. Some states have attempted to standardize the use and wording of parentheticals. See, for example, the Administrative Office of the Courts, The Maryland Reporters' Manual (1982).

[16] I discovered this example while doing a close comparison of my transcript with both my stenotype notes and the audio recording I routinely made of each job I took. Like other reporters who use two systems of recording, my paper tapes were the official record of the proceedings and thus, I did not always refer to the audiotape while typing the transcript. This accounts for the fact that errors of the type discussed here could appear in a transcript.

that I am aware of in what entered the record. (If it had, I would have been more ready to hear "management" as a hypercorrect form.) But as a general rule, the influence of perceived social characteristics is very strong in creating a climate for what hearers "hear." A witness who holds a Ph.D. in philosophy, for instance, will likely be heard by all listeners, including reporters, to ask, "Where are you going?" using full forms of the verbs, in spite of the fact that in normal speech, even for well-educated speakers of Standard English, the "are" disappears, leaving the actual spoken phrase "Where' you goin(g)" (with or without the final "g"), which is how the high school dropout will tend to be heard to say it.

For all speakers, however, whatever their perceived categories, court reporters, knowing that the finished form of the record is a written one, regularly and unconsciously follow the literate orientation of their profession, and edit most of the common phonological variances of spoken language into the form that is expected in the written version. Changes from "gonna" to "going to," "hafta" to "have to," "ever'" to "every" are examples of this type of unconscious editing which, generally speaking, passes unnoticed, and is noncontroversial. It is the conscious editing—that which is perceived as "correcting"—that is the most irregular, and occasions much argument in and out of the fields of law and reporting. It is with some justification that it can be considered discretionary.

The fact is that reporters are trained to edit. There is no real consensus in the reporting field about how much editing should be done, but the view expressed in an educational publication of the National Shorthand Reporters Association (NSRA, 1962, p. 26) is as follows:[17]

7.   To edit or not to edit is not the question; every reporter does it in greater or less degree. It is well settled that the reporter should make every effort to eliminate obviously bad grammar from his transcript. The only questions are—whose utterances shall enjoy the privilege of being edited? and how bad must grammar be to warrant the reporter's departing from a strictly verbatim report? These are the questions that each reporter must answer for himself. Some judges and lawyers like to be edited and some do not.

Note that this quotation makes the following points: (1) editing is done as a matter of course; (2) editing is differential as to speaker; (3) editing is ad hoc to the situation and reporter, and what the reporter knows about the intended reader (lawyer or judge); and finally, (4) sophisticated readers of transcripts are aware of the options of editing. Taken together, these points suggest that the National Shorthand Reporters Association (NSRA) guidelines implicitly recognize the points made earlier in this chapter that "strictly verbatim" is in practice neither an attainable nor a desirable standard.

---

[17] The most recent reprinting of this text, which also contains the Budlong references, is 1982. This would seem to indicate that the NSRA still subscribes to all positions taken in the original edition.

The observation by the NSRA that some judges and lawyers like to be edited and some do not highlights the fact that there are at least two classes of courtroom speakers: (1) lawyers and judges, some of whom like (i.e., expect) to be edited and some who do not; and (2) witnesses, whose likes and dislikes are immaterial. This necessitates the application of different standards of editing to the two classes. Witnesses are members of that class who as a rule do not "enjoy the privilege of being edited." Their speech is thus less likely to have informal or ungrammatical speech forms rendered by the court reporter into Standard English, although even here one can find apparently contradictory prescriptions in standard court reporting publications. One widely distributed manual of the NSRA quotes the following advice (Hotchner, 1971, p. 7):

8. The sworn testimony of witness [sic] is, of course, reproduced exactly as given.

In the NSRA text on English, a different point of view is presented (Budlong, 1962, p. 4):

9. No one will deny that such errors [false starts, bad grammar, and repetitions] on the part of lawyers should be corrected; and in the opinion of the writer it is entirely permissible that they be *corrected in the testimony of well-educated or expert witnesses*. (Emphasis added).

This attribute of being "well-educated" plays an important part in the operation of a verbatim standard. In the same article, Budlong goes on to write, under the heading "Judges and Lawyers are Supposed to be Educated Men" (4):

10. Another important thing to remember is that all judges and most if not all lawyers are men of education, and they will resent having attributed to them in stenographic reports ungrammatical and carelessly-phrased remarks. Witnesses often are illiterate, and as a rule they do not see the reports of their testimony. The average judge or lawyer is apt to consider a slightly edited report of his utterances a more faithful report than one which is photographically literal.

The elements which bear on conscious editing as mentioned in these quotations above (8, 9, and 10)—status of the speaker in relation to giving sworn testimony, level of education, and probable readership of the record—all affect class membership, and thus the standard of verbatim which is applied. One result of class membership, however, which is nowhere in the literature made explicit, is that in the case of witnesses, application of the verbatim standard is unilateral. Witnesses have no say in trial records as to how their speech is represented.[18] Lawyers and judges, on the other hand, belong to that class of courtroom speak-

---

[18] This is not true of the deposition procedure (giving of pretrial testimony under oath, usually in civil cases). Witnesses have the right in deposition to read their testimony after it is typed, and offer written changes which, however, must be justified.

ers which enjoys editing privileges that extend from being supplied with corrected versions of their literary quotations[19] to more subtle alterations that "give just the right touch at the right spot" (NSRA 1962, p. 2).[20] Furthermore, they can, and do, make their wishes known.

A corollary issue to the existence of differing classes of speakers is whether or not ungrammaticality is considered to be information. The consensus among both court reporters and counsel, as expressed in the literature and the research I have done, is that it is information if a *witness* is ungrammatical; it is not information if the ungrammatical speaker is a lawyer or a judge. This notion is apparently influenced by the status of witness speech as sworn testimony which, as evidence, must not be altered, while the utterances of speakers not under oath—although their language may indeed be crucial to the issues of the case— is not under the same constraints in being recorded and transcribed.

The implication here is that sworn testimony must be represented more faithfully, be more "verbatim," than unsworn colloquy, but again this precept is clouded somewhat by the issue mentioned earlier of a reporter's perceptions of a model of English appropriate to a speaker. Sworn or unsworn, educated speakers are expected to use grammatically correct speech, and accordingly, for some reporters on some occasions, the speech of some witnesses is rendered by the same rules applied to lawyers. In most cases, however, the speech of witnesses is perceived as more sacred, with the concepts of sworn testimony, evidence, content, and grammaticality all seen as tied together. The result is that editing of their testimony, if done consciously at all, is kept to a minimum, consonant—as in all other editing practices of whatever kind—with the *sense* of the utterance. The fact that it is the sense of the utterance that matters, and not its presentation, is crucial to preparation of a record, and is indicative of the belief of the legal world that speech is for information, and information is content, not context, of speech. Since the purpose of the record of legal proceedings is to transmit and preserve information in a clear and usable form, it is not surprising that features of individual speech style such as false starts, hesitation sounds, pauses, and so on are often considered peripheral and unimportant as opposed to meaningful.[21]

---

[19] Both NSRA-accredited schools which I attended advocated this policy, each, in fact, suggesting that a copy of Bartlett's *Quotations* was a necessary part of any court reporter's working library.

[20] The full quotation is: "Editing should be deft and inconspicuous. It should give just the right touch at the right spot, with as close adherence as practicable to the *exact words* of the speaker. The reporter should never forget that he is concerned with the discourse of another, rather than his own." (NSRA 1962, p. 2).

[21] As one federal judge put it, when questioned about transcripts that were verbatim to the extent of including the two contextual features of hesitation sounds and pause indications (Walker, 1981, p. 51): "I wouldn't stand for it. The court reporter would be interpolating." Since interpolate means to "insert additional or false material into a text" (American Heritage Dictionary, New College Edition), this implies that he, like many another native speaker of English, ignored the reality of these features and regarded them as noninformation. As noninformation, in the literate view, they have no place in a transcript.

When this happens, when idiosyncrasies of personal style are viewed as uninformative, the tendency even of those reporters who hew to a "strict" construction of the verbatim concept is to edit.

This was demonstrated in a fairly conclusive way by the published report (Greenwood, 1983) of a recently concluded study by the Federal Judicial Center of alternative reporting systems in the federal courts.[22] Since the proposed alternate system of electronic recording is widely viewed in the court reporting field as potentially threatening to the existence of their profession,[23] and since accuracy was an important issue in the study, the assumption could be made that an especially stringent effort on both sides would have been made to record everything that was said in as much detail as occurred. "Verbatim" could be expected to be construed as strictly as possible. Yet the results showed that in a random 680–page subsample of 2,483 proofread pages (out of a total population of 35,630 pages), there were 6,951 discrepancies[24] between the master audiotapes that were used as controls, and the resultant transcripts (Greenwood, 1983). Of the 13 "categories of error" assigned to identify these discrepancies for analysis, four dealt explicitly with omissions and accounted for 42 percent of the "errors" made. Of this speech which was generally described as omitted, 46 percent was designated as "verbal tics" and "false starts", contextual categories generally regarded by the reporter, as I have shown, to be noninformative. This would seem to be an impressive indication of how ingrained is the practice of filtering out whatever is considered by the hearer to be noninformation, with the resultant unconscious skewing of a "strict" verbatim concept. The explanation for this is connected to the fact that the features omitted in the test, contextual as well as phonetic variations of speech, are generally regarded as mere errors of perfor-

---

[22] The testing of electronic recording as a possible alternative to stenographic recording was mandated by section 401 of the Federal Courts Improvement Act of 1982 (96 Stat. 25,56–57) and was conducted in 12 project courts. The protocols and results are reported in Greenwood, 1983.

[23] The NSRA hired lobbyists to press the cause of stenotype reporting; issued legislative/regulatory alerts (e.g., Alert, 10/16/83) to its members on the progress of the test. Articles in the house organ, National Shorthand Reporter (NSR) appeared often, and continue to do so as of this date (fall, 1984).

[24] The ratio noted in the text of the Federal Judicial Center report (Greenwood 48) of 680 pages to 6951 discrepancies would seem to translate roughly to 10 "errors" per page. But these figures are misleading for two reasons. First, each page studied represented a summary of discrepancies from *both* electronically and stenographically produced transcripts of a matched portion of the proceedings. Second, variations in document design (margins, spacing, transcription conventions, etc.) create differences in the number of pages needed to represent the same extracted portion; i.e., what might take one page for one transcriber might take one-and-a-half or two for another. This means that the true ratio would be at least 1360 (680 × 2) to 6951, or at the most, an average of 5 "errors" per "page." This is, of course, still a noteworthy number of deviations, but most of them (89%) were found by a panel of jurists and lawyers to be of no consequence. The FJC report was silent as to the significance of the remaining 11% which were considered to be important—i.e., nothing was said as to what type of discrepancy had what potential legal consequence.

mance that are neither germane to the proceedings nor a reflection of the speaker's underlying grammatical competence. This makes more understandable the
alteration of such features, whether by omission or by "correction" in the notes
and/or transcript, since it is the message and not its presentation that is seen as
crucial. As one reporter phrased it, speaking for her firm's policy as to representation of these performance "slips":

11.   When we know what they're saying (i.e., meaning), we put that down
      (Walker, 1981, p. 25).[25]

In other words, in the verbatim reporter's view, form should reflect meaning,
and it is the reporter who takes the crucial steps in matching one to the other. It is
the reporter who makes decisions about when and whether to edit—about how to
represent the speech of the speaker—based on his or her own training, and
beliefs, and the desires, if known, of the prospective reader. The guiding principle, of course, is always the literate legal tradition of what constitutes information, modified by the awareness that while the purpose of the record is to
preserve the event, the purpose of the transcript is to make the record available
for consumption.

And therein lies the explanation, the justification, of the verbatim concept in
the American institution of law: the constructs of information, event, and consumption. What a verbatim record is expected to supply, through the agency of
the court reporter, is a "correct statement of the testimony taken and proceedings
had" (28 U.S.C. §753(b)(1976). It is *information* in the form of testimony, not
words alone, that is to be translated from the oral to the written form. Testimony
involves words which are attributed to a certain speaker in a certain time and
certain space, with speaker-intended meaning attached. And the words, time,
space, and speaker all meet in the *event* which is to be preserved in a *consumable*
form: the written record of the legal proceeding. Understanding the verbatim
concept then, requires an appeal not to the dictionary and its literal definition of
"word-for-word," but to the customs and expectations of its users. It is an
operational definition that expects not a mechanical reproduction of every word
spoken, but a faithful representation, rather, of the events that are considered by
the legal world to be information. Such a requirement necessarily renders a
literally constituted "verbatim record" a contradiction in terms.

In the beginning of this chapter I said that the court reporter would figure
prominently in the discussion, since it is through his or her understanding of both
language and task that "verbatim" finds its definition. In this claim lie the
elements which link language and institutional power. It is through the power of

---

[25] Dialect features are particularly susceptible to this practice, "idear," "aks," "goin'," being
rendered as "idea," "ask," and "going," respectively. On this subject of dialect, Budlong (1962,
p. 5) writes: "It goes without saying that the testimony of ignorant or illiterate witnesses should be
literally rendered, but literalness should not extend to the point of dialect if the language has a
reasonable equivalent in ordinary English words. After all, the shorthand reporter is not a novelist."

the institution that the occasion for discourse arises at all, that classes of speakers are delineated, that event and speech are preserved. And it is the need for preservation of the event that occasions the reporter's presence. As the official interpreter of the legal institution's constructs with relation to the proceeding being memorialized, the court reporter acts as a language broker between the oral event and its written representation. And it is his or her concept of "verbatim" which provides the filter through which what one *says* becomes what one *said*. This is a potentially powerful observation, particularly in view of the fact that the filter does not operate in like fashion for all who must pass through it.

There are, of course, practical implications which flow from this fact, one of which is that if, as a pilot study which I carried out in 1981 suggests, readers make judgments about speakers' credibility based on their speech as represented in writing, then a differential treatment of courtroom speakers in a transcript might prove to matter. The questions are, however, to whom? And how critically? My own research has suggested the answers to those questions, but further inquiry needs to be made. The issues involved are complex, and made more so by the fact that human agency is involved. What is important here and now is to separate myth from reality in relation to the verbatim concept in the institution of American law. Only by recognizing what in fact is involved can what is hoped for be achieved.

REFERENCES

Cases and Statutes
United States v. Craig, 573 F.2d 455 (7th Cir. 1977)
United States v. DiCanio, 245 F.2d 713,715 (2d Cir. 1957)
United States v. Perkins, 498 F.2d 1054 (D.C. Cir. 1974)
United States v. Piascik, 559 F.2d 545 (9th Cir. 1977)
United States v. Smith, 433 F.2d 149,151 (5th Cir. 1970)
Herron v. United States, 512 F.2d 439 (4th Cir. 1975)
Stephens v. United States, 289 F.2d 308 (5th Cir. 1961)
Caffrey v. Chem-Ionics Corp., 419 P.2d 809,811 (Wash. 1966)
In re DLF, 176 N.W. 2d 486,488 (S.D. 1970)
28 U.S.C. §753(b)(1976); Federal Courts Improvement Act of 1982, Public Law 97–164, §401, 96
    Stat. 25, 56–57 (1982).

Articles and Texts
ALERT (Legislative/Regulatory). (October 16, 1983). Vienna, VA: National Shorthand Reporters
    Association.
American Heritage Dictionary, New College Edition. (1975). New York: American Heritage Pub-
    lishing Company.
Bieber, S. (1976). *Let verbatim be your guide.* In NSR National Shorthand Reporter, April 1976, p.
    27–29. Vienna, VA: National Shorthand Reporters Association.
Budlong, P. E. (1962). *Editing court proceedings and speeches.* In Professional Education Series:
    English, p. 4–14. NSRA.

Federal rules of appellate procedure. (1975). In *Federal rules of civil procedure.* p. 149–180. Mineola, NY: The Foundation Press, Inc.

Greenwood, J. M., et al. (1983). A comparative evaluation of stenographic and audiotape methods for United States district court reporting. Washington, DC: Federal Judicial Center (typescript edition).

Gumperz, J. J. (1977). *Sociocultural knowledge in conversational inference.* In M. Saville-Troike (Ed.), *Georgetown University round table in language and linguistics* (p. 191–211). Washington, DC: Georgetown University Press.

Havelock, E. (1963). *Preface to Plato.* Cambridge, MA: Harvard University Press.

Hotchner, S., C. S. R. (1971). *How to take a good deposition.* In *Deposition form book* (Rev., p. 5–9). Madison, WI: NSRA.

Lakoff, R. (1981). *Literacy in a non-literate age.* In *fforum III,* 1. (p. 13–14). Ann Arbor: MI: The English Composition Board.

The Maryland Reporters' Manual: Administrative Office of the Courts. (1982).

McArdle, G. C., M. D. (1981). *Not quite what the doctor said.* In *Verbatim, The Language Quarterly.* (Reprinted in January 1982 NSR National Shorthand Reporter, p. 49. Vienna, VA: NSRA.)

Professional English Series: English. (1962). Vienna, VA: NSRA. (Fourth printing, 1982).

Punctuation for Shorthand Reporters. (1971). Madison, WI: NSRA.

Walker, A. G. (1981). *Transcription conventions: Do they matter? A sociolinguistic study of a legal process.* Unpublished manuscript. Georgetown University.

Walker, A. G. (1982a). *Patterns and implications of cospeech in a legal setting.* In Robert DiPietro (Ed.), *Linguistics and the professions* (p. 101–112). Norwood, NJ: Ablex.

Walker, A. G. (1982b). *Discourse rights of witnesses: Their circumscription in trial.* Sociolinguistic Working Paper No. 95. Austin, TX: Southwest Development Laboratory.

Waltz, J. R., & Kaplan, J. (1982). *Evidence: Making the Record.* Mineola, NY: The Foundation Press, Inc.

Whitford, W. (1898). *Defective hearing or mishearing in its relation to shorthand writing.* In *The Phonographic Magazine,* Cincinnati, Ohio. (Reprinted in January 1982 NSR National Shorthand Reporter, p. 46–49. Vienna, VA: NSRA.)

11. Some Functions of Spatial Positioning and Alignment in the Organization of Courtroom Discourse*

Susan U. Philips
University of Arizona

The purpose of this paper is to consider some ways in which the nonverbal context of speech provides information about the social organization of discourse, which in turn is used in making sense out of courtroom speech. We will consider how spatial positioning and alignment, and changes in positioning and alignment, provide information regarding the communicative roles of participants and changes in communicative roles, particularly changes associated with the boundaries of speech events. It will be argued that the ability to make inferences about communicative role and to use those inferences in interpreting utterances depends on several different kinds of knowledge. Besides knowledge about courtroom-specific positioning and alignment, which if known by the observer, will facilitate the interpretation of courtroom speech, knowledge of general *cultural* patterns in the United States and knowledge of general *human* patterns relating positioning and alignment to communicative roles also facilitate such interpretation. At the same time, the relation between courtroom specific organization of nonverbal behavior and more general cultural patterns in the organization of nonverbal behavior, including status differentiated patterns, enable us to see the ways in which the legal system participates in a wider cultural system for the organization of talk.

SPEECH EVENT

The term ''speech event'' has for some time served as an anchoring concept for those interested in explaining patterned variation in language use through reference to features of the social context in which speech occurs. In Hymes' (1972) discussion of the concept of speech event the term referred to activity bounded in space and time from the point of view of members of the culture whose activity it was. The type of activity that might come to be labeled as a speech event and the criteria used by members of a culture to define when such a thing had occurred (including when it began and ended) was treated as that which was to be deter-

* An earlier version of this paper was presented at the 1977 American Anthropological Association Meetings in Houston. I am grateful to Jean Florman for drawing the figures of courtroom spatial organization to scale.

mined through the investigation of members' behavior and knowledge. But it was clear that some aspect of speaking itself ought to be criterial, otherwise the event could not properly be seen as a *speech* event.

One key question to be answered (Hymes, 1964) was: How are various societies similar and different in the way in which they define communicative events, and why? The salience of cognitive concerns, that is, a concern with the difference between the "emic" criteria used by a native speaker and the "etic" criteria that an investigator would begin research with, is apparent in such a question. The concept of speech event, like the proposed dimensions of speech events (e.g., channel, code, participants) that could be relevant in defining them, was intended as a starting point. It was intended as an etic investigative device to be used in initiating inquiry that would eventually yield emic descriptions, which in turn would expand the etic framework of investigation (Hymes, 1964).

For the most part, that concern with the difference between the investigator's and the members' perspective has not been maintained in descriptions of cultural differences in language use. Although we tend to assume that the activity described, for example, a greeting (Irvine, 1974), or a 'kabary' (Keenan, 1974) constitutes an isolatable event from the natives' point of view, it is not this assumption that is explicitly treated as to be demonstrated in the description. Often, we are satisfied that the activity in question can be labeled, with either a native term or a term from our own language.

While the cognitive concerns reflected in Hymes' writings have not often been explicitly addressed by people doing ethnography of communication, the interest in speech events has continued (e.g., Duranti, 1983; Irvine, 1979). There has been some confusion in the use of the concept, however, in part because it was deliberately given no operational definition to begin with, but has been applied as if there was one. This has led to a situation where the same speaking activity (e.g., "the dozens" in black culture) has been referred to as both a speech act and a speech event, without attention to the sense in which it might be both, or why one term rather than the other should apply.

Although Hymes drew the term speech act from Austin's discussion of the accomplishment of actions through utterances (Austin, 1965), and intended to retain the sense of performance suggested by Austin, he identified the speech act as something that occurs within a speech event. Thus a speech event could be made up of a number of speech acts, although it could also consist of a single speech act (Hymes, 1972). The speech act in this way has come to be viewed as a unit within a larger unit, which raises the possibility of cultural variation in the internal organization of speech events. There has been little agreement among ethnographers of communication in decisions regarding the level of the organization to which to apply each term. One reason for this is that even clearly bounded speech situations, for example, a classroom or courtroom, are part of larger interactional systems that vary in complexity, and vary in the complexity of their internal organization.

What applications of the term speech event often *do* have in common is that regulation of interaction is routinized and predictable with express norms regarding who can talk when about what, a boundedness, and an internal sequestial structure (e.g., Philips, 1974; Sherzer, 1974; Irvine, 1974; Duranti, 1981).

In American society, activity in prototypical public settings for various public institutions relies on positioning of participants for evidence of expected and actual speaker-hearer roles, and on often abrupt coordinated changes in the positioning and alignment of participants as evidence of *boundaries* to interactional units—units of the sort often called speech events in the literature.

Here we examine these functions of positioning and alignment in a group of procedures in an Arizona state court of general jurisdiction. But we will argue later for similar functions of positioning and alignment in all societies.

A criminal defendant's experiences with and in the courts begins with the Initial Appearance, where the defendent is informed of the charge against him or her. This is followed by the Arraignment, the Trial or the Change of Plea, and the Sentencing. The trial itself ideally consists of a jury selection, opening statements by prosecution and defense, presentation of evidence, closing statements by prosecution and defense and the jury decision. Each of these activities is in turn comprised of smaller units of activity.

In practice each stage of the proceedings for the criminal defendant except the trial are held in bunches. Thus in a given session a judge will ''do'' two dozen initial Appearances, while later a series of Arraignments will be held at a daily time. This is true of Sentencings and Changes of Plea as well. As we will see, the procedures form a class, both behaviorally and conceptually, in their shared pattern of use of positioning and alignment.

POSITIONING AND ALIGNMENT

When the positioning of those present in a bounded speech situation is considered in isolation from other sources of information, as in Figure 11.1 (Positioning), it is evident that positioning in itself does not provide very much information about the organization of interaction. It is possible to see mainly that each individual is closer to some than to others. This might lead us to infer those who are closest to one another are most likely to be engaged in communicating with one another, if we consider that as the range or distance between parties increases, the difficulty in exchanging information increases because of the range limits of our eyes and our ears. However, where all parties are within 75 feet of one another, as can be assumed here, it is also possible that all persons are involved in a single focused encounter, and mutually regulating their behavior vis-a-vis one another.

When information about the direction in which the bodies of participants are facing, that is, their alignment, is added to our information on positioning, as in Figure 11.2 (Positioning and Alignment), the number and composition of interactional groupings possible is considerably reduced.

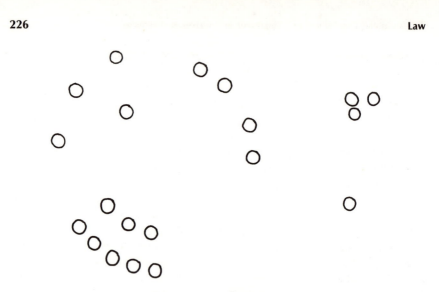

Figure 11.1.   Positioning

Those in the top part of the diagram, in groupings A, B, and C, have mutual visual access to the fronts of one another's bodies, except for the possibility of interference from E who can constitute a visual blocking of access between persons in grouping A and persons in groupings C orB. The people in these groupings are aligned so as to be more able to communicate with individuals in *other* groups, rather than with those with whom they are facing in the same direction. In other words, those in grouping B cannot communicate with one another as readily as with those in grouping A or C. This is because members of

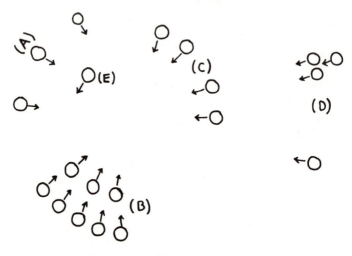

Figure 11.2.   Positioning and Alignment

the *same* grouping do not directly face one another. Those who face one another have mutual access to one another's sensory receptors and signaling sources because both our receiving and our sending sources are oriented from the front of the body. The eyes and the ears face forward. The mouth projects voice from the front, and facial expression and gesture are visible primarily from the front of a person's body.

Those in grouping D in the lower part of the diagram (Figure 11.2) lack visual access to the fronts of the bodies in grouping C and those in grouping C can't see those in grouping D at all within the 180 degrees visual sweep they can make by turning their necks. Grouping D's access to B and E may be further blocked by C.

Those who face one another are more likely to direct speech to one another because they have maximal access to one another's sensory receptors and signaling sources. It is true that the ears are omnidirectional, and can pick up sounds from all around a person, so that one can hear people facing away from one, either in front or behind. But the importance of visual information in the regulation of talk, particularly talk in a speech situation where more than two people are present, has become increasingly evident. We use our eyes to locate a speaker, to distinguish her or him from others, because we make sense out of talk partly through knowing "who" it is that is speaking.[1]

When we locate a speaker, we inform that person that we are attending by our gaze; hence, speakers look at addressees to determine where they are looking. In brief, we determine who is paying attention to who visually.

We also determine when a speaker is coming to the end of a turn in part through information sent and received in the visual channel (Duncan, 1972; Kendon, 1967). And finally, we recognize that gesture and facial expression convey information that modfies our interpretation of a speaker's speech. For all of these reasons, we usually face the people we address with speech, and almost always face those who respond to us, that is, who *exchange* speech with us.

When we consider an actual situation in which the particular positioning and alignment considered could occur, as in Figure 11.3. (Civil Trial), a diagram of an arrangement that could occur in an Arizona trial, and we know who actually talks to whom, some further insights into the role of positioning and alignment in the organization of interaction may be added. First, except for members of the public who comprise the audience in this scene, and the court recorder, those whose view of others might be blocked are elevated. The second row of the jury is elevated, as are the witness, the judge, and the clerk; the judge is highest of all.

It does not follow from this, however, that all who have visual access to one another talk to one another. It is only where there is a direct line of mutual visual

---

[1] Those who have transcribed tapes of multiparty conversations know how difficult it can be to identify speakers on the basis of voice quality, and when we decide who is the speaker on the basis of who has said what in the past, we are imposing our theory of who is likely to say what on the data.

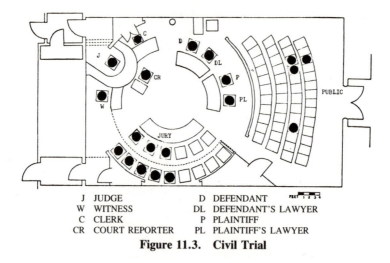

J   JUDGE   D   DEFENDANT
W   WITNESS   DL   DEFENDANT'S LAWYER
C   CLERK   P   PLAINTIFF
CR   COURT REPORTER   PL   PLAINTIFF'S LAWYER

Figure 11.3.   Civil Trial

access that a mutual exchange of talk occurs to any extent. In other words, the
bulk of talk flows between witnesses and lawyers, and the judge and the lawyers.
It is true that the talk is for the benefit of the jury, and it is interesting to note that
lawyers asking questions of witnesses, or addressing juries have license to roam
from their allocated position, so that they may directly face the jury at whatever
distance they choose. But in fact, when questioning a witness, a lawyer far more
often faces and gazes at the witness than at the jury. Witnesses often have
difficulty facing and gazing at jurors, in answering questions posed by lawyers.
Their tendency is to face the lawyer who posed the question.

But one cannot assume that those most directly facing one another at the
closest range will, in fact, talk to one another. The clerk does not as a rule engage
in exchanges of talk with the lawyers as a part of official courtroom proceedings;
the defendants do not engage in dialogue with the judge or the witness; and the
court reporter rarely speaks to anyone during court proceedings.

Positioning and alignment alone do not tell us who will actually talk to whom
in a given speech situation (although once we know who talks to whom, we can
predict who will speak on the basis of positioning). Instead, positioning and
alignment indicate the varying degrees of visual and auditory access persons
have to one another, and thus the degree of probability that they will exchange
talk with one another.

We infer the likelihood of particular sender-receiver relations in part on the
basis of awareness of biologically-based limitations on sending and receiving
relations. Our expectations here are also based on culture-wide principles of
spatial positioning and alignment in relation to communicative roles in public
institutional scenes. Thus in the church, the classroom, and the courtroom the
person controlling and regulating the activity (be it teacher, judge, or minister)
has his or her back to a wall, often with secret exits used only by him and a few

privileged helpers. She or he faces those whose participation is being regulated, often in a position elevated over that of others, and facing the door through which "the public" comes. The official representative of the institution who controls the interaction is thus in the maximal position of visual and auditory access to all present in the situation, as well as entries and exits.

CHANGES IN POSITIONING

In turning now to a consideration of shifts or changes in spatial position, I will attempt to demonstrate that even in a courtroom, where positioning seems relatively fixed, a good deal of shifting goes on, and this shifting is correlated with boundaries of interactional units.

First of all, in the Arizona state courts of general jurisdiction, the stages of a legal case are separated in time. Thus the units of interaction that a criminal defendant can be involved in, discussed earlier, do not follow immediately one upon another for a given defendant. Those who are necessary participants to the entire sequence of procedures—that is, those who are positioned before the bar—all eventually leave the courtroom after a given stage has ended, and reassemble for the next stage at a later date. This is the change of positioning of the greatest magnitude that signals the boundedness of the interactional units which constitute a criminal proceeding.

Second, as a comparison of Figure 11.3 and 11.4 (Initial Appearance), indicates, stages can differ in the basic positioning of participants, so that when parties leave and return for a new stage of criminal proceeding, this new stage may also be signaled by a change in positioning.

Figure 11.4 is a diagram of the first court procedure encountered by a criminal defendant. As indicated earlier, a number of defendants appear in court at the same time for this procedure. This first stage is referred to as the Initial Appearance. While the sequence of events comprising the Initial Appearance varies from state to state, in the court session diagrammed here, the County Commissioner, functioning in the position of a judge, was informing defendants of the charges against them, appointing lawyers for those who did not have lawyers and could not afford to hire them, and either setting bail or allowing the defendants to be freed from custody without bail. Note in Figure 11.4 that the prisoners sat in the jury box, a sheriff's officer sat in the witness box, and the lawyers sat apart from their actual or prospective clients.

The spatial arrangement of a criminal trial, a later stage, is similar to that diagrammed in Figure 11.3, and here the positioning is obviously quite different. The differences in positioning between Figures 11.3 and 11.4 are related to differences in the roles that are relevant for a given stage (i.e., a jury has no function in an Initial Appearance and there are no witnesses), and to differences in the relationships among participants.

I do not mean to suggest that the spatial arrangement for each stage of the

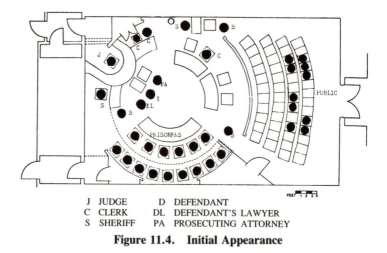

J JUDGE   D   DEFENDANT
C CLERK   DL DEFENDANT'S LAWYER
S SHERIFF   PA PROSECUTING ATTORNEY

Figure 11.4. Initial Appearance

criminal proceeding is unique. The arrangement I have seen at sentencings is basically the same as that diagrammed in Figure 11.4, except that the state/ prosecution lawyer does not stand before the judge during the sentencing. My point here is that in addition to a positional shifting of going away and coming back associated with junctures between stages in a criminal proceeding, there will also sometimes be a rearrangement of participants at the next stage.

In addition, within a given court session, repetitions of the same stage or unit of activity can occur, and the beginning and end of each repetition is also marked by positional shifts. For example, when a defendant is brought before the judge, as in Figure 11.4, his name is called and he moves from a seated position in the jury box to a standing position just in front of the judge. He is joined there by his lawyer on his left, and by the prosecution lawyer on his right, and all three face the judge. When all three move away from this positioning, the Initial Appearance is over for that particular defendant, and the process is repeated with a different defendant. Even though the same lawyer may repeatedly represent the state, that lawyer repeatedly returns to the lawyers' table when the defendant turns away from the judge, only to come before the judge again after the next defendant comes before the bench. This same pattern of positional shifting also occurs when defendants are sentenced, when they are arraigned, and when they plead guilty.

In the Arizona State Court of Appeals, several appeals will be heard in a single session, just as multiple Initial Appearances or Sentencings occur in a single session in the lower courts. The spatial arrangement of the Court of Appeals courtrooms is similar to that in the trial courts, and here too the spatial replacing of two opponent lawyers with two more marks the end of one appeal and the beginning of another.

In these various courtroom proceedings, then, the beginnings and endings of repetitions of the same named speech event or unit are marked by changes in the position of some, but not all, of the participants who assume speaking roles.

Positional changes are also associated with junctures between smaller units of interaction within the stages that have been mentioned thus far. For example, among defendants making their Initial Appearances before the court, those who already have lawyers experience a slightly different proceeding than those who do not have lawyers. When those who have lawyers go before the bench to be charged, their lawyers are by their side (literally) from the time they are initially so positioned, and they are not questioned about their financial solvency. Defendants who do not have lawyers initially stand before the judge with no one to their left, while they are questioned about whether they can afford a lawyer and asked if they want one appointed. Only after they have indicated they want a lawyer does the public defender move to stand to the defendant's left, at which point the judge initiates a new topic of questioning. In this way, the point at which a defendant acquires a lawyer, and the point at which the lawyer may engage in exchange of talk with both client and judge is marked by his arrival before the bench, even though both the public defender and the judge, and possibly the defendant, know before this occurs that this lawyer will be appointed.

The testimony of a given witness during a trial is similarly marked by the witness's change in positioning from a seat in the public area to a seat in the witness box, at the beginning of the testimony. And the end of that testimony is marked by the departure of the witness from the witness box.

In these examples of positional shifts, the changes that occur take place when there is a change in the specific individuals who must engage in an exchange of talk. The initiation of these exchanges is associated with a change in positioning that facilitates or increases the mutual visual and auditory access of those involved in the exchange.

There are several reasons why such shifts in positioning are viewed by participants as marking boundaries of interactional units. First, they are correlated with cessation and initiation of exchanges of talk, and the changing of positions itself creates a hiatus in the flow of talk.

Second, where old parties to talk "leave" and new parties to talk "arrive," the talk involving the new parties cannot build on or refer back to the talk that has gone before, where it is assumed that the new parties have not heard what went before, so the structure of the talk itself must change.

Finally, the fact that such shifts do signal junctures for reasons already given means that they can stand for or signal a juncture, even when shifts in positioning are not strictly necessary to accomplish visual and auditory access that will be sufficient for successful communication. In other words, positional changes are used as a framing device (Goffman, 1974) to convey to those present that a juncture is occurring. Consider, for example, the shifts in positioning that occur during the oral arguments of an appeal. Each lawyer has her or his own table, with the appellant's lawyer on the left and the appellee's lawyer on the right, and they take turns standing before the podium between them when they speak to the judges. It is not really necessary for them to stand, or to stand in the middle, for the judges to see and hear them. But these changes in positioning signal the initiation of different stages in the oral argument.

Positional shifts are basically motivated by changes in the role relationships among those present in the same speech situation. Since such changes in role relationships often accomplish junctures in speech activity, the positional shifts required by the changes come to be associated with the occurrence of junctures. Given this association between positional shifts and junctures, such shifts may be used to convey junctures where role relationships change, even though no positional shift is necessary to accomplish the change. In other words, positional shifts can be used iconically to stand for an interactional juncture.

We are all equipped with the same sensory receptors and signaling sources so that we must be within a certain range of one another and face-to-face to gain visual and auditory access to one another. In all societies some rearrangements of who communicates with whom that require changes in positioning to achieve mutual sensory access will also initiate a new context for speech, if only because the shared basis of understanding is altered as those who exchange speech changes. This creates a juncture. Our shared biological make-up, then, creates a likelihood of cross-cultural similarities in the interpretation of the relation between changes in spatial positioning and the social organization of talk.

At the same time, here too we find that cultural models of boundary marking in large scale events in American society also contribute to our ability to comprehend and participate in such events. Thus, changes in positioning that mark discourse unit boundaries in churches, classrooms, and courtrooms often involve everyone beginning and ending, coming and leaving at the same time, so that junctures are sharply marked. In other cultures, such boundaries are not always so sharply marked (Philips, 1974).

There are also nonuniversal expressions of *status differences* reflected in the pattern of movement, which hold for a variety of public situations. Thus the judge stays in one place, the spatial position of control, while lawyers and their clients pass through. In a similar manner, students pass through a teacher's classroom so that a new group arrives each year. And a common bureaucratic pattern in American society is one in which the bureaucrat stays in one place and serves a line of clients one by one.

CONCLUSION

In some settings such as the courtroom, then, positioning and alignment and their changes provide important evidence to others of participants' communicative roles in relation to one another, and thus of which pieces of speech can be interpreted as *related*. This evidence is interpreted using awareness of both culturally and biologically conditional constraints on communication.

REFERENCES

Austin, J. (1965). *How to do things with words.* New York: Oxford University Press.

Duncan, S. (1972). Some signals and rules for taking speaking turns in conversations. *Journal of Personality and Social Psychology, 23,* 283–292.

Duranti, A. (1981). The Samoan FONO: A sociolinguistic Study. *Pacific Linguistics,* Series B, vol. 80. Canberra: Department of Linguistics, R. S. Pac. S. Australian National University.

Duranti, A. (1983). Sociocultural dimensions of discourse. In Teun A. van Dyke (Ed.), *Handbook of discourse analysis.* London: Academic Press.

Goffman, E. (1974). *Frame analysis.* New York: Harper and Row.

Hymes, D. (1964). Toward ethnographies of communication. *American Anthropologist, 66* (6) Part 2, 1–34.

Hymes, D. (1972). Models of the interaction of language and social life. In J. Gumperz & D. Hymes (Eds.), *Directions in sociolinguistics* (pp. 35–71). New York: Holt.

Irvine, J. (1974). Strategies of status manipulation in the Wolof greeting. In R. Bauman & J. Sherzer (Eds.), *Explorations in the ethnography of speaking* (pp. 167–191). New York: Cambridge Unversity Press.

Irvine, J. (1979). Formality and informality in communicative events. *American Anthropologist, 81,* pp. 773–790.

Keenan, E. O. (1974). Norm-makers, norm-breakers: Uses of speech by men and women in a Malagasy community. In Bauman & Sherzer (Eds.), *Explorations in the ethnography of speaking* (pp. 125–143). New York: Cambridge University Press.

Kendon, A. (1967). Some functions of gaze-direction in social interaction. *Acta Psychologica, 26,* pp. 22–63.

Philips, S. (1974). Warm Springs Indian time: How the regulation of participation affects the progression of events. In R. Bauman, & J. Sherzer (Eds.), *Explorations in the ethnography of speaking.* New York: Cambridge University Press.

Sherzer, J. (1974). Namakke, Summakke, Kormakke: Three types of Cuna speech events. In Bauman & Sherzer, *Explorations in the ethnography of speaking* (pp. 263–282). New York: Cambridge University Press.

12. Some Linguistic Contributions to a Criminal Court Case

Roger W. Shuy
Georgetown University

In 1980 I was asked to assist the defense attorneys in a criminal case involving a prominent politician and two associates who were being charged at the same time together with him. The case grew out of scam-type operation conducted by the FBI in which 106 surreptitious audio tape recordings were made by undercover agents of the FBI. These tape recordings were of several group meetings involving the men being charged, in conversation with one or more of the FBI undercover agents and representatives. There were also tape recorded telephone conversations.

Since the government's operation was primarily to gather incriminating evidence about labor officials involved in skimming money from medical and health insurance programs, the taped evidence also included many conversations between FBI undercover agents and other people not involved in this case. Although such conversation might not, at first, seem relevant to the defense of the three men charged in this particular case, it will be shown that these recordings also played a crucial role in their defense. The government provided typed transcripts of all the conversations on tape, totaling approximately 2,800 pages of text.

In court cases which involve tape recorded evidence, there is a public predisposition toward guilt. The reasoning is emotional, not intellectual. It runs something like this: "If the FBI suspected that these men are guilty and succeeded in getting tape recorded evidence to that end, the defendants are probably guilty. If there is talk about deals, there must be deals. If some of the speakers on the tapes agree to accept money for illegal purposes, then they all must be doing so." No juror would admit this, of course, but the emotional set is there. The job of the linguist, then, is to determine exactly who said what to whom and when and then to make this very clear for the jury to see and hear.

Perhaps it should be made clear at this point that the role of the linguist or any other expert witness in lawsuits is not to take sides, to defend, or to prosecute. It is critical that such witnesses make no promises and exhibit no favoritism, even when the evidence seems to be against their clients. The expert witness is compromised by anything short of integrity with the data and analysis. If the linguistic analysis of tape recorded data is valuable, it should be the same analysis regardless of whether the prosecution or the defense uses the service. In this case, as in all others, the first job of the linguist is to teach the lawyers what

234

it is that can be found in the data and to then let them determine how such information can or cannot be used. Good attorneys, of course, are partial to their clients but good attorneys also understand that expert witnesses are useless to them unless they are allowed to be objective and impartial.

In this particular case, the FBI made use of a convicted criminal in an insurance fraud in another state, one Bob Susce,[1] to discuss other possible insurance frauds in the Southwestern United States. For his plea bargain he was to wear a body microphone and tape record his conversations with various labor officials and politicians. He worked with two undercover FBI agents on most occasions but often he worked alone. In addition, the FBI tape recorded various telephone conversations which these three men made and tapped the telephones of the persons whom they singled out for further scrutiny. The result was a mass of tape recorded data, spanning eight months of time and involving many people. When the FBI obtained what they considered sufficient data for incrimination, indictments were made. The trial in which I was involved was the result of one such indictment. Three men were tried together in this case, a prominent politician and two lawyers in private practice who formerly had been employees of that state and who, in this case, had been hired as consultants by Mr. Susce and his associates to assist them in determining how the state insurance bidding could be reopened so that the company they pretended to represent, The Big City Insurance Company, could get the state insurance contract. In fairness, it should be noted that Big City Insurance had no knowledge of this FBI operation. Susce's approach was to say that he represented the home office of Big City in Chicago and that he had the authority to pare down Big City's bid by over a million dollars. The enticement that he offered was that he would split such savings personally with the persons who would help him get the bids. To show his good faith, he would offer such persons a smaller amount of money up front (between two and ten thousand dollars) which he would refer to as peanuts and promise whatever additional money such persons might need to use on other officials or for expenses.

My problem, as a linguist, was first to determine what sort of analysis to perform on this massive amount of data covering eight months of time, involving about 50 people in a number of different conversations. Several kinds of analysis could be ruled out immediately. Phonological analysis, for example, would not yield the patterns which could be most useful to the jury in understanding what was happening. Even a comparison of the written text to the actual tape recordings was not particularly relevant since the scripts in this case were, unlike other cases on which I have worked, quite accurate. Large scale syntactic analysis also was not necessarily productive on this corpus. For example, if this had been a contract dispute, where the structure of the syntax might show ambiguity or

---

[1] The names of the actual participants and corporations in this case have been changed to preserve anonymity.

alternative interpretations of the text, a careful syntactic analysis might prove more helpful. Since the important issue in this case concerned the structure and meaning of actual conversation, I decided to analyze the conversations as a group for any common attributes.

As it turned out, most of the face-to-face conversations shared a common structure. They all tended to lead toward the making of a proposal followed by actions taken about the proposal. It became clear that if the conversations involving the defendants were to show anything different about their language behavior, such behavior should contrast to that of other speakers in the same kinds of conversations. This type of analysis, then, blends some features of familiar contrastive analysis procedures with what has become known as speech event analysis. It also became clear that what was not said and done could prove to be as interesting and useful as what *was* said and done. But to make any sort of contrast of this sort, it was first necessary to describe what the speech event was. By examining all of the proposal or contract types of conversations in this text, I determined a structure of such events which is shown in Figure 12.1. This analysis shows that the contract or proposal conversation, a great deal like a business meeting, contains seven phrases, from beginning to end, in which a problem is identified (why I am here), a proposal is offered and responded to, a completion is accomplished, and an extension of further work together is discussed.

Figure 12.1 offers a model which accounts for all the conversations of that type in the body of data presented by the FBI as evidence in this case. After the greetings phase, a problem is presented by the first party. It is usually a request for help of some sort. During this phase the first party checks on the other's authority and control to determine whether or not he or she is the appropriate person to follow up with a proposal. The next phase is the proposal itself, usually for services or products of some sort. Money is discussed and promises are made. Often at this phase, conditions are rechecked or new ones are introduced. If things are going well, some type of intimacy is established, often with anecdotes, stories about mutual friends, and even with in-group language behavior. Both parties can engage in such checking and rechecking. Out of the proposal phase grows the completion phase, in which an offer is accepted or rejected. If made, this is signaled by a handshake, the signing of an agreement or verbal expressions such as "It's a deal." After this completion, usually there is discussion about further extensions of the relationship now established, frequently involving other possible deals. This phase is followed by a frequently extensive closing phase in which further anecdotes and stories are exchanged and it is culminated with a conversational closing.

Since no sociolinguistic analysis of such a business meeting is available in the literature, this analysis may provide the groundwork for future research. This is not to say that the proposal conversation is the only kind of business meeting but, rather, that it is a routine or type of business meeting which is a member of that

Figure 12.1.   Structure of a Proposal Conversation

Phases	1st Party	Topics	2nd Party
introduction	greetings		greetings
		-mutual friends -establish authenticity -flattery	
problem	establish problem		respond to problem
		-request help -check conditions and control of other party	
proposal	present offer		consider offer make conditions
		-service -products -payment -promises -money discussed	

	recheck conditions,
	  control,
	details
			recheck conditions,
			  control, details

		-establish intimacy
		  with stories; in-
		  group language	

completion	complete contract
	  offer
			check conditions
			  of offer

		-handshake -contract -''it's a deal''	accept/reject offer

extension	extend business
	  relationship
			extend business
			  relationship

		-plan other deals	
close	closing		closing
		-tell stories	

category. As such, it fits the ''minor genre'' type suggested originally by Hymes (1975) and extends Goffman's notion of supportive and remedial exchanges (1971). The proposal conversation, as a minor genre, is a part of the culture of business exchange which differentiates ad hoc improvisation from predictable, patterned sequences. Since the complete proposal conversations of several individuals follow exactly the model structure shown in Figure 12.1, it is taken as the norm of this genre. The "natural" speech which could be expected in this genre is thus culturally predictable, at least for the American society. As such it was possible to use this genre model as a touchstone with which to compare other conversations, particularly those involving the defendants, to determine whether or not they were actually participating in a proposal event.

The next task was to determine how the various people with whom Mr. Susce spoke responded within this framework. Figure 12.2 shows how the model worked with a Mr. George Howard, one of the early conversations in this body of data. Susce introduces his problem, how to get Big City Insurance business in the state, checks Howard's control over a Mr. Gordon, a person in power there, and asks how he can develop a business relationship with Howard (having first given indirect clues that there was something in this for both of them). Howard opens the door to the next proposal phase by indicating that he has other ways of doing business than the company he works for. In the proposal phase, Susce offers $2,000 up front with a promise of a 50-50 split, along with the condition that he deal only with Howard. Howard responds by saying "Keep talking" and offers the condition of each deal being individual and then checks the authority of Susce to handle things at Big City. This phase is followed by a clear completion in which Susce gives Howard $2,000, shakes hands, and says, "Its a deal." Howard refuses the money four times, then finally accepts it and replies that they have a deal. Howard then extends their future relationship by suggesting that there are 50 people he can send Susce and names a few specific organizations that he can set up for this operation. It is worth noting that there is no ambiguity or lack of specificity in this proposal conversation. Each phase is followed in sequence and the terms are explicit and clear. This same pattern can be noted in other conversations in this corpus, all of which happen before Susce meets the defendants in this case. One labor leader, Mr. Tom Wilson, includes in his extension the fact that he is a close friend of the politician and that he knows two lawyers who can help him figure out how to get the insurance business for that state. Twelve days later, a meeting takes place between Bob Susce, Tom Wilson, and the two lawyers, Fred Smith and Al Reed. Figure 12.3 displays how this proposal conversation differs from that of the other proposal conversations that have taken place thus far.

This particular conversation contained 50 topics, of which 17 were introduced by the defendants, Smith and Reed, and 33 were introduced by Susce and Wilson. The topics introduced by Smith and Reed were all related to the insurance business in the state, or small talk topics about football and local personalities. Susce and Wilson also introduce topics about small talk but their recurring recycled topic of getting the politician is clearly their common thread. A topic is recycled as a signal that it has not been resolved to the satisfaction of the person initiating it. The topic of getting the politician involved in this operation was first introduced indirectly by Susce, then directly seven times throughout the conversation as topics numbers 10, 11, 17, 19, 27, 29, and 42, indicating a

Figure 12.2. Proposal Conversation With Mr. Howard

Phases	Bob Susce Topics	George Howard Topics/Responses
introduction	-mutual friends ⟵—————	greetings
	-famous friends	
	-credentials	
	-flattery	
problem	to get the state business →	I will just have to work out some-thing, Bob, where you could visit with some trustees.
	checks control: Do you control Mr. Gordon?	He'll go along with a lot of the things I recommend.
	How do you and I develop a rela-tionship?	have a public relations firm . . . and I do business other than what I'm doing here.
proposal	$2,000.00 now 50-50 split of com-mission →	Keep talking
	conditions: -I deal only w/you -$4,000/mo. possible	conditions: -case by case basis -can you handle Big City Insurance politics?
completion	Here's $2,000.00 Let's shake hands We have a deal? →	rejects four times, then accepts
		We have a deal.
extension		-50 people I can send you -District in Tennessee -contacts -Boston
close	closing	closing

strong interest on the part of Wilson and Susce to obtain resolution of this topic. In ordinary conversation we do not impose upon our conversational partners by talking about the same thing over and over again. It is also interesting to note here that the resolution of that topic does *not* come from the persons to whom it is presented for resolution. Wilson, the proposer, resolves his own topic as a directive two times near the end of the conversation (topics 29 and 42). The FBI's case against Smith and Reed charges them with conspiring to bribe a public official, yet the structure of this proposal conversation shows them to assent only to the fact that Wilson has agreed to his own resolution to try to get

Figure 12.3.   Proposal Conversation With Mr. Smith and Mr. Reed

Phases	Susce	Wilson	Smith	Reed
introduction		greetings	greetings	
problem		to get this insur-ance busines		
	who controls?———————————→			-If anybody is a strong per-son . . . its a staff man. -Gives over-view of state insurance.

Topic 10
| The politician controls the dental pro-gram ——————————→ | | | | -Legislative au-thorization has to be sought. The politician is not some-body who would be in-volved. |

Topic 11
| T. R. Murphy takes his or-ders from the politi-cian | | | | He's a valuable man. He's the politi-cian's right hand man. |

Topic 17
| We'll have to meet the politician ——→ | | | Don't count on anything happening | |

Topic 19
| We should go to the pol-itician ——→ | | | You don't have any-thing to lose even if he says he doesn't want to | |

Figure 12.3. (*Continued*)

Phases	Susce	Wilson	Smith	Reed
			get involved in it.	
	Topic 27 Shouldn't we get the politician?			I don't think the politician is the key.
		Topic 29 We'll get the politician.		You can do without the politician at all.
		Topic 42 We're gonna get the politician.		Alright, but it's going to be a problem.
completion		NONE		
extension		NONE		
close	closings		closings	

the politician to apply pressure on the persons responsible for reopening insurance bids, a perfectly legal thing for him to do provided that benefit accrues to the state by his doing so. In addition, as Figure 12.3 points out, there is no completion phase to this conversation, no agreement on a deal, no handshake, no binding contract. There is also no extension phase, the agreement to join in further work of this nature. There is no quid pro quo and no discussion about what one party will do for the other for money.

In contrast to the proposal conversation with Mr. Howard and with other persons, there are only noncommital responses from Smith and Reed about the proposals which Susce and Wilson were actually making. One can only presume that Susce and Wilson wanted Smith and Reed to agree that the politician was the key person to get involved in this and to offer their services, for money, to do so. Even if they had done so, which they did not, there would be considerable doubt about whether this could be considered conspiracy since there was no way that they could know what Susce and Wilson's intentions of bribery were.

It should be borne in mind here that the concern of the defense attorneys was that the jury, knowing that Smith and Reed were charged with such crimes, would not be able to keep track of times and events which were tape recorded and that they would confuse Susce and Wilson's intentions with those of Smith and Reed. Earlier, taped conversations between Susce and Wilson, who was an unsuspecting dupe in this case and who did not know that Susce was really working for the FBI, had revealed that Wilson felt that he could get Smith and Reed involved in the crime. The problem for the defense was then one of helping the jury, through visualization of the sort provided here, to sort events out and to focus on the critical parts of the mass of tape with which they were presented.

The next important conversation for the jury to consider took place 16 days later. In this meeting, the now well-established structure of the proposal conversation was violated. In this meeting there was no problem stated, no proposals made, no completion, and no extension. The speech event here was that of the client interview. At the close of the earlier meeting, Susce and Wilson asked Smith and Reed to check on some things related to Big City's being able to get the insurance bids reopened. (It should be pointed out that such activity is perfectly legal, resembling more the work of a lobbyist or an investigator. Phrases used by Wilson included expressions like "find out how it's wired" and "help us know what the deal is." Such expressions eventually were used by the prosecution to infer that illegal activity was involved somehow.) This conversation included 26 topics, 17 of which were introduced by Susce and Wilson and 9 by Smith and Reed. Sixteen topics related to the task of finding out how to get the bids reopened and other Big City Insurance concerns. All of the other nine topics were small talk and greetings. One topic was the payments of money by Wilson to Smith and Reed for legal work that they had done for him in a different consulting role related to a school issue in a local suburb, where Wilson was a member of the school board. Although some of the topics are about getting the politician involved in reopening the insurance bids, in the last topic, Wilson brings up plans for his meeting with the politician and asks for Smith and Reed's advice on meeting strategies. Wilson's exact words are, "Bob and I . . . let me tell you what our plans is and you guys help us with this." It is worth noting here that Wilson has difficulty with his personal pronouns throughout all conversations but, in this case it is clear whose plans these are (not Smith and Reed's). Again, the defense strategy was to call attention to the pronoun references, out of all the morass of less relevant conversation, and to mark it in the minds of the jury so that it would not be forgotten. It should be noted that I was not made aware of exactly what the charges were and that I was led to this analysis of the conversations by first determining the structure of the commonly recurring speech event, the proposal meeting, and by comparing such proposal meetings with *each other*. What was *not* present in the first proposal meeting with Smith and Reed were significant marked features of that type of meeting. The *second* meeting with Smith and Reed was so different from the common proposal meeting that it could not be classified as a proposal meeting at all. In this case, the speech event was more like other kinds of speech events such as the doctor–patient interview or, in this case, the lawyer–client or advisor–client conversation.

The conversation with the other defendant, the politician, was treated in much the same way. His first meeting with Susce and Wilson was an eight and one-half minute meeting. It followed the format of the common proposal meeting with some notable exceptions which easily could be missed or forgotten by the jury. I have already noted that as Wilson is encouraged by Susce to take over more and more of the leadership in such meetings, Tom Wilson frequently becomes confused about which persona he actually represents. This confusion is clearly evident in his use of pronouns. In a tape recorded meeting between Susce and Wilson alone, Susce encourages Wilson to be the quaterback in their meeting with the politician. Susce knows that his job is to get the FBI operation going well because soon he is going to have to go to jail for his earlier conviction. Of course, Wilson is totally unaware of this. This confusion of pronoun referencing needed to be called to the jury's attention because the proposals made by Wilson and Susce, in their meeting with the politician, can be clearly differentiated by their use of pronouns. For example, when a person says, "I fire you," that person is using *I* to mean, "I in my role as boss" and not necessarily "I personally." Likewise, when a person says "I love you," it is not generally regarded as a statement involving corporate responsibility. Figure 12.4 points out the actual text of the beginning of the proposal-making in this conversation.

Note that it begins by Moore representing himself in a statement which is interrupted by Susce, who sees an opportunity to direct the conversation to the topic of money, and says to Wilson that they should get into that right now. Wilson understands and asks Susce's permission to play quarterback. Wilson

Figure 12.4.   Proposal Conversation with the Politician

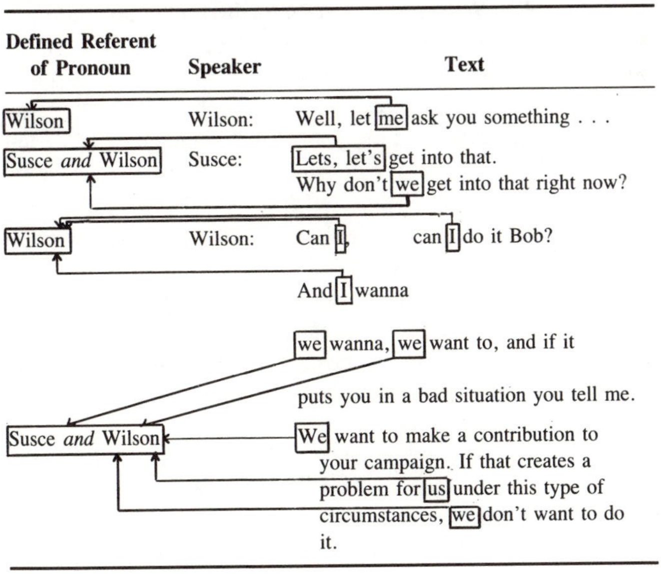

then begins the proposal with *I*, then switches to *we*. This is critical because if the contribution is from Tom Wilson alone, the contribution is perfectly legitimate and clear. If it is from Wilson and Susce, it is unclear exactly who it is coming from, possibly from Big City Insurance Company. If it is from Big City and the politician can be seen to be helping Big City reopen the insurance bids, then the contribution could be seriously questioned in terms of ethics, if not legality.

Having seen how crucial the use of pronoun references can be in a meeting of this sort, it is now instructive to examine *all* of the proposals made in this conversation, including one which precedes the one shown in Figure 12.4. Figure 12.5 outlines these proposals, along with the politician's actual responses. In terms of linguistic analysis, Figure 12.5 employs both topic-response analysis and pronoun reference analysis.

Five different proposals are made in this brief passage. Susce proposes that if the insurance bids can be reopened, the state will save a million dollars. The politican agrees that this is good and agrees to help reopen the bids, following acceptable procedures. Wilson follows with an offer of a campaign contribution from an unspecified *we*. The politician defers this offer saying "Let's take care of this thing first (the first proposal, to save the state a million), *then* let's think about a contribution." Undaunted by the deferral, Tom Wilson then changes pronouns and asks if he personally ("I, Tom Wilson," appositionally clarified) could make such a contribution. The politician agrees (this is, by the way, perfectly legal). At this point, Wilson turns to Susce and says, "Give me the deal." Susce's voice then counts out, "One, two, three, four, five." Later, when Wilson retells the event to other undercover FBI agents, he points out that Susce had handed him five thousand dollars from his pocket. While the money is on the politician's desk, Wilson then redefines the politician's agreement to the legality of a personal contribution by changing the pronoun to *we* and by upping the ante in amount. The politician's response was *not* to Wilson's proposal to the upped-ante, but to Susce's first proposal, to save the state money. Analysts of conversaion have long recognized the politician's strategy here as a redirect to a topic more appropriate to the conversation. The politician's response is about the announced or official purpose of the conversation. It is also likely that he was quite aware of the nonverbal event which had just taken place. After Wilson offered a personal contribution, he turned and got the money from Susce. This physical event could well have defined for the politician the reference to *we* in this proposal—enough, at least to cause him to become very cautious and to try to divert the topic back to the appropriate one. Wilson responds to the politician's response with "That's all the commitment we want out of you." Susce adds, "Okay, that's all we want." The politician then verifies the meaning of his response with, "I think that's what part of my job is—to try to save the state."

Susce then comes in as quarterback and, with very specific language, indicates that there will be a savings of 1.2 million and that he intends to keep half and give the other half to the politician. The politician clearly rejects this pro-

Figure 12.5. Proposals Made in Meeting with the Politician

Proposals: Susce and Wilson			Responses: the Politician
Insurance Proposal to save the state money	Campaign Contribution	Offer to Split commission	
Susce: There will be a savings of approximately a million dollars			. . . anytime you can save the State a buck by God, I'm for it.
	Wilson: We want a contribution to your campaign		Let's get this thing, and try to take care of it first . . . and uh, uh, then, then, then, uh, then let's think about that.
	Wilson: Could I, Tom Wilson . . . give you a contribution?		Oh, sure.
	Wilson: We will put, I will, in your whatever you want to run. $100,000 going in and we can prepare to put a half a million		Anytime you can show me where you can save the state money well, by God, I'll go to battle for you . . . I think that's what part of my job is, . . . try to save the state.
	Wilson: That's all the commitment we want out of you.		
		Susce: There's $600,000 every yr. I'm keeping 600 and 600, whatever you want to do with it to get the business.	. . . our only position is we don't want to do anything that's illegal or anything to get anybody in trouble and you all don't either.
			And this is as legitimate as it can be because anytime somebody can show me how we can help save the state some money, I'm going to bat for it.

245

posal and once again returns to the official, announced topic of saving the state a million dollars. He recycled the topic of saving the state money four times during this part of the conversation.

Topic recycling as a means of indicating the intention of speakers in a conversation played a rather important role in analyzing these tape recordings. One last example of such recycling is worth noting in this meeting with the politician. Shortly after the exchanges noted in Figure 12.5, the politician's administrative aide who was also present in this conversation, notes that the campaign contribution will have to be reported. Wilson responds that he would like to be told *how* they intend to report. This could mean several possible things. It is possible, in that state, to report campaign contributions to several different agencies. Wilson could have been referring to this. More likely, however, is that Tom Wilson was concerned whether they would report the contribution as from him personally, from the labor group he heads, from Wilson and Susce together, from Big City, or from some other source. This could be of great concern to him if it were reported as from his labor group since the politician is a conservative and labor seldom supported him. The interruption pattern of this conversation is also interesting since Wilson and Susce appear to have different agendas about the reporting question and, of course, the politician and his aide hold still a different position. Figure 12.6 reports the sequential conversation as it happened but sorts it into three agenda columns, again for the sake of jury understanding and clarity. Note here that Susce is talking only about *not* reporting it. Wilson is not raising the issue of whether it should be reported but, instead, *how* it will be done. Each interrupts the other to direct the conversation toward his own position. Susce interrupts to try to convince the politician not to report it. Wilson interrupts Susce *and* the politician to direct the politician to respond to his direction, acknowledging that it will *have* to be reported. Then he recycles his request that it not be reported until the politician talks to him. The politician's "no, no, no" is a positive response, indicating that he won't report it until they talk. In all, Wilson requests assurance that the politician talk to him before reporting it six times. The politician agrees four times.

In the proposal conversation between the politician and Susce and Wilson, there is no completion phase which indicates that the politician has agreed to do something for money. This contrasts sharply with other taped conversations provided by the FBI in which other individuals *do* agree to accept money for specific activities in the completion phase. In fact, there is no completion phase in this conversation. Nor is there an extension phase.

This summary of the analysis which I performed on the tape recorded data provided by the FBI constituted the major portions of what was offered to the defense attorneys for their clients. The paradox of all applied linguistics is that we must call upon our scientific training to perform our analyses but not to explain it in too much detail to people without linguistic training. In the case of

Figure 12.6. On Reporting the Contribution

Susce Why Report It?	Wilson How to Report It	Politician & Aide It Will be Reported.
		But you know that it'll be re-ported
	You tell me how you want to report it now so I'll know what's gonna happen.	
Why do you have to report it?		Well, we need . . . I don't . . .
Why do you have to report it?		. . . want to get into no damn tax . . .
	Why don't you do this . . .	Well, . . .
You can report it later on, a year from now. Put it away . . .		
	You guys devise a way to do it, alright?	
. . . cause we're talking about . . .		
	. . . and let me know how you're going to do it. What I want you to do though, is you devise some way, if you got to report it, if that's what you got to do. But you guys don't do it till you talk to me . . .	
	. . . So I know where the hell I'm at, OK?	. . . No, no, no
		Yeah right. Because you know we don't want to have, we don't want to do something where you're gonna find out (unt.)
	I don't want you to get me strung out. You guys figure out how to do that.	I know, don't worry.
		Alright, we'll be in touch with you, sure will. Appreciate it.
	You do what you want to, OK? Don't do nothing till you let me know.	

work in court cases, we must establish our authenticity as scientists without confusing either lawyers or juries with it. This calls for an entirely different form of presentation to juries than we would usually make to other linguists who we are trying to impress with our linguistic knowledge and rigor. When linguists are to appear as expert witnesses in court, we must establish our credentials in the predicate of our testimony, noting our achievements, publications, awards, and so on, in a way which would be totally inappropriate at an academic conference or meeting. This may seem like self-serving puffery but it is the way the courts work. Early in the expert testimony we must indicate the outline of our analysis and methodology, but in terms which a jury can understand. It is permissible to say that we use, as in this case, such procedures from linguistics as contrastive analysis, referential analysis, and topic-response analysis, but not go into detail about them. It is more important that a jury understand that these are acceptable analytical procedures than it is for them to know all the facts about such approaches that we as linguists know.

The date for my expert witness testimony in this case was scheduled, and on the evening before I met with the defense attorneys, we went over my proposed testimony as, in this case, a summary witness.

Although there was no unanimity among them, the five defense attorneys decided at that time that their advantage in the trial to this point was so great that they did not need to use my expert witness. (They did use some of my charts and ideas in their summary arguments.)

Ironically enough, the defense lawyers agreed that if they were behind or doubtful about their position in this case, they would have most certainly used my testimony directly. But being ahead, as they assumed they were, they decided not to chance the possible negative effects of cross-examination. Their predictions proved to be correct when the jury found the politician, Smith, and Reed all not guilty.

The title of this paper is "Some Linguistic Contributions to a Criminal Court Case." In this case, the contributions were more formative than summative. Despite my letdown of not being allowed to perform that which I prepared, I feel that a contribution was most certainly made. This case suggests, in fact, that there are ways in which linguists can contribute to a criminal case, or perhaps to any kind of lawsuit, which are more consultative than performance oriented.[2]

---

[2] I have done both and, whatever thrill I get from the courtroom performance, the strain is very great and the risks are many. In short, there is also benefit to be had from the satisfaction of contributing only in a behind-the-scenes fashion. One side benefit, for example, is the rich source of natural language data which was obtained by the FBI's surreptitions tape recordings. It would be utterly unethical for a linguist to obtain language data in such a surreptitious fashion. Since it exists, however, it can provide a useful body of information for us to understand a great deal about how language is used in natural settings. The speech event of the proposal conversation may be studied in other ways, but it is unlikely that it will be able to be found in such richness or abundance and with fieldwork supported and carried out by the federal government.

One way in which my analysis was used by the defense attorneys was in preparing their clients for direct and cross-examination. In cases which involve tape recorded data of the actual events, the courtroom testimony of the accused can be refreshed by playing the tapes and reading the transcripts. A defendant's testimony on the witness stand about his or her language was clearly not as good as his or her use of language in the actual event. This situation is a great deal like the comparative usefulness of actual data with self-report data. And it is at this point that perhaps the greatest significance of tape recorded evidence will be seen: people use language in real life situations better than they are able to recall what they did and still better than they are able to recount what it is that they said. The value of taped evidence, in this case, can be clearly seen as an advantage for the innocent. This is, of course, not surprising to linguists, but it has tremendous implications for courts of law. Despite the fact that juries are predisposed to view taped evidence as incriminating, such evidence is far superior to the traditional self-report data of courtroom testimony. The courts have not yet realized how powerful such tape recorded data actually can be. One task for the linguist is to help them.

REFERENCES

Goffman, E. (1971). *Relations in public*. New York: Harper.
Hymes, D. (1975). Folklore's nature and the sun's myth. *Journal of American Folklore*, 88, pp. 345–69.

Author Index

Italics indicate bibliographic citations.

Subject Index

A

abortion, 59–60
alcoholism, 30, 31, 38, 40, 41
alienation, 26, 41–42
allergies, 57, 58
attribution
  control of, 179–181
  frequency of, 171–173
  positive and negative, 173
  psychological testing and, 176–181
  role of placement meeting and, 170–171, 173
  school psychologists and, 171–173, 175
  special education teachers and, 170–173
  theory of, 164–165, 167

B

birth control. *See* contraceptives

C

capitalism, 26, 27, 31, 34
collusion, linguistic, 123–128, 136–138
contraceptives, 3–8, 12–15, 19–23, 29–30
  abortion and, 60
  continued user of, 13–19
  hazards of, 20–22
  intra-uterine, 8, 10–12, 14–15, 20–22
  new users of, 8–13
  non-prescription, 11–12, 21
  oral, 3, 6–8, 19–23, 29–30
criminal cases, linguistics and, 246, 248–249

D

decision process, 104–108, 110–113, 140–141
  in education, 140–141, 143–148
  of Eligibility and Placement Committee, 144–148, 161–162
  governmental funding and, 144–145
  lay and professional role in, 157–158
  learning disability and, 181–184
  reports and, 148, 151, 153, 157–158
  teacher's role in, 146, 150–156, 158
decisions, medical
  alcoholic patient and, 30–31
  economic factors and, 43, 65–68, 72–73
  ethics and, 49–55, 71, 73, 74
  inadequate information and, 68–69

informed consent and, 52, 54–55
in interests other than patient's, 69, 71
pain and, 65–66, 71
patient's preference and, 64, 65, 67
of resident physician, 61–62, 71–72
depression, 29–32, 34, 95
discourses. *See also* language
  collusionary examples of, 128–133
  on contraceptive use, 9–12, 14, 16–18, 29–30, 37–38
  on decision formulation, 104–106
  dental, 84–89
  of depressed woman, 29–33, 36–48
  criminal disclosure during, 92, 105, 119
  feminist ideal of, 198–199
  formal, 109
  of liberals, 199–201
  of mole surgery patient, 61–63
  personal disclosures during, 110–111
  with pregnant patient, 59–60
  psychiatric referral during, 43–44
  of radicals, 199
  rights and obligation of parties in, 110–111
  role of small talk in, 86–87, 108
  screening process during, 110–113
  of strept throat patient, 57–58
  of telephone counselors, 105–106, 108–114, 116–120
drugs, prescription
  birth control pills as, 34, 37, 41
  for relief of pain, 64–66, 70–71
  for strept throat patient, 48–49, 64, 69–70
  tranquilizers as, 34, 47–48

E

emic and etic criteria, 224
ethnography, 7, 56–57, 93, 97, 224
evidence, tape recorded, 234–235, 244–247, 249

F

feminism
  defusing of, 196–197, 200
  education and, 192–196, 200
  equal opportunity and, 192–193
  fetishism and, 193

persuasion, (*cont.*)
   negative attitudes, 79–80, 82
   partisan strategy and, 85–88
   political implications of, 83
   reality and, 88–89
   small talk and, 86–87
pharmaceutical companies, 21, 69–70
power, exploitation of, 4, 5, 21–23, 26–29, 33–35
   by collusion in conversation, 128–133, 136–138
   by dentists, 79–84, 89
   in education, 158–161
   by government funding, 144–145
   and organizational decision making, 107–108, 110, 113, 159–160
propositional analysis, 129, 134
prostitution, 92, 99, 101, 103, 112
psychiatric needs, 43–44, 91–93, 95, 101

Q

questionnaires, 56
quiddity, 102–104

R

reports, 148, 151, 153, 157–158, 172
research methods, 6–8, 57, 92–97, 166–167
research surveys, 6–8
residents, medical, 56, 61–64, 66–67, 71–72
role reversal, 194–196

S

school psychologists attribution and, 171–173
   evaluation authority of, 153–154, 156, 170
   role of, 145–148, 152–153
   technical status of, 158–162
   transcript of meeting with, 148–151, 158, 180–181
science, 8, 20, 26–29, 35–36
screening processes, 110–113
sexism, 22, 35, 187
   education and, 192–196, 200
   policy statements and, 187–190, 193, 197–199
   Queensland Statement and, 190–191, 195–196, 199–200
   role categories and, 191–192
   role reversal and, 194–196
sexual problems, 98, 101, 116–117
special education teachers, 170–173
students, 128–133, 141–143, 153–157, 165
   case studies of, 168–169

suicide, 41, 91, 100
surgery, 61–64, 66–67, 71–73

T

teachers, 131, 141, 143
   attribution theory and, 164–165, 167, 172–173
   decision making by, 146, 150–155, 158
   of special education, 150, 156, 158, 170, 171
   women's careers and, 194–196
tests, 176–179
topic recycling, 246
transcripts, 9–12, 14, 16–18, 57–58, 61–62. *See also* discourses
   of alcoholic mother, 36–46
   of court cases, 206–207, 209, 211–213
   of decision making process, 105–106, 116–120
   of dental patients, 79, 81, 82, 84–89
   editing of, 215–218, 220
   electronic recording of, 206, 219, 235
   of Eligibility and Placement Committee deliberations, 147–151, 158–159
   of hyperactive woman, 46–48
   idealized forms of, 213–214
   informational construct of, 218, 220
   literacy of, 210, 214, 218, 220
   of Maria, 59–60
   of procedural positioning by Rosa, 131
   recording techniques of transcription, 211–212
   of school psychologists interviews, 148–151, 158, 180–181
   sworn testimony in, 218
   tape recorded evidence as, 234, 244–247, 249
   of teacher's placement referral, 173–174
tranquilizers, 34, 47–48
treatment
   dental, 80–82
   non surgical, 22, 33, 47–48, 58–59, 64–65
   (*see also* drugs, prescription)

W

wholistic medicine, 35
women
   education and, 192–196
   health care and, 4–6, 20, 22–23, 33–36
   as new patients, 57
   role reversal and, 194–196
   scientific repression of, 27, 29
   sexual equality and, 192

the pole of formal talk, that is, the pre-allocation, according to some "formula," of rights and obligations regarding certain turns and turn types (Sacks, Schegloff and Jefferson, 1978, pp. 45–47; McHoul, 1978); these formal elements are, in the cases at hand, "superimposed" on, or rather achieved through, ordinary conversational devices such as recipient-invited stores or disclosures and the like. Notwithstanding, these formal elements comprise oriented-to interactional lineaments of the telephone counseling conversations, through which the talk is adjusted to the organizational and problem-oriented relevances.

The differential allocation of participation rights and obligations generate and distribute a "social identity contrast," as McHoul puts it, of "client" and "counselor," a contrast which operates over and above the "caller"- "called" identities. Many features of the talk are addressed to this contrast, and to specific, asymmetrical distributions of (and rights concerning) knowledge. These "formal" features are typically found in formal-organizational or institutional contexts, and indeed work to impart the organizational or institutional character to those settings—especially since, as we have noted, these settings may well feature some asymmetry of knowledge.

The examination of the formal elements of what we might call "organizational talk" brings us, perhaps, to some of the core considerations in the ethnomethodological examination of authority in relation to this particular organization. Based on our data, we would not wish to treat "authority" as an overall characterization of the counselor-caller relation *in toto*. This relation is, to be sure, a formal-organizational one but it would perhaps not be wise to regard the authority in that relationship as having a single, undimensional, zero-sum character, such that the counselor has authority to the precise extent that the caller lacks authority. Nor would we want to treat authority as invariably a *diffuse* capacity (though it is indeed a capacity).

Instead, as the analysis below will indicate, it is better to proceed more fastidiously by examining authority in its prepositional forms, namely in terms of "authority *to* (say, perform some given activity)." In the analysis it will be found that the counselor has the authority or right to, for example, decide on the relevance of a given problem to the Lifeliners, while the caller has the authority or right to decide whether to reconstrue his/her problem. Sometimes the obverse of these issues of authority is that of obligation, which limits authority in some cases more than others. Reference to particular instances is crucial in these considerations; moreover, one can not divorce or decontextualize the work "going into" the arrival at some provision, some decision or construal—this being largely descriptive work involving, *inter alia,* membership categorization, formulation-decision pairs, and so on.

Moreover, one can not divorce or decontextualize the descriptive and other work "going into" the arrival at some decision or construal from its implementation—work again involving membership categorization, formulation-decision pairs, and the like. In other words, we can not divorce the implementation of (say) a decision from members' constructions of grounds for that decision, grounds that for members, give that decision its "authoritative" character.

In declining to treat authority as necessarily a diffuse or undifferentiated property of organizational relations, we are perhaps placing limits on a Weberian notion of legitimate bureaucratic authority, which is, at least in part, based on the acknowledged expertise, experience, or knowledge of the official vis-à-vis non-incumbents of that bureaucracy. However, as we have noted elsewhere in this paper, members themselves may on occasion question, criticize, and assess the officer's expertise in relation to particular performances, and so on, and in this sense it is members (rather than analyst) who "circumscribe" Weber's characterization. This is particularly (though not exclusively) the case in the organization we are examining; the asymmetries are not so marked as in, say, courtroom cross-examinations, police interrogations, and so on. However, some aspects of Weber's observations on the bases of the legitimation of authority are perhaps preserved in the notion of "rights" I have used below, bearing in mind that these rights are oriented to by members and are part and parcel of members' practices in making sense of (say) organizational settings. We may now proceed with a preliminary and merely indicative unraveling of various instances of "authority to," remembering that the initiation of some of these instances falls within the proper ambit of the caller. Additionally, we need to ensure that our analysis of instances of "authority to" preserves the interactional nature of their deployment.

In the counselor's case, s/he has knowledge concerning the proper application and mobilization of the organization's resources to specific cases. The "client" categorization is, by contrast, the locus of (say) knowledge concerning a personal problem which s/he knows on his/her own behalf and over which s/he has rights concerning its disclosure.[21] It is within and through this distribution of rights and obligations that attempts to achieve organizationally-proper-help-in-this-case come to fruition or to nought, as the case may be. Interlocutors arrange their talk so as to display its character as talk in accordance with this distribution of rights and obligations, and, reflexively, the distribution can work as a sense-making template in accounting for the nature and course of the call and in monitoring and tracking the various particularities of the call. In this sense, they are constituents of the organizational resources whose uses are outlined by Bittner (1974). Our outline of some of the relevant "formal" features comprises a highly preliminary gross characterization. It is certainly not exhaustive and simply points to a line of analytic enquiry.

A first jointly oriented-to feature of the calls under consideration is that the counselor may legitimately seek to elicit a disclosure from the caller. This, in a yet-to-be explicated sense, may be projected from the counselor's opening utter-

---

[21] Owing to limitations of space, I have not been able to address this issue of (knowledge concerning) the client's problem(s) at any length.

ance. It is also more straightforwardly evident in utterances such as line A11, and also in instances such as:

1. Co. Hello Lifeliners can I help you?
2. C1. I don't know what to do with myself
3. Co. Well what seems to be the trouble then?

One way of highlighting the boundedness of a disclosure-elicitation rights to the category ''counselor'' is by imagining a possible situation where the *caller* asked the question in line 3. Such a situation would doubtless come off as implausible, absurd, insolent, presumptuous, incompetent, or as a joke or ''put-on.'' It is difficult to conceive of a real situation in which this might happen; certainly I have no instance of this in many hours'-worth of recorded data.

A second jointly oriented-to feature of the calls is that the caller has the right to disclose a problem or propose a solution (e.g., getting in touch with a marriage bureau as in A17–21). The caller's right has its obverse in the counselor's obligtation to listen to the disclosure if and when made. This right is very much a counterpart of the first feature outlined above. These rights, as with the other rights we are examining, are ''paired rights.'' In other words, the fact that the caller may elicit a disclosure simply serves as an orienting template for an array of members' practices which weave actions into interactions. It should not, however, be inferred that the list of features given here preserves some necessary temporal ordering of the mobilization of rights in the calls. Instead, the paired rights serve to distribute and inform activities amongst interlocutors and this distribution may take many specific sequential forms. In addition, we have the whole issue of ''getting to'' the disclosure, where—even in the sparsely-structured example above, we have a caller—initiated predisclosure item on line 2. Consequently, what I have termed ''paired rights'' may be diffusely present throughout the call, such that it can be used as a sense-assembly template for entire blocs of talk.

A third jointly oriented-to feature is that the counselor has the right and obligation to decide on the relevance to the Lifeliners of the proposed problem (or solution)-as-presented. Indeed, the tentativeness and guardedness with which callers frequently preface their problem-disclosure attests to their orientation to this right, as in ''. . . . well I'll put it to you anyway but I don't suppose there's anything you can do, erm.'' This and many other examples in the data presented here evidence the ''candidacy status'' of the proposed problem or solution, such that a refusal by the counselor is anticipated or provided for as a distinctly possible next action. The negative form of the request on line C2 also displays such candidacy status, where the proposed activity presented is a possibility whose actualization is to be decided upon—as it is in lines C5–7—by the counselor *qua* incumbent of the organization. A corollary of this is that the counselor can also decide on the order of relevance of the problem/solution as construed, for example, whether the Lifeliners can help directly or whether they can at least refer the caller to some agency such as the police, welfare office, and so on. The making of such referrals and recommendations may also be seen as the Lifeliners' "proper business" even though dealing with the "problem itself" (e.g., tracking down an alleged criminal) may not be a proper concern *per se* for the Lifeliners. The ability to recommend or refer to another organization may, however, be a valuable "fall-back" resource for a counselor who may not be able to deal directly with some problem. Of course, the kinds of referrals the Lifeliners may properly make is also an issue, as Extract C shows.

A fourth oriented-to feature, paired with the third feature, is that the caller has the right to request "guidelines" as to the organizational relevances of the Lifeliners, as in A2–4. The caller, here, does not try to stipulate guidelines on his/her own behalf. One of the few things a caller can do in this regard is to attempt to construe a particular problem or solution as relevant to the Lifeliners' work, and here the above comments on candidacy status characteristically serve to diminish various perlocutionary effects (disaffiliation, etc.) of such a construal.

A fifth oriented-to feature is that the caller has the right to reconstrue his/her problem if, when, and where that becomes relevant, for example, when a first candidate—relevant construal is turned down by the counselor. The right to reconstrual allows the interlocutors to extend the call and the search for help, and allows the caller to transform the presentation of a problem in such a way that it might putatively be adjudged to be more in line with the Lifeliners' organizational relevances. In lines A18–21, for example, after the caller's first proposed activity ("looking for a girl") is turned down by the counselor, the caller reconstrues the activity on lines 20–21, where the Lifeliners are asked to put him in touch with an agency which, one assumes, could do this.[22] In Extract C we have a problem (possible difficulty in contacting a prostitute)-cum-solution construal on line 3 which, when the counselor turns it down, occasions a projected reconstrual (line 4) which is "cut off" in overlap by the counselor's utterance indicating inability to help. Instead of the Lifeliners putting the caller in contact with a prostitute in either of the two senses projected by the caller, the caller is invited (line 7) to reconstrue yet again (perhaps, for instance, on a sexual problem, loneliness, and so on, which the first two construals may then retrospectively be held to gloss, or gloss over). Here, then, we have a paired right here, where the counselor may invite or elicit a reconstrual rather than just wait for one to occur. Again, we should talk of a "candidate" reconstrual elicitation; as line C7 shows, if the elicitation "fails" it could transpire that it serves as a preclosing item instead.

A sixth oriented-to feature of the calls is that the caller may choose to close

---

[22] There is also, of course, a strong element of "motive work" here, that is, that the caller's "intentions are honourable," Reconstruals, as transformations, may work to make visible these previously invisible, or at least ambiguous, matters.